The Friends of th

has been helping clerg,
years. The Corporation, in its present form, carries on a
tradition of giving to the clergy and their families which
started over 150 years ago.

In 1999/2000, the Corporation made grants of £920,000 to
nearly one thousand clergy and their dependents in need.

These grants have provided help towards:
- holiday breaks - school clothing - funeral expenses
- help during the trauma of marriage breakdown
- resettlement and retirement
- undergraduate maintenance - relief from debt

To maintain this tradition, it relies on **your**
continued generosity.

**You can help us by making a donation – or by
remembering the Corporation in your Will.
Parish donations are equally gratefully received.**

*For further information on how you can help, or if you know
someone who needs our help, please contact the Secretary:*

The Friends of the Clergy Corporation
27 Medway Street, Westminster, London SW1P 2BD
Telephone: 020 7222 2288 Email: focc@btinternet.com
or visit our website: www.friendsoftheclergy.co.uk
Registered Charity No. 264724

THE
CHURCH PULPIT
YEAR BOOK
2003

*Sermons for Sundays, Holy Days,
Festivals and Special Occasions
Year B*

edited by Dr J. Critchlow

CANTERBURY
PRESS
Norwich

© Canterbury Press 2002

*First published in 2002 by the Canterbury Press Norwich
(a publishing imprint of Hymns Ancient & Modern Limited,
a registered charity)
St Mary's Works, St Mary's Plain,
Norwich, Norfolk, NR3 3BH*

www.scm-canterburypress.co.uk

British Library Cataloguing in Publication data

A catalogue record for this book is available
from the British Library

ISBN 1-85311-0487-1

Typeset by Rowland Phototypesetting Limited,
Bury St Edmunds, Suffolk
Printed in Great Britain by
St Edmundsbury Press Limited, Bury St Edmunds, Suffolk

Editor's Preface

Now entering its hundredth year, the *Church Pulpit Year Book* probably holds by a fair margin the record for the most sermons of any extant publication: and the 'Day of the Sermon' is by no means over. Bernadino of Siena used to say: 'If you are given the choice between the communion and the sermon, choose the latter.' However strange this may at first sight appear, it is nevertheless true that in the communion one is feeding one's own soul, while in the sermon one is seeking to feed many other souls. Whether we operate a one-to-one ministry, or preach to thousands (and through the *Church Pulpit Year Book* the 'thousands' grow into 'millions'), we are sharing the message of God – and making a difference.

Today, that difference is being made with the advantage of a century of prayer and dedication, the steady increase in reader-demand being in itself an affirmation of the value of the *Year Book*'s writers over the years. Within the past year, my predecessor, the Revd. Francis Stephens, went home to the Lord. For seventeen years, Francis not only brought deep spirituality and theological expertise to his work, but also shrewd humour and the ability to stimulate further study and exploration. If indeed Charles Wesley was divinely inspired when, near the point of death, he told his brother: 'I believe it will be all activity', we may imagine Francis even busier in glory than when he was on earth!

A Christian in China struggling to translate the Gospel of John into one of the many dialects of the country, could find no word in the language to render 'Comforter'. Then one of his employees came to him, asking for time off to go to his sister who was in despair at the loss of her child. 'I want to go to help get her heart round the corner,' he said. And the translator had the answer to his problem. Let us pray that we may use these sermons with God's grace, to help hearts round the corner and on to God – and to him be all the glory.

J.C.
Corpus Christi, 2002

Clergy – St Luke's is your hospital

and your treatment here is FREE!

S T LUKE'S offers free treatment to Church of England ordained Ministers, active and retired, their spouses and dependent children, Ordinands, members of Anglican religious orders, Church Army officers, overseas Missionaries, and priests from Anglican Churches abroad. If you need a consultation with a consultant surgeon or physician, just send us a letter of referral from your GP. *The consultation, and any further treatment carried out in the Hospital, are entirely free.*

St Luke's, one of London's most up-to-date acute hospitals, is the laity's gift to the clergy. For over 100 years it has been financed by voluntary subscription, and treatment is provided by some 220 of the country's leading Consultants, who give their services free. It is a fine example of Christian stewardship in action. (And it helps the church too, because our aim is to get you back to your ministry as quickly as we can!)

St Luke's
HOSPITAL FOR THE CLERGY
Caring for those who care for others

14 Fitzroy Square, London W1T 6AH
Tel. 020 7388 4954. Fax. 020 7383 4812
E-mail: stluke@stlukeshospital.org.uk
Website: stlukeshospital.org.uk
Registered Charity 209236

If you would like to know more, telephone, or write to, our Medical Secretaries on 020 7388 4954.

And remember - if you think you might need us, we want to hear from you!

CONTENTS

Unless otherwise stated, the readings are taken from *Calendar, Lectionary and Collects* and are for Year B – the year of Mark – in the Revised Common Lectionary.

xi

SERMONS FOR SAINTS' DAYS and SPECIAL OCCASIONS

A helping hand for clergy families

Are your children eligible?

The Corporation of the Sons of the Clergy takes its name from its foundation, over 300 years ago, by a group of clergy sons. It exists to provide grants to Anglican clergymen and women, serving or retired, and their families, in times of need.

These grants are to help with expenses in a variety of areas. They include help with the costs of school and university education, maintenance and childminding for single clergy who have dependent families, and the cost of removal and resettlement. There are also grants at times of bereavement, and, after retirement, with expenses such as heating, house maintenance and repairs.

If you or someone you know needs our help, please send for a leaflet which gives details of all our grants. And, if we cannot help, we may be able to suggest someone who can.

Founded 1655

On the other hand, if you are in a position to help us, we would be enormously grateful for a donation or bequest. That would enable us to help our clergy even more!

Corporation of the Sons of the Clergy
1 Dean Trench Street, Westminster, London SW1P 3HB
Tel. 020 7799 3696. *Reg. Charity 207736.*

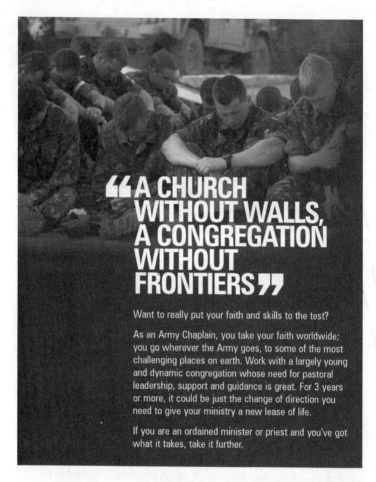

"A CHURCH WITHOUT WALLS, A CONGREGATION WITHOUT FRONTIERS"

Want to really put your faith and skills to the test?

As an Army Chaplain, you take your faith worldwide; you go wherever the Army goes, to some of the most challenging places on earth. Work with a largely young and dynamic congregation whose need for pastoral leadership, support and guidance is great. For 3 years or more, it could be just the change of direction you need to give your ministry a new lease of life.

If you are an ordained minister or priest and you've got what it takes, take it further.

Contact the Deputy Chaplain General, MOD Chaplains (A), Trenchard Lines, Upavon, Pewsey, Wiltshire. SN9 6BE

ARMY
CHAPLAINS

www.army.mod.uk
The Army is committed to Equal Opportunities.

First Sunday of Advent   1 December 2002
Principal Service   **The Best of Beginnings**
Isa. 64:1–9; Ps. 80:1–7, 17–19; 1 Cor. 1:3–9;
Mark 13:24–37

'Grace to you and peace from God our Father and the Lord Jesus Christ.'
1 Corinthians 1:3

Unmerited favour
What better way to begin a new year, than by accepting and rejoicing in the *grace* (unmerited favour) and *peace* of God? As we review the past year: what has gone right, what has gone wrong, where we have advanced in our spiritual journey, and where we have either trodden water or backslidden – the everlasting promise of divine grace and peace is still on offer. Thank God, *Someone* is constant, in this ever-changing world! We can surely echo the schoolboy's prayer: 'Lord, thank you for being you – 'cos if you weren't, we wouldn't half be in a mess!'

Ongoing grace and peace
From out of his infinite store, God is constantly making available *more* grace and *more* peace – for it seems to be part and parcel of the human condition, to need more as life advances. And however long we spend today, at the beginning of a new Church year, in looking back, we MUST also look forward. Our lives may be going through a dark patch just now, with a future that seems threatening and even hopeless – or we may currently be experiencing one of God's 'blissful moments', when things are going well – or we may just be emerging from a period of pain or stress, and feel drained of both physical and spiritual stamina. No matter our condition, God's grace and peace are there for the asking:

> *When you come to Jesus weary, broken-hearted,*
> *A Friend you'll find as gentle as a dove;*
> *Rest your tired and aching body, soul and spirit*
> *In the tender arms of everlasting love.*
>
> *For he's promised to be there for us, for ever,*
> *Just a breath, a sigh, a tearful prayer away,*
> *Bringing peace and love, restoring us for service,*
> *If only we will let him have his way.*

1

For those he loves, he never leaves abandoned,
Though days there are when everything goes wrong,
When we try to do our best, but lose direction,
And trouble stops us breaking into song.

'Come unto me, and I will give you respite!'
The promise is as sure as when 'twas made;
His grace and peace are there just for the asking,
As certain as his arms where we are laid.

My Jesus, Lord, I come to you in weakness,
Give me your grace to fight my whole life long.
I come to you in sorrow, give me joy, Lord;
I come to you in sickness, make me strong.

Help me to pray, and not to do things my way,
To ask and seek and knock upon your door;
For you have promised help, Lord, and I need it.
Give me a heart to pray and praise you more.
(This hymn can be sung to the tune 'Galway Bay')

'God is faithful'

God is faithful (v. 9), Paul assures the Corinthians – Christians who were, like us, struggling to keep faith themselves in a world entranced by glamour, immorality and self-indulgence. God is faithful, with a patience that is nothing short of phenomenal towards the struggling Christians of today. We can do nothing to earn his patience – but at times it seems we do everything to try it.

A new year

Can we try to make this year our best so far? Can we allow God to rule – really rule – in every aspect of our lives: to go his way, and not our own? Can we allow – in deed as in word – that he really does know best? It means taking a big, bold step into the unknown, but the first step is the biggest. Every time we give God best, he will respond with an assurance designed to make our next move easier. Being human, we can get cold feet; we can complicate life beyond endurance – but that's not God's problem.

Lord, I *intend* to lead a new life. I know your grace and peace are available to help me honour this intention. When other matters bid for my attention, nudge me, Lord, and remind me of your promise.

Suggested hymns
Hark! a thrilling voice is sounding; Lord, speak to me, that I may speak; The advent of our King; Thy way, not mine, O Lord

First Sunday of Advent *Second Service*
An Open Invitation Ps. 25; Isa. 1:1–20;
Matthew 21:1–13

'Come now, let us argue it out, says the Lord; though your sins are like scarlet, they shall be like snow; though they are red like crimson, they shall become like wool.' Isaiah 1:18

Arguing with God?
Well, the AV invites us to 'reason it out'. Either way, it's an invitation to get serious with God, to the extent that we involve him in the intricacies of our lives as though our lives depended upon it, which they do. But it is an arguing (reasoning) to be undertaken not for its own sake, but as a means of discerning God's will and then acting in accordance with that will: the best of New Year resolutions anyone can ever make.

Making a God-space
God is here, everywhere – in the rush-hour queues on the M25, or the crowded commuter train, or at the church bingo sessions on a Friday night. And he may very well choose such a busy situation in which to make his will known; but in general we need a quiet corner for the 'God-space' in which our failings can be brought before the Lord, and our situation argued out in order that he may go to work on us and lead us to an understanding of his plans: 'For surely I know the plans I have for you, says the Lord, plans for your welfare and not for harm, to give you a future with hope' (Jeremiah 29:11). There, in the quietness, wherever we make our God-space, God will (if we dare to ask him) show us more of ourselves. Unless we follow his reasoning (for who else knows what is in us, in the 'self' we may hide not only from

3

others but from ourselves), we shall not be able to work out what he has already worked into us, for his glory.

Who are we?
Two thousand years ago, one Man walked the earth whose life was so God-centred, so single-minded, so full of integrity and truth, that he could declare with justification: 'Whoever has seen me, has seen the Father' (John 14:9). 'The Father and I are one' (John 10:30). Yet his followers make life much more complicated: so often we present one person to the world, another to God – and where *is* the real 'me'? Do I know myself? We may, in fact, skirt round the issue: the person we show to others may suit us just fine; the one we show to God may be less easy to live with, because God being God has a habit of reminding us that he knows us better than we know ourselves: the time we drove through the red light . . . the under-charged bill we didn't query . . . the unfranked stamp we peeled off and used . . . *silly* little things? Hey, God reminds us, let's argue it out!

A dramatic colour change
When we have taken on board the fact that *every* sin is scarlet in God's eyes, but that he is waiting and willing to effect a dramatic colour change in our lives, from the guilt of scarlet to the innocence of pristine white – then our good *intentions* are well on the way to real implementation. As we argue ourselves before God, he will show us more of who he knows we are, and what he is wanting to make us, and what he knows we can be. Reasoning with God, coming into his presence with assurance and yet humility, is a way of learning more about ourselves and about him. And, judging by most conversations, the favourite subject of most of us is ourselves.

A tremendous ask
A tremendous ask, at the start of a year? More than that, it is the challenge of a lifetime. One day, perhaps, we shall see just how much hangs on the way we meet this challenge.

Thank God we still have time to meet it.

Suggested hymns
A charge to keep I have; Commit thou all thy griefs; Sleepers, wake! the watch cry pealeth; The Lord will come, and not be slow

4

Second Sunday of Advent   8 December 2002
Principal Service   **Against the Odds**   Isa. 40:1–11,
Ps. 85:1–2, 8–13; 2 Pet. 3:8–15a; Mark 1:1–8

'Finally, all of you, have unity of spirit, sympathy, love for one another,
a tender heart, and a humble mind.' 2 Peter 3:8

Contrary to nature?

Isn't it asking an awful lot – even too much – in the frenetic run-up
to Christmas, to follow Peter's advice? It's hard to bite back the
sharp retort, and to see instead the light of God's Spirit in the
other; hard to find time and effort to show sympathy, when we're
trying to fit three days into one; hard to break into our so-
important schedules, to show someone else we care; hard to hug
and kiss, when all we really want to do is tell them to get lost; hard
to check ourselves at every wrong step, and say, 'Lord, forgive'.

But this advice comes from one who knew the anguish of failing
to ask forgiveness quickly, of denying his Lord in his hour of need,
of putting his foot in it so often that his name in the gospels is a
by-word for impetuosity. If Peter could grow in God's 'grace and
knowledge' (2 Peter 3:18), there's hope even for us.

In communion

Living in communion with God is like living in community: we
are not alone for any length of time. We may believe we are – but
sooner or later God will disabuse us of that notion. Living in
community means that eventually our rough corners are smoothed
off – but sometimes only after a long, painful process of abrasion.
We come to realize that hitherto-cherished luxuries like privacy,
independence and self-assertiveness (though we may prefer to call
this individualism), must go. God is always here: we may claim
privacy from others, but not from him. He doesn't prevent us
deciding for ourselves, but he asks us to be dependent on him.
He has created us as individuals – so that in doing his will our
God-given names will identify us as his, in his Book of Life (Revelation 3:5, 6).

Laying down one's self

Isn't this turning the prevailing climate of the world's advice completely topsy-turvy (cf. Acts 17:6)? We deny ourselves, to discover
ourselves; more precisely, to discover our God-given mission.

How would we wish God to see us? Can we work towards this end? We can be certain others will notice the difference; we can be doubly sure that God will. And the more we check that unruly thought or word, the more we open the door for God to work mightily in our lives. Never let anyone catch you saying: 'Oh, I don't ask for mighty miracles! All I want is to get by without sinning!' No one has ever yet 'got by' without sinning: sin slams into every life. It's not the presence of sin that trips us up – it's the caving in to sin. And not to expect God to work mightily in our lives is more stupid than asking the Yangtse River to flow backwards. God is *almighty*. He doesn't work on any other scale. He thinks big. He acts big. Let's live by his standards, not ours.

A life of overcoming
As Christians, we're in big business – the overcoming business: overcoming disunity with unity, impatience with sympathy, hate with love, cruelty with tenderness, pride with humility. Soon we shall be worshipping again a little Child who showed us how to overcome larger obstacles than we shall ever have to face. He came with a simple message: 'Don't just learn what I teach; go and put it into practice!' (cf. Luke 10:37).

Well, now's our chance. We may not get another.

Suggested hymns
How firm a foundation; Judge eternal, throned in splendour; When a knight won his spurs; Ye servants of the Lord

Second Sunday of Advent *Second Service*
Holy Encouragement Ps. 40; 1 Ki. 22:1–28; Rom. 15:4–13
'For whatever was written in former days was written for our instruction, so that by steadfastness and by the encouragement of the scriptures we might have hope.' Romans 15:4

Love for the word
How much does the word of God mean to us? If the house was burning down and we could grab only one item, would it be the Bible? Do we carry a bible in the car, the pocket, the handbag? Or

have we made a bible out of something else – the Filofax, the laptop, the mobile phone? Watchman Nee, the great Chinese Christian preacher and teacher, used to read nineteen consecutive chapters of the New Testament daily: that was the whole of the New Testament every fortnight, along with a rigorous schedule of ministry. This dedication to study meant that when Nee was imprisoned for his faith, he had a wealth of scriptural encouragement already memorized beyond the reach of his communist guards.

Every day is 'Bible Sunday'

The Book of Common Prayer's collect for today, long observed as Bible Sunday, urges us to 'read, mark, learn and inwardly digest' God's holy word. We can, like Watchman Nee, make a Bible Sunday of every day, reading the Bible either to a set plan, or as the Spirit moves us – studying, memorizing, cross-referencing, discussing it with others, sharing its inspiration and message. God alone knows how desperately modern folk are in need of his word, though few of them would admit it. From John Wycliffe and William Tyndale, to J.B. Phillips and Dom Henry Wansbrough, scholars have devoted their lives (and on occasion lost them) in defence of the English Bible, until we have a wealth of versions from which to gain divine encouragement. Their work and dedication has given us a hope that in the words of God are spirit and life (John 6:63) for everyone – not merely for Greek, Latin or Hebrew scholars.

The availability of scripture

Tyndale and his ilk made the scriptures available to millions in the English-speaking world. Do we take their dedication and sacrifice for granted? If so, we have a problem that needs to be taken to God. If not, how are we, in turn, making the scriptures available to others? We hold, between the pages of Genesis and Revelation, a great responsibility. When Jesus was giving his last instructions to the men on whom his hopes for the Church rested, he didn't tell them to erect breathtakingly beautiful buildings – nor even to celebrate the eucharist every Sunday – but to 'go into all the world and proclaim the good news to the whole creation' (Mark 16:15), for the End of the world will come when every nation has been told (Matthew 24:14; Mark 13:10).

Well, how are we doing? The two thousand or so most widely

spoken languages now have the Bible (or at least part of it) – but this earth has over six thousand languages! The average of one new translation for every year since Christ ascended is not the most stunning of records. We have a lot of work to do.

Even this one, Lord?
So, what can *I* do? I can't speak any other language, or fly across the world, or backpack across China with Bibles to far-flung places. Perhaps not, but the ministry of *prayer* is available to us all: prayer each day, quality time, regular, dedicated prayer – for translators, missionaries, printers, carriers, preachers and teachers of the precious word. Never belittle the power of prayer, which can make the Internet seem outmoded in its scope.

A mountain to move? No, a whole range of mountains to get this world evangelized. Take it in prayer to God, who has undertaken to kick the 'im' from 'impossible' – and, while he's doing that, will give us all the encouragement we need to move those mountains.

Suggested hymns
God is working his purpose out; Hills of the North, rejoice; Lord, thy word abideth; On Jordan's bank the Baptist's cry

Third Sunday of Advent 15 December 2002
Principal Service **Sent from God** Isa. 61:1–4, 8–11; Ps. 126 or Canticle: Magnificat; 1 Thess. 5:16–24; John 1:6–8, 19–28
'There was a man sent from God, whose name was John.' John 1:6

Today's four-letter word!
SENT! John did not decide, out of the blue, to become an eccentric troglodyte in the desert, with a message almost no one wanted to hear or could understand. He was *sent* – by God, on a specific mission. The execution of his mission was more important than anyone's response to it. God knew, before John was born, that few would listen, and fewer still take up the challenge. But because of

John's preaching, no one would be able to say later that scripture had not been fulfilled (cf. Isaiah 40:3f.).

> *So send I you, to labour unrewarded,*
> *To serve unpaid, unloved, unsought, unknown;*
> *To bear rebuke, to suffer scorn and scoffing,*
> *So send I you, to toil for me alone.*

> *E. Margaret Clarkson*

What a contract!

Only the Almighty could formulate such a contract of employment! But then, only the Almighty can guarantee perpetual tenure of service. Many who sign up to God's contract will seek for an early release; just a few will accept his proffered grace to see it through. John the Baptist's life shows us that we cannot rely on physical means, nor human support. If we are to be of use to God, we need to let him supply the means. He is unlikely to go bankrupt or lose interest. But for our part, can we meet his conditions?

> *So send I you, to leave your life's ambition,*
> *To die to dear desire, self-will resign,*
> *To labour long, and love where men revile you,*
> *So send I you, to lose your life in mine.*

God's encouragement

Take heart, it's not all grit and grind! God's encouragement can leave the rest of the world standing. Only a sadist would call for unremitting suffering – and God is LOVE. Read the gospels, to see how the joy that Jesus kept in view sustained him through his earthly ministry: the love of his friends, the joy of bringing healing, wholeness and the good news of the kingdom to others; the gradual building up and coalescing of his mission team: 'I watched Satan fall from heaven like a flash of lightning!' he told the seventy, on their return *with joy* from their first mission (Luke 10:18, 17). When was the last time we took joy in the thought that our ministry was toppling the Devil off his pedestal?

The world's distractions

The world's distractions probably impact more at this time of year than at any other; pressures mount as budgets are stretched, the days are dark, winter's cold sets in, and everyone tries to cram a

9

week into half the time – for the modern Christmas is weighed down with extraneous busyness.

Watch it! Jesus warns, as he reminds us of the seed that was lost to success, because it was choked by growth inhibitors (cf. Luke 8:14).

A fine example
A man was sent from God, to prepare for the Saviour of the world. John's mission is our mission, too. If Christians don't prepare others for the Saviour's second coming, who will? And, since we have Christ's word that he will come when this earth has been given a worldwide chance, when every nation has been given the opportunity to hear and receive the gospel message – surely our mission is clear.

Like John, we have been *sent*.

Where are we going?

> So send I you, to hearts made hard by hatred,
> To eyes made blind because they will not see,
> To spend, tho' it be blood, to spend and spare not –
> So send I you, to taste of Calvary.

Suggested hymns
Be thou my vision; Go, tell it on the mountains; On Jordan's bank the Baptist's cry; We have a gospel to proclaim

Third Sunday of Advent   *Second Service*
Energized for Duty   Ps. 68:1–20; Mal. 3:1–4:4; Phil. 4:4–7

'But for you who revere my name the sun of righteousness shall rise, with healing in its wings. You shall go out leaping like calves from the stall.' Malachi 4:2

Inspired by joy
Confined to barracks during the long, cold winter, come the first spring sunshine, calves released from their stalls kick and prance with a superabundance of joy at tasting freedom at last. So Christians, brought out of the dark confines of sin and grinding slavery

to Satan, emerge into the fresh air of God's service with an energy that is supernatural, supercharged for duty. Like the little calves, we quickly discover that life in God's free air is not all warmth and sunshine; but the spiritual energy which God has invested in us is not dependent on physical factors. Let us remember this – on bad days as well as good.

Winged healing
We are not here to avail ourselves of precious oxygen for our own selfish benefit, but to bring to others from God an even greater healing than fresh air. The wings (rays) of Christ's glory penetrate atmosphere, flesh and mind, to heal where human medicine cannot reach: to heal the whole person, to fit us for duty and witness. This was the healing light that came to a world in a darkness more dreadful than night. That the world in general either took no notice, or actively opposed the light, made no impact: Jesus continued his ministry unmoved by opposition, not deflected by praise or blame from his purpose of saving the world. God asks for our allegiance – but if we deny it, his purposes will still go on. We are vital to his mission, in that our names are written in his Book of Life. But those names can be expunged, and there will then for ever be an accusing lacuna, a space unfilled by anyone else, for each of us is irreplaceable.

Mother love
As the calves revel in their sunny freedom, their mothers watch over them with affection tinged with concern for their welfare. So Christ enjoys our delight in his service, while giving us the tender love of a mother (Luke 13:34). We take up our cross – perhaps of sorrow, poverty, ridicule, sickness, misunderstanding or misrepresentation – yet God has undertaken not to overwhelm us with Angst (1 Corinthians 10:13). He is greater than the greatest trial – and in his strength we, too, shall leap over difficulties, with a greater, more powerful energy than even a calf released in the spring. Just as a mother watches over her offspring, to see that their impatience and enthusiasm do not run riot, so God is watchful that we don't wear ourselves out before our time. We may think we are exhausted – but no one whose body has been made 'a temple of the Holy Spirit' at baptism can exhaust the indwelling power. We may come to the end of ourselves, but not of God. His power still has a long way to go, when we are ready to call it a day.

Strength in joy

The more we take joy and delight in God's service, the greater
will be our power to serve – to preach, heal, teach and pray; to
worship, and to help and join with others in worshipping the Lord
who has brought us healing in his wings. Are you downhearted,
for one reason or another? Do you doubt at all the power of God?
Then remember this: Christmas is coming. God didn't *need* to give
us a reason to celebrate.

But, out of sheer love, he chose to.

We can negate this love that made the world, and died to save
it. But one day he may ask us to give a convincing reason for our
negation.

Suggested hymns

Give me oil in my lamp; O come, O come, Emmanuel; The Advent
of our King; The Church of God a Kingdom is

Fourth Sunday of Advent 22 December 2002
Principal Service **'Here Am I'** 2 Sam. 7:1–11, 16;
Canticle: Magnificat or Ps. 89:1–4, 19–26;
Rom. 16:25–27; Luke 1:26–38

*' "For nothing will be impossible with God." Then Mary said, "Here
am I, the servant of the Lord; let it be with me according to your word."
Then the angel departed from her.' Luke 1:37, 38*

Mission impossible?

Imagine it: you have just been told the impossible will happen,
and that you – a virgin – will conceive and bear a child. The fact
that he will be no ordinary child is subsumed under the sheer
impossibility of the conception anyway. The more we try to understand Mary's reactions to the angel's news, the more remarkable
she seems. Who else would have coped so well with such a com-
pound shock as to respond: 'Let it be with me according to your
word'? To what was this young girl committing herself? To
becoming *Theotokos*, Mother of God.

'Here am I'
Eight hundred or so years before, God had asked for a volunteer prophet, and Isaiah had risen to the challenge with 'Here am I; send me!' (Isaiah 6:8). Now it's Mary's turn, though Gabriel is not in the business of asking, rather *telling* Mary what she is to be, and what is to happen. The pace has quickened over the centuries: the time to which Isaiah had looked forward is now about to come to pass.

Time for action
So in our own lives a time of waiting and preparation sooner or later gives way to the fulfilling of dreams, the implementation of plans – and, perhaps gently, perhaps forcibly, events which had seemed to be a long way off, take shape. We may welcome them with Mary's equanimity – or they may take us by surprise. How flexible does the Lord find us, in his service? Are we willing to lay a cherished plan aside, for God's choice to take precedence? How do we cope, when the Lord nudges us out of a comfortable, long-established pattern? All the members at the centre of the Christmas story were to experience God changing their lives: Mary and Joseph, the shepherds, the Magi, Simeon and Anna – even Herod and the childless, grieving mothers of Bethlehem.

We do not know why these people, from a wide range of society and culture, were chosen by God: after all, the Saviour of the world could have come in a million other ways. That this particular way was chosen as God's best should give us much food for thought – yes, even while the preparations for a modern Christmas threaten to monopolize our lives.

Saying 'Yes' to God
Saying 'Yes' to God is no easier in today's world than it was two thousand years ago. There are so many ways of avoiding it. We don't need to give the Lord an outright denial: the lukewarmness of the Laodicean church (Revelation 3:16) has many modern counterparts. Advent is a good time to examine the state of our spiritual enthusiasm: is it at white-hot heat for God and the things of God, as it was when we first came to him? Or have we watered it down to a more conventional, convenient, easygoing, *insipid* Christianity? Or perhaps we *are* fervent, zealous, wholehearted? But do we put service for God before love for him? For example, one can attend ostensibly Christian meetings every night of the

week, at which the discussions include anything but God's worship, praise, prayer and adoration. Administration, expertise, management and their ilk are important, but only as the practical spin-offs from the spirituality of the Church. A praying church is a powerful church. This Christmas, let's set aside quality time for prayer to move us into the centre of God's will, where Mary so obviously was.

Suggested hymns
Come, thou long-expected Jesus; I, the Lord of sea and sky; Lo, he comes with clouds descending; The Advent of our King

Fourth Sunday of Advent *Second Service*
Why Has This Happened? Ps. 113[131];
Zech. 2:10–13; Luke 1:39–55

'And Elizabeth was filled with the Holy Spirit and exclaimed with a loud cry . . . "Why has this happened to me, that the mother of my Lord comes to me?"' Luke 1:41–43

Lord, Why?
The times we ask it! But in our case isn't it so often because something has gone *wrong*? Elizabeth's question was from a different standpoint: 'Why is it that such a wonderful thing has happened to me?' It didn't occur to her to take good news for granted. What patience the Lord must have with those who accept all that is good with an equanimity that borders on the nonchalant – yet who are quick to complain as soon as anything goes wrong! – who accept a bonus as their right, and blame God for everything else!

Wow! Of course we're not as bad as that (all the time) – but there are times when we come perilously close.

Full to the brim
Elizabeth had already enjoyed the miracle of conceiving in her old age; now she is filled to the brim with delight at Mary's news. God is being so generous! There is not a trace of envy that Mary's is the greater miracle. With Elizabeth's genuine humility and love, we can see how Mary would joy in staying with her to help for

the next three months. Goodness attracts goodness – which is doubtless why God chose these two women for such important roles.

Spirit-prompted
Note that it was God's Spirit working in and through Elizabeth that vocalized her joy. There is no justification in scripture for seeing the Holy Spirit as 'the strong, silent type' – strong, perhaps – but silent? No! Advisedly, Bishop Dudley-Smith has transliterated Luke 1:46 into: 'Unnumbered blessings, give my spirit voice.' It is the mission of the Spirit to let the light of God shine out from his people; to let the good news be broadcast through his people. If by any chance a Christian goes through life unrecognized as such, then that person has negated the title of Christian. With the Holy Spirit as our energizing, divine implantation, we cannot be 'Christians incognito' and yet retain integrity.

Never too late
'Oh, I can't expect things to improve now!' We might have even said this ourselves; but there should be no room for such hopelessness in a God-fearing, God-praising heart. Elizabeth, old as she was, had the courage and faith to accept great things from God. Whatever our situation, God reserves the right to ask us to accept improvement. The athlete at full stretch, on hearing the gun that signals his final lap, knows that if he 'kicks on', he can tap into strength and speed he thought were gone. The Lord who made us knows to the nth degree what we can do – which is almost certainly more than we think.

Two women
Though Christmas is almost upon us, can we take time in these days crammed with so much else, to consider the two women at the centre of the drama: one, old but still resiliently determined to delight in her walk with God – the other, young, unmarried, yet pregnant with the world's Saviour. See them together, and in their combined faith, trust, hope and love take heart that God is still offering to do great things for those who are his.

Suggested hymns
Amazing grace; Hark, the glad sound; Tell out, my soul, the greatness of the Lord; To the Name of our salvation

Christmas Eve (Tuesday)   24 December 2002
Morning Eucharist   **God Has Remembered**
2 Sam. 7:1–5, 8–11, 16; Ps. 89:2, 21–27; Acts 13:16–26;
Luke 1:67–79

'Thus [God] has shown the mercy promised to our ancestors, and has remembered his holy covenant.' Luke 1:72

A timely reminder?

How often do we – in the nicest way and with the best of intentions – give God a reminder in our prayers, when he seems to have been slow in answering our requests? – for all the world as if we believe God's memory isn't quite what it once was! Oh, Lord, we've blown it – yet again! And, yes, there are many times when God appears to have forgotten our so important, so imperative needs. But he always comes through with an answer (perhaps not the one we've been looking for) IN TIME – *his* time. Abraham waited for Isaac for twenty-five years; his descendants had waited for a Saviour for much longer; but the Saviour came, for God will always honour his promises – without being reminded.

The promises we make

As we celebrate the coming of the promised Saviour this Christmas, may we, too, review the promises we've made – to others, and to God. Have we kept them all, or are there some still outstanding? Christmas is a good time for remembrance and restitution. Fallible humans do make – and break – promises; but so long as God gives us the grace of time, we can make amends. For his part, he will fulfil all that he has promised – and no one has promised, or can promise, more than the Almighty. There are over seven thousand divine promises in the Bible. We can be confident that God will keep every one; but he will not keep those that *we* have made: we must take responsibility for our own promises, though the Lord will help us to keep them if we ask him.

Here he is!

Here today is the One who was promised! Why has he come? Because he was needed. To whom has he come? To all who will accept him. For how long has he come? For as long as it takes. Where is he now? In the hearts of his followers.

What a catechism for Christmas! But it is only in the proportion in which we see beyond the Child-in-the-manger, that we can realize the Christ-in-the-world; only as we identify him in our hearts, that we can share him with others; only as we take on board the urgency of his coming, that we can become white-hot with energy to evangelize the world.

Christ for the world
But no, it's too much to take in just now! With parties, entertainment, extra services, carols, and all the Christmas rush! Let's consider evangelizing the world some other time! To which God replies, as we look at the Child-in-the-manger: 'I made a covenant, to sustain this world until salvation has come. I have remembered this covenant – for you. This Child-in-the-manger will only come again when his good news has been spread worldwide. That was the promise he made, when he returned to heaven' (Matthew 24:14; Mark 13:10). Jesus is still remembering. Are we? How many folk are we reaching out to, who are once again celebrating a Christmas without Christ? If we ignore them, they will have a holiday without holiness – but we shall have a Christmas without challenge. The choice shines out at us, from the purity of the Christ-child's eyes.

'See,' says God, ever so gently but persistently, 'I have remembered!'

Suggested hymns
A great and mighty wonder; Earth was waiting, spent and restless; O Jesus, I have promised; There's a light upon the mountain

Christmas Eve *Evening Prayer* **All that We See**
Ps. 85; Zech. 2; Rev. 1:1–8
'The revelation of Jesus Christ, which God gave him to show his servants what must soon take place; he made it known by sending his angel to his servant John, who testified to the word of God and to the testimony of Jesus Christ, even to all that he saw.' Revelation 1:1, 2

John of Patmos

Does it seem strange to think about an old man on the little isle of Patmos, on Christmas Eve? Yet John, in a way, was also celebrating Christmas – for Jesus came to him in exile, as he had come in Galilee, with a vision, a message, a challenge and a hope. John was on Patmos as a punishment for witnessing to Christ; we are here today, also because we acknowledge Christ in our lives. As John, we are presented with the vision of the Child, the message of love, the challenge of witnessing, and the hope that our celebrations are a foretaste of greater things to come.

Christian in a pagan world

John's visions are thought to have been received around AD 95. The Domitian persecution of Christians (AD 81–96) was rife, and those who refused to worship the emperor were banished to quarry stone on Patmos. Perhaps John had been allowed 'time off' on 'the Lord's Day' (Revelation 1:10), and had retreated to a quiet place for prayer. Whatever the conditions, he was receptive to God's word: it was new, startling, and full of meaning for the seven church communities to whom John would later send copies (Revelation 2 and 3). As we come to worship this Christmas at our eucharists and carol services, we shall hear words so familiar that they may wash over us. May we resolve not to let them escape; for Jesus has told us, they 'are spirit and life' (John 6:63). Just now, they are encapsulated in a Baby – and each of us can hold a baby; surely, then, we can keep a firm hold on God's words.

Angels in a dark world

The Greek word *angelos* means 'messenger'. God used angels to deliver his messages at the first Christmas – to Zechariah, Mary, Joseph, the shepherds, the Magi ... just as he sent word by an angel to John on Patmos. But today angels are not redundant: as of old, they come in a variety of shapes, sizes and situations; and, as we Christians are called to be the messengers of the gospel to a largely pagan world, we, too, have angelic business. We are God's light in the world (Matthew 5:14). How are we shining? Will anyone this Christmas know the meaning of the season because of us?

Getting the word into print
John was told to 'write in a book' what he saw (Revelation 1:11), even as earlier prophets had been instructed (e.g. Habakkuk 2:2). Do we share God's written word with those whom we cannot contact face to face? Do we write it as a personal *aide memoire*? In China, where many Christians still do not have easy access to a Bible, portions of scripture are copied and shared – often across vast distances – with far-flung, remote hill communities.

The precious scriptures
The Cambridge cricketer-turned-missionary, C.T. Studd, would use his Bible so much, he needed a new copy every year. How much better was such enthusiasm than the lukewarmness that allows God's word to gather dust on a shelf! This Christmas, as we reflect on John's exile which gave us our Book of Revelation, may we also reflect that the best gift we can give is this same word of God.

Suggested hymns
It came upon the midnight clear; Joy to the world, the Lord is come; Of the Father's love begotten; When came in flesh the incarnate Word

Christmas Day (Wednesday)
25 December 2002   *Midnight or early Eucharist*
The True Light   Isa. 52:7–10; Ps. 98; Heb. 1:1–4[5–12]; John 1:1–14

'The true light, which enlightens everyone, was coming into the world.'
John 1:9

Light into darkness
There are Christians across the world who will be celebrating Christmas in bright sunshine, with temperatures higher than an English summer ever knows. Yet the Light that came to Bethlehem at Christmas, two millennia ago, went far beyond the brightest sun. But it was not a physical light – and most people, comfortably ensconced in a human, physical way of life, didn't notice it. The

Light of the world came without cataclysmic shock, fanfare or demonstration. Yet it has outlasted earthquake, war, pomp and circumstance, and continues to change lives and history with a resilience and mystery that puzzles non-believers.

The Light of Christ is stronger by far than the darkness of evil. Communism, fascism, Marxism – any -ism one cares to mention – has failed in the face of Christ's Light. Why? Because this Light is God himself: the energy, the force, that in the beginning brought order out of chaos, physical light from physical darkness, and life out of inertia. Because of its inherent, dynamic power, it could afford to come as it did – as a helpless, dependent Child. Yet for all its fragility, a Child that God would protect until his mission had been accomplished.

The force of Christ
This force, veiled as a Child today, meets us with no abatement of dynamic energy – for (unlike the shepherds) in the eyes of the Christ-Child we can see a simple horizontal and a vertical that crossed at Calvary; and at their crossing remains the *titulus*: 'Jesus of Nazareth'.

'This I have done for you – what are you now doing for me?'
Such is the force of the challenge that greets us in the joy of Christmas. It's not a joy that merely invites us to 'eat, drink and be merry' – but 'celebrate and witness'. You have joy today? Share it! You've met Christ today? Share him! You've heard his challenge? Do something about it! Yes, in the middle of all your Christmas 'arrangements', take Christ – the reason for the season – to someone else. When once the force of Christ has met up with a believer, life notches up into overdrive, other folk notice, mountains begin to move, the impossible becomes possible!

A real Christmas
In the realization that Christmas is not just about celebrating the birth of a child, comes real spiritual growth. We broaden our perception, widen our parameters – use a variety of descriptions – to flesh out our realization that the Child-in-the-manger is so much more than what he appears to much of the world: he is life, light and love: *this* is God's Christmas gift – for the whole world.

We can show this life, as the Holy Spirit in us energizes us for gospel service; we can show this light, by bringing Christ to homes and lives darkened by sin and ignorance of the things of God; and we can show this love by showing others we care.

We *can* – even at Christmas.

Suggested hymns
Hark! the herald angels sing; Love came down at Christmas; O come, all ye faithful; O little town of Bethlehem

Christmas Day   *In the day: Principal Service*
Let's Go Now!   Isa. 62:6–12; Ps. 97; Titus 3:4–7; Luke 2:[1–7]8–20

'When the angels had left them and gone into heaven, the shepherds said to one another, "Let us now go to Bethlehem and see this thing that has taken place, which the Lord has made known to us."' Luke 2:15

Stand not on the order, but go – now!
The thrill of the angelic message, the song of the heavenly choir, gave the shepherds confidence to leave their sheep and hurry into Bethlehem. We don't know how long they took to find the Child, in a town packed to the doors with more folk than it was built to accommodate – but we can be sure that, having given them the news, God would speed their progress. What energy would we expend, to act on what we believed God was saying today? Would our work, our daily commitment, take second place? Would we seek caveats, insurances and the like, before going beyond the point of no return for God?

If the shepherds had not been obedient to the message, God would doubtless have found someone else. For all we know, there may have been other angels, other recipients, who may or may not have responded positively; but the shepherds' reaction has been preserved by St Luke, as a challenge to all who would meet the Christ-Child this Christmas. We know our daily work will be waiting for our return – but while we worship the child, he will give us his present, his personal Christmas gift, for us to take out into the world. Jesus loves us for coming to greet him – but he has a heart large enough to love all those who either don't yet know him or don't want to know him. He could send legions of angels to evangelize these millions; instead, he has chosen us as his messengers. Let us pray that we take out from worship the message he wants us to share.

God's choice
In a Bethlehem crammed to the walls with home-grown residents as well as incomers, God chose to go out to the fields, where simple men were on watch with their sheep. It would not be the entrepreneurs of the town, keeping late hours to bolster their profits – nor yet travellers dog-tired and fast asleep after their journeys – who would be receptive to the news of the Saviour's birth; but working men, on night duty under the stars. One perhaps would have expected the news to come first to the priests at the local synagogue – or local government officers at Bethlehem's town hall . . . even as today, we here in church this morning may regard ourselves as prime messengers for Christ. Let us reflect that God may have many modern counterparts of the shepherds in view as prime messengers this Christmas.

God's way of working
God's way of working, as at the first Christmas, so often continues to be to entrust the humblest folk with his most important work! By the world's standards, it's a topsy-turvy method of operating – but it is the Almighty at his most magnificently unfair. If he chooses us for a particular work, it is not because of any virtue we possess, but because he can see in us a willingness to be used. Let us get rid of the notion that we have uniquely qualified ourselves for his purpose. Remember: by the normal recognized physical standards, Mary and Joseph had not even 'qualified' themselves to have a child.

Lord, please use me as and when you want – not invariably as I believe I ought to be used.

Suggested hymns
Christians, awake!; It came upon the midnight clear; Unto us a Boy is born; While shepherds watched their flocks

Christmas Day *Second Service*
The World's Saviour Ps. 8; Isa. 65:17–25; Phil. 2:5–11

'Therefore God also highly exalted him and gave him the name that is above every name, so that at the name of Jesus every knee should bend, in heaven and on earth and under the earth, and every tongue should confess that Jesus Christ is Lord, to the glory of God the Father.'
Philippians 2:9–11

The whole earth?
Salvation on a worldwide scale? St Paul sees it in even wider focus, including heaven and the underworld. As St Peter wrote, God does not want 'any to perish, but all to come to repentance' (2 Peter 3:9). Yet Jesus came as a child, to his own people who rejected him (John 1:11), and he returned to heaven, leaving the building of his Church in the hands of a few disciples. What a miracle, that this Church did not founder then and there! but that, two millennia on, it continues to grow! It teases the imagination out of thought, to attempt to visualize the redeemed hosts of heaven, and the (as yet) unsaved souls of hell: difficult enough to envisage the Church Militant here in earth among the millions of (as yet) unevangelized and unconverted.

Tell it out!
To acknowledge the Christ-Child as the Saviour of the world, without making any effort to share him and his gospel with the world, is to fail in our mission. On the first Christmas, it was the mission of Mary and Joseph to provide for the birth; the shepherds' mission to worship Jesus and then to spread the news; the Magi's mission to present their gifts and to take news of the Saviour back to their homeland.

What is our mission this Christmas, but to do likewise: to come to the manger; to worship and adore the world's Saviour; to present our gifts – the time and talents, the best of ourselves we have to offer – and then . . . ? For each of us, God will give unique opportunities to bring the Christmas message to others. If we did *nothing else* – went to no parties, decorated no trees, baked no cakes, roasted no turkeys . . . if the only work we did this Christmas was to share the gospel, would we not bring a smile to the face of God? It is very difficult to bring divine priorities to bear on a modern, commercialized Christmas – but it's not impossible.

Combustible energy

The world's celebration of Christmas – with its emphasis on 'holi-day' rather than 'holy day', its commercial hype beginning even before the summer is over, and its entrepreneurial fervour ensuring inflated prices for weeks beforehand, followed by a plethora of 'sales' – too often means that its self-generated combustible energy burns out before the true Christmas has begun. Christians tend to get swept along by the commercial currents, and the major-ity of carol and crib services are now held before 25 December.

It may be difficult for us to turn the tide, but it's not impossible. And the challenge to present Christ to the world doesn't end on Twelfth Night: it meets us every day of the year. Can we take time, this Christmas, to identify ourselves – as the Church Acquiescent, Compliant – or truly, divinely Militant here in earth?

Suggested hymns
Go, tell it on the mountain; On Christmas night all Christians sing; Silent night; What Child is this?

First Sunday of Christmas   29 December 2002
Principal Service   **Spirit-prompted**   Isa. 61:10–62:3; Ps. 148; Gal. 4:4–7; Luke 2:15–21

'And because you are children, God has sent the Spirit of his Son into our hearts, crying, "Abba! Father!" So you are no longer a slave but a child, and if a child then also an heir, through God.' Galatians 4:6, 7

SO!

SO we are now no longer grinding along through life with slave status, but walking tall in the power of God, as heirs to the king-dom of everlasting life! With this little word 'so', Paul emphasizes the reason for Jesus' coming: our salvation. We could not have saved ourselves: the initiative, chock-full of love, had to come from him. Even now, we are only children in the faith. We need the prompting of the Spirit to get in right standing every day with God. Of old, the prophets and righteous folk saw God as 'Almighty Lord Jehovah'. When Jesus came, he showed us a more intimate side of God: 'Call him "Father".' And after his ascension, as he had promised (John 14:26), his Spirit was for ever reminding preachers like St Paul: 'Call God "Father" (Abba)!' Like salvation, we could not cope with calling the Almighty by so intimate a name ourselves: but God's Spirit doesn't have the word 'impossible' in his vocabulary.

Walking tall
It would be tragic if Christians were to carry on as though we were still slaves: to give folk no inkling of our true status in God; to deny others the chance of seeing what the Lord is doing for us, in us, through us – and what he can do for them. He gives us his best. Only our best should be good enough for him. He gave his most cherished possession on that first Christmas. What are we bringing to him in return? We can love our neighbours fervently, and spend quality time in helping them; but our love for God should come before even this service for others. Once we have put God first, the other will follow. If we put others before God, we shall end up in a spiritual tangle, and it's hard to walk tall when one's tangled up!

Friends of Christ
Jesus could not have made God's abolition of our slavery clearer than when he told his disciples: 'I do not call you servants any longer . . . but I have called you friends' (John 15:15). Yet we must take account of his earlier words: 'You are my friends if you do what I command you' (John 15:14). We are no longer slaves, but we are under orders. We can 'go out free' (cf. Exodus 21:5; AV), if we choose – but if we do, we shall forfeit the friendship of Jesus and the privilege of calling God 'Father'. The beautiful paradox is that God's service is perfect freedom: freedom *not* to choose Satan's way.

A new man
Does it seem too good to be true? Does our past insist on rising up and accusing us, over and over again? Do we ever feel like the centurion who sent word to Jesus: 'Lord, I am not worthy to have you come under my roof' (Matthew 8:8)? Then just remember how Jesus responded to what faith the man did possess, and how he healed his servant. Remember, too, the 'purple past' of Paul – how he had victimized the earliest Christian believers prior to his conversion. The overpowering love of the Spirit working in him could afterwards encourage him to say: 'There is therefore now

no condemnation for those [including himself] who are in Christ Jesus' (Romans 8:1)!

Can we, as we worship the Christ-Child of Christmas, approach his manger – yes, with awe, wonder and humility, but also walking tall, in the full assurance that his love has given us a fresh start: as his friend, not his slave.

Suggested hymns
Child in the manger; Father God, I wonder how I managed to exist; Jesus, hope of every nation; Love came down at Christmas

First Sunday of Christmas   *Second Service*
Called for Service   Ps. 132; Isa. 35:1–10; Col. 1:9–20 or Luke 2:41–52

'For this reason, since the day we heard it, we have not ceased praying for you and asking that you may be filled with the knowledge of God's will in all spiritual wisdom and understanding, so that you may lead lives worthy of the Lord, fully pleasing to him, as you bear fruit in every good work and as you grow in the knowledge of God.' Colossians 1:9, 10

Job description
This is some job description! Does it make you quake in your shoes? Take heart – if God did not believe Christians could measure up to his standards, he would not have set them. We cannot come close to these heights in our own power – but in partnership with the indwelling Holy Spirit, yes, we can do it! When Paul told the Philippians, 'I can do all things through him who strengthens me' (Philippians 4:13), he wasn't being sinfully boastful, but was giving God the glory for working in and through him.

Not by might . . .
It's a power veiled in 'spiritual wisdom and understanding' (v. 9). Christians don't evangelize by force, but through the power of God's love. The further we press into the will of God, the more our wisdom and understanding develop (courtesy of the Holy Spirit), and the more God changes our lives for the better. We may not be conscious of the change – but others will notice it, and

be attracted to its source. And how do we press into God's will? With the determination and single-mindedness at the back of Paul's declaration to the Philippians: 'Forgetting what lies behind and straining forward to what lies ahead, I press on towards the goal for the prize of the heavenly call of God in Christ Jesus' (Philippians 3:13, 14). Paul had heard the call of God, and he was not going to heed any other. When once God has intervened in our lives (not necessarily in such a dramatic way as in Paul's Damascus Road experience), we, too, shall not wish to hear any other voice.

The Child's voice
His call at Christmas is the frail, yet insistent, voice of a Child: the same voice that called the shepherds and the Magi; the voice that, forty days after his birth, was to identify the Saviour of the world to Simeon and Anna, despite the daily temple crowd of worshippers, entrepreneurs and the busyness of offering of sacrifices. And unless we become as little children, frail yet insistent in our desire to know God better – his will and way and word – we shall not be much further forward in our spiritual journey when this Christmas season is over.

Knowing more
How has our knowledge of God advanced in the past year? If we cannot tell, then probably the progress has not been great. Where do we seek him? In his word, in worship, in a Bible group, in sharing with others, in private prayer? If we are completely open to his guiding, we have the opportunity of learning more of God in every circumstance and situation – every one!

Giving thanks
Giving thanks to God for guidance at every step keeps our heart open to his will. It allows him to show us more of himself. It also deflects us from navel-gazing. God may very well extend our self-knowledge, but that is not our reason for living: learning more about him very definitely is. We could do worse than follow Paul's example, and retreat for even a short time to a quiet place alone with God: 'When God, who had set me apart before I was born and called me through his grace, was pleased to reveal his Son to me, so that I might proclaim him among the Gentiles, I did not confer with any human being ... but I went away at once

27

into Arabia, and afterwards I returned to Damascus' (Galatians 1:16, 17).

Suggested hymns
God is working his purpose out; Immortal, invisible; Jesus, hope of every nation; Thou didst leave thy throne

Second Sunday of Christmas (*or* The Epiphany, if transferred from 6 January, q.v.)
5 January 2003   *Principal Service*   **The Only Son**
Jer. 31:7–14; Ps. 147:12–20; Eph. 1:3–14;
John 1:[1–9]10–18

'No one has ever seen God. It is God the only Son, who is close to the Father's heart, who has made him known.' John 1:18

Coming alongside
From birth to death *and beyond* Jesus, in coming alongside us in every situation we are likely to face (and even some that we, personally, are not), has made God known, has shown us what a God of love and compassion is like. We can study the gospels, and from first to last read 'God the Father' for 'God the Son'. We can read there how Jesus affirms this oneness: 'Whoever has seen me has seen the Father' (John 14:9). We can meditate on the beautiful Proper Preface for Trinity Sunday (*Book of Common Prayer*):

Who art one God, one Lord; not one only Person, but three Persons in one Substance. For that which we believe of the glory of the Father, the same we believe of the Son, and of the Holy Ghost, *without any difference or inequality.*

With the coming of Jesus, God is no longer unknown or unknowable.

True identity
Identity is very important. Without it, we create all sorts of problems for ourselves. And during his earthly ministry, Jesus repeatedly challenged people with his identity. At one point, the Jews tried to

stone him. Jesus rounded on them: 'Can you say that the one whom the Father has sanctified and sent into the world is blaspheming because I said, "I am God's Son"? If I am not doing the works of my Father, then do not believe me. But if I do them, even though you do not believe me, believe the works, so that you may know and understand that the Father is in me and I am in the Father' (John 10:36–38). On another occasion, he asked the disciples: 'Whom do men say that I the Son of Man am?' (Matthew 16:13; AV).

Who do *we* say that Jesus is? What is he to us, in our lives? How do we describe or show him to others? Well, perhaps it is easiest at Christmas: after all, everyone loves a baby. Yet we cannot approach the Christ-Child as did those who were closely involved in the first Christmas – for they didn't know the Man of Galilee, the Man on the Cross, nor the Resurrected and Ascended Christ. Jesus means so much *more* to us – doesn't he?

The 'Jesus walk'
But as we share Jesus with others, Christmas is a good place to start. God as Man did not invade the world by force (as he very easily could have done); he came in the most natural way possible; but the impact that his life – and death – made, continues to grow. We, too, can walk the Jesus way, ministering quietly and perhaps even thinking we are making little headway; but the seeds of even the lowliest ministry, with Christ at its heart, can eventually produce a rich harvest. No matter if we ourselves don't see the harvest; others will, and so will God. Giving him of our best each day, making the most of every opportunity he sends – this is walking the way Jesus walked, according to the gospel accounts: never rushing, never dawdling, always with the overriding purpose: to proclaim the good news of the kingdom.

St Paul had a word for it: we are *ambassadors* for Christ (2 Corinthians 5:20). We are not on this earth for any other reason. If we are at all doubtful as to whether our lives are showing Jesus, or ourselves and our own importance, to the world, it's not a bad exercise to reflect on how our obituary might read, were we to cross the Divide just now.

God willing, we still have time to amend the record!

Suggested hymns
Lord, who left the highest heaven; O little one sweet, O little one mild; Once in royal David's city; You laid aside your majesty

Second Sunday of Christmas *Second Service*
A Living Sacrifice Ps. 135; Isa. 46:3–13; Rom. 12:1–8

'I appeal to you therefore, brothers and sisters, by the mercies of God, to present your bodies as a living sacrifice, holy and acceptable to God, which is your spiritual worship.' Romans 12:1

Laying down our will

God has given us free will – probably the most exciting yet danger-ous of his gifts; are we, then, to relinquish it back to him? So Paul seems to say: a 'living sacrifice' is just that – letting God have his way, both when it's congenial to us and when it is not. Often by the way we rebel at laying down our will one would imagine that God is so sadistic and tyrannical, as always to demand the *worst*! Whereas our Father of love is willing, waiting, wanting to give us always his best! Even circumstances that seem fraught can develop into something beautiful for him (cf. Romans 8:28).

Service for God

We may not agonize too long over alternatives that are clear-cut, with God's way on the one hand, and the world's way on the other. But how about when several ways of serving God are pre-sented? How do we discern the right way? How can we be sure which decision will result in the greatest blessing – for us, for others, for God? Well, we can pray, and fast – even seek counsel of a proven Christian. But there will be times when we make the decision we believe to be best, and subsequently discover that one of the alternatives would have been better. We get a blessing – but, Oh, Lord, if only . . . ! And there we are, a bit further along God's learning curve; and each time he teaches us a bit more about how to divine his will.

Take it gently!

Remember how Jesus presented his own 'living sacrifice' – not only in the mighty act of Calvary, but little by little, right from the time of his miraculous conception, when he sacrificed his life of glory for the constrictions and restraints of human life. As his ministry developed, so the sacrifice grew: a misunderstanding here, the threat of stoning there; a betrayal, a denial, the torture . . . The sacrifice deepened, until it had accomplished the will of God. Ours is not a sacrifice on the same scale; there will never need to be a sacrifice to match our Lord's; but day by day, if we are open to God, he will ask us for a little more of the 'I and me and mine' that, until we knew Christ, seemed all-important.

Goodbye, self!

Someone has said that humility (being open to God) is not only thinking lowly of oneself, but not thinking of oneself at all. Paul puts his finger on it, at the end of our reading, when he says that one of God's gifts to us is compassion (Romans 12:8). What characterizes the compassionate, but cheerfulness? The person who has forgotten self, who is operating as a living sacrifice to God, is cheerful; there is no room in an unselfish heart for gloom. Even with the agony of Calvary before him, the author of Hebrews tells us that Jesus' *joy* kept him going (Hebrews 12:2). As Nehemiah had discovered centuries before, it's the 'joy of the Lord' that is our strength (Nehemiah 8:10). It gives us the unselfishness to show compassion to others, rather than looking for it from others to satisfy our self-interest.

> *Except I am moved with compassion,*
> *How dwelleth thy Spirit in me?*
> *In word and in deed,*
> *Burning love is my need;*
> *I know I can find this in thee.*

> *Albert W.T. Orsborn, 1886–1967*

Suggested hymns

God be in my head; Lord, who left the highest heaven; Love is his word; You laid aside your majesty

Eve of the Epiphany *Evening Prayer*
'I Am He' Pss 96, 97; Isa. 49:1–13; John 4:7–26

'The woman said to him, "I know that Messiah is coming (who is called Christ). When he comes, he will proclaim all things to us." Jesus said to her, "I am he, the one who is speaking to you."' John 4:25, 26

The Lord's patience

Patience (long-suffering, Galatians 5:22; AV) is a gift of the Holy Spirit, and is thus (divinely, theoretically) in each of us; but our practical application of it comes nowhere near the level of patience Jesus showed – with his disciples and with others he met, such as this Samaritan woman. She had imbibed the theory all right; she knew what was expected of the Messiah. Yet when he came and did tell her 'all things' (John 4:29; AV), when he even met her face to face, she did not recognize him! How often Jesus may have wondered: 'What will it take to get them to believe?' Well, he answered that question himself, in the parable of Dives and Lazarus: 'If they do not listen to Moses and the prophets, neither will they be convinced even if someone rises from the dead' (Luke 16:31). And how right he was!

The Sunday service

We can attend worship each Sunday, we can sing the truth, hear it read, share in the sermon, then pray about what we have heard – but we cannot *compel* anyone else to believe it! What will it take to effect a parochial, national, even worldwide revival? The sobering answer is: more prayer, more Christian energy, more seeking of the will of God, than is going on at present. Christ's second coming, according to the gospels (Matthew 24:14; Mark 13:10) is scheduled only when the whole world has had the chance to hear the gospel. How zealously are we looking and working towards this end? Folk are not going to receive and believe it *in toto* – but God is waiting until they have been given the opportunity of accepting it. Only Christians (like us) can give the world this chance: non-believers are not going to spend any time in getting the work under way.

Telling it true

Because Jesus made the most of his opportunities to evangelize, for instance, when the Samaritan woman came to the well she was encouraged to return to her community and broadcast the news: the first Christian missionary – a woman, and a Samaritan into the bargain! What should we have done, in Jesus' place? Gone to sleep until the disciples returned? Asked the woman for a drink, and left it there? When strangers join us for Sunday worship, how do we show Christ to them? Do we make them want to go and tell their friends they've found Jesus here? Do they come back? If not – why not? 'When a man is tired of London, he is tired of life,' said Dr Johnson. With even more reason, one can say: 'When we are so preoccupied with life, that we fail to notice God, there is no real life in us.' On this first Sunday of 2003, let us resolve not to try God's patience as do those with unseeing eyes and unhearing ears (cf. Matthew 13:15f.). God always keeps his lines of communication open; if we have our own receiver switched off, he is not to blame.

Encouraging response
At first sight, the Samaritan woman may not have seemed the world's most receptive example, especially as Jesus knew her shady past. But she quickly demonstrated a willingness to dialogue, and proved in the end a worthy missionary. Let us (who certainly don't know everything about anyone) not give up before we have explored the reason for any opportunity given by God. Once missed, it may not be repeated.

Suggested hymns
As with gladness men of old; Breathe on me, Breath of God; Give me oil in my lamp; The people that in darkness sat

The Epiphany   6 January   *Principal Service*
Overwhelmed with Joy   Isa. 60:1–6; Ps. 72:[1–9]10–15; Eph. 3:1–12; Matthew 2:1–12
'When they saw that the star had stopped, they were overwhelmed with joy.' Matthew 2:10

Mission accomplished
Journey's end, with mission accomplished, was surely ample cause for joy. These *literati* from the Orient had travelled with one eye on the road and the other on the star. They had met a ruler suffering from paranoia (v. 3) in Jerusalem, who seemed to know of a King but not of his whereabouts – but the star had led them to the object of the enterprise, so their joy could have full rein.

Today's Magi
As we gather round our Christmas cribs, with today's addition of
three kings with gifts (and often a red-robed camel, superciliously
observing the sheep outside the stable), what impact do they
make? What have these Magi to say to us today? They brought
costly gifts. How much does our love for Jesus mean? They
brought meaningful gifts, tailored to the recipient. Do we bring
Jesus our finest talents, our prime time – or just what is left at the
end of the day? They came a long way. How far do we go, or are
we prepared to go, in the service of our Lord? They asked for
nothing in return, save the privilege of kneeling in adoration before
the Child. Are we always asking Jesus for things? Are there times
when we simply take delight in being in his presence? Oh, don't
these Magi challenge us, in ways we may not feel like coping with,
so soon after the frenetic season of Christmas!

Revelation
It was enough – *amply* sufficient – for the Magi to worship the
Child, and then return to their homeland. That they were securely
in the will of God is seen by their obedience to God's message as
they slept, to return by a different route and so avoid Herod (v.
12). Do we take notice of the stuff that dreams are made of? We
should. God's messages today come in many ways, and dreams
still fall short of a purely medical, clinical diagnosis.

Overflowing joy
Some churches are cold, others nicely heated; some are large,
others small; some are 'high', while others are 'low'; yet none of
these criteria really matter. The crucial factor is: does the church
(i.e. the Christians in it) welcome newcomers, grow in fervour,
love each other and take great joy in witnessing for Christ? It has
been said that today's Christians are sadly lacking in the ability
to be joyful. Who, then, will ever be encouraged to come to Christ
through us? Who have we encouraged to come to worship in the
last year – or have we kept the joy of the Lord to ourselves? In
some countries there is still an official ban on Christian evangelizing; would there be a greater willingness to defy that law, were
such a thing operative in the Britain of 2003?

Time and effort

As we reflect on the time and effort expended by the Magi in their determination to seek and find Jesus, inevitably the contrast between them and the Jews is pointed up: while 'his own people' largely ignored him, or (as in the case of Herod) actively opposed him, Jesus attracted *literati* from a distant land. He was later to warn the Jews: 'Many will come from east and west and will eat with Abraham and Isaac and Jacob in the kingdom of heaven, while the heirs of the kingdom will be thrown into the outer darkness' (Matthew 8:11, 12).

With the Week of Prayer for Christian Unity not far away, can we become more aware of what Christians of other denominations, other countries, may be trying to tell us?

Suggested hymns

Brightest and best; Earth has many a noble city; O, worship the Lord in the beauty of holiness; The people that in darkness sat

The Epiphany *Second Service* Glory Revealed

Pss 98, 100; Baruch 4:36–5:9 or Isa. 60:1–9; John 2:1–11

'Jesus did this, the first of his signs, in Cana of Galilee, and revealed his glory; and his disciples believed in him.' John 2:11

Shining out

It was a glory that could not be hidden. Thirty or so years before, the shepherds and the Magi had been drawn to it; now, at Cana, light is beginning to dawn on the disciples, that in the carpenter's Son is a power and an energy not of this world. Jesus acted, and his glory shone out to such an extent, that it called forth belief from his disciples: not, St John implies, from everyone within sight and sound, but from those nearest to him in spirit.

Our spiritual impact

And we, as ambassadors for Christ: what impact for him are we making on others? Seeing us, hearing us, do they want to see and hear more? Are they encouraged to ask further about this power pack we seem to have within us? Does our life and witness point them to Christ? We are his present-day disciples – commissioned to spread his gospel whether we wear a clerical collar or not.

The right time?
Jesus seemed at first reluctant to begin the series of 'signs' which were to characterize his ministry, and to provoke not only wonderment and approval, but also criticism and animosity. Yet his mother, who had patiently waited for thirty years from his birth, for once disregarded his remonstrance, and virtually ordered the action to begin.

Is there a 'time' for us to notch up into a higher gear in our ministry? Unlike Jesus, who knew his timetable in advance, we live each moment only by the grace of God, kept by our Father in ignorance of everything that lies ahead. St Paul, faced naturally with the same situation, realized that to hang about waiting for 'the right time' was not the right way – for Timothy (to whom he was writing) or for us: 'I solemnly urge you: proclaim the message; be persistent whether the time is favourable or unfavourable' (2 Timothy 4:2).

Oh, holy Joe!
This isn't to say that God is in the business of recruiting a team of holy Joes who are so confoundedly earnest that they're a positive turn-off to those around them. Notice that this first miracle of Jesus took place at a celebration, and its effect was to prolong the jollity rather than curtail it. Whether it's on the golf links or at the garage; in the library or at a luncheon party; on holiday or at home – we can get the Lord's gospel out of our hearts into someone else's – if we choose.

Filial regard
We do not know how Jesus would have reacted, if the order given to the servants had come from anyone but Mary. He was thirty or so years old, but although he had obviously not been willing to make a public declaration of his power, he acquiesced with grace and rose to the occasion. Today, when some sons (and daughters) attain the so-called 'age of independence', obedience to their parents tends to wane. Jesus gives us a wonderful example of the honour due to our parents for as long as they (and we) live (cf. Exodus 20:12).

Father, I place into your hands; Jesus, good above all other; Songs of thankfulness and praise; The race that long in darkness pined

Baptism of Christ   (First Sunday of Epiphany)
12 January   *Principal Service*   Two Baptisms
Gen. 1:1–5; Ps. 29; Acts 19:1–7; Mark 1:4–11

'[John said], "I have baptized you with water; but he will baptize you with the Holy Spirit."' Mark 1:8

Acknowledged by Christ
The water-baptism of John was not to be eclipsed by the greater Spirit-baptism of Jesus. Our Lord underlines the importance of John's mission by offering himself for baptism by water; but John was open and humble in his insistence that he and his baptism were of lesser importance.

In water-baptism, our sins are symbolically washed away; we lose them (and nothing becomes them like the departing!). In Spirit-baptism, we gain something: we gain the divine implant of energy and power that will sustain and impel us in this life, and also see us across the Divide into the next. Such an understanding not only makes it clear which baptism is the greater, but also illustrates the need for both in the life of every Christian. To use a secular example: water-baptism is similar to the price for a ferry ticket; Spirit-baptism, to the boat that actually carries us from one shore to the other.

The need to be willing
It is surely significant that John is not on record as having taken his message into the heart of Jerusalem, or even into the country towns like Bethlehem and Nazareth. He seems to have concentrated his ministry in the wilderness regions and the Jordan valley. Folk came out from Jerusalem and the towns, to hear him; his *modus operandi* at least ensured a degree of motivation and commitment on the part of his hearers. Jesus, on the other hand, although spending some time in quiet places, seems to have exercised a fair

amount of his ministry in Jerusalem and towns such as Capernaum and Nazareth.

Surely this shows that there is scope for both forms of ministry. In our own time, we hear of evangelists in America, Korea and parts of Africa, drawing a million or more participants to Christian rallies, crusades or conventions; at the other end of the scale, some ministers spend most of their lives preaching to congregations of fewer than ten, in team or group ministries in rural England.

For our sakes

Strictly speaking, Jesus had no need to undergo John's water-baptism. The Son of God had no sin that needed washing away – symbolically or otherwise. But with voluntary humility he did it for our sakes: just as he washed his disciples' feet; just as he went to Calvary. His was a laying down of the will, so that we had an example to follow. Even John was nonplussed in the face of such humility, but he did as he was (oh, so gently) commanded to do, and baptized the Lord who stood before him. Let us keep this beautiful picture in mind, when folk try to tell us baptism is unnecessary or not for them. If the outward sign of God's cleansing from sin is not accepted, we may well query the presence of an inward desire to be cleansed.

Spirit-filled

When does 'baptism with the Spirit' take place? Many would say, in the sacrament of confirmation, which in the Eastern (Orthodox) Church occurs immediately after water-baptism, and in the Western Church usually some years later. Yet there are many in the nondenominational churches who take a less stereotyped view. Certainly, if a person is 'filled with the Spirit', others sit up and take notice, because things begin to happen: God's blessing is experienced, healings take place, some begin to praise 'in tongues' ... Even in strictly liturgical settings, we are finding God's Spirit is being manifested in ways undreamt of years ago. Let us, as this year 2003 advances, not be afraid to be open to what God is doing in our midst. He will then involve us more and more in his mighty work.

Suggested hymns
Be thou my vision; Filled with the Spirit's power; How sweet the
Name of Jesus sounds; O Breath of life, come sweeping

Baptism of Christ *Second Service*
What God Has Made Ps. 46[47]; Isa. 42:1–9;
Eph. 2:1–10

'For we are what he has made us, created in Christ Jesus for good works,
which God prepared beforehand to be our way of life.' Ephesians 2:10

Take no credit!
The world loves 'a self-made man', almost as much as he loves
himself; and the same is true of the feminine of the species. But
God says, 'Just remember, I made you – in the beginning, and
right on from there. I gave you what it's taken to get you where
you are today!' So give God the glory – and, if you can't, take a
long, hard look at where you veered off the track. God made us,
in the likeness of Jesus, for 'good works'; works which redound
to his glory, not ours. If you feel like a square peg in a round hole,
there is one answer; you are not where God has made you to be.
Take a long, hard look at where you veered off the track.

Forward planning
God has 'prepared beforehand' our way of life. It's here, somewhere; all we have to do is seek his will in finding it. Each of us
is an individual, and God doesn't categorize us into an 'A' or 'B'
stream; he has been to the trouble of planning a tailor-made path
through life for each and every one. Many, if not most, choose to
stream themselves, joining the easy flowing current along the
broad river to hell. It's an undemanding passage – no need to
make oneself ill over the question of sin, or forfeit time that could
be spent in riotous living, or going to church . . . A good, easy life
– until the end.

But we, with sin to confess, a life to live, a soul to save, and a
gospel to share . . . we have a much more exciting time, now and
in prospect! But all the way, in every circumstance, let's give God
the glory. Left to our own devices, we'd only make it to hell.

How surprising!

Isn't it often the case that when something has turned out right –
a terminally ill patient has been healed, or an impending disaster
has been averted, or a person has walked away from an accident
unscathed . . . we say: 'How amazing! Isn't medical science
wonderful! What a good thing the wind veered, or the rain came,
or the fog lifted! Wasn't (s)he lucky!'

Yes, even Christians do it! And then we wonder why God
doesn't work (more) miracles nowadays! We are what he has made
us. Oh, Lord, keep this truth always before us.

A daily review

Human memories being the fallible things they are, it does help
to have a daily review of what God is doing in our lives. Our
Father in heaven likes to be appreciated and thanked, even more
than do our earthly fathers. As this new year extends, can we
resolve to be more diligent in our gratitude for all he is doing for
us, and through us? And then he'll do some more.

His way, our way

One of our modern hymns runs:

> *There is only one God,*
> *There is only one King;*
> *There is only one Body,*
> *That is why we sing:*
> *Bind us together, Lord . . .*

> *Bob Gillman*

Following today's text, we could add: 'There is only one Way.'
But there isn't, is there? Not yet, at least. There is only one *true*
Way – and that is Jesus. But each of us comes to God in our own
way. If our way is the same as his, we make contact with him. If
it isn't, we don't. It is that simple. That is why regular daily prayer
is so vital – why regular daily study of the scriptures is so essential.
If we don't know (or ask) God's will, we shall not find his way.
To know his will and way, we need his word.

In the words of the Prayer Book collect for Advent 2 (Bible
Sunday), let us 'read, mark, learn and inwardly digest' his word
– and to him be all the glory.

Suggested hymns
Lord, thy word abideth; Spirit of God, unseen as the wind; Thy way, not mine, O Lord; To God be the glory

Second Sunday of Epiphany   19 January
Principal Service   **Following Our Leader**
1 Sam. 3:1–10[11–20]; Ps. 139:1–6, 13–18; Rev. 5:1–10; John 1:43–51

'The next day Jesus decided to go to Galilee. He found Philip and said to him, "Follow me".' John 1:43

Confounded by simplicity?
The call was so simple. Jesus had prepared no three-volume manual of instruction, no chunky Filofax. Just the simplest of commands, and Philip followed. Then, as we read on, we find that either Philip already has a good grasp of the old messianic prophecies, or that he quickly receives instruction, for it's not long before he in turn is finding Nathanael and encouraging him to come to Jesus. Philip doesn't hug his new-found privilege to himself.

The spread of the gospel
The Christian Church has not spread at a uniform pace over the last two thousand years. From the outset, growth has at times been very gradual (as in this reading today), at other times quite remarkable (as on the Day of Pentecost, Acts 2:41). So today, in a country parish in the English shires, an infant will be baptized; across in Korea, over a million will attend a single service. In some areas, the Church may seem to be treading water, or even losing ground, while in other parts it is growing at a rate of knots. But, viewing it on a worldwide scale, the Christian Church has not ceased to spread since its foundation: a tribute not so much to the individual Philips or Peters or Pauls, but to the grace of God working through them.

The nature of the challenge
What sort of challenge do we need to give of our best? Danger? Unpopularity? Privation? We can expect all these, if we answer the

call of Christ. Why, then, don't more people take up the challenge? Surely for the reason that called forth the sad observation of Jesus: 'If they do not listen to Moses and the prophets, neither will they be convinced even if someone rises from the dead' (Luke 16:31). Some simply don't want danger, unpopularity or privation – though they should know that they can expect some, if not all, of these anyway. Others believe that to be a Christian means they will have to 'give up' much of what they think makes life worth living. God never asks us to give up anything that will harm us. Yet others feel the invitation of Christ is so simple that there must be a catch in it somewhere.

Not by our might, but by God's free love
We can do nothing to earn the right to follow Christ – still less earn a ticket to eternal life. And this bothers some people, who feel uneasy about accepting a free gift. Surely we can tell such folk that though salvation is free, discipleship does not come cheaply. The Christian life is one of constant overcoming; as soon as one hurdle is behind us, another is in view. Yet the sting is taken out of the battle, in that God has made available all the resources we need to finish the course victoriously. Unlike a secular bank account, where we can draw out in excess of what we need (and run the risk of depleting our reserves), God gives us grace to meet the needs as they present themselves: and the Almighty stands in no danger of bankruptcy.

The first big step
The first step to Jesus is the biggest. That is not to say the road from then onwards gets easier all the way – but it takes a unique combination of courage and faith to 'declare for Christ', 'be born again', 'accept Christ' – there are many ways of describing it. Only when we have taken this step can we lead another towards following. And what do we say when they ask 'Why should I?' Surely we need to be prepared to give personal testimony; to say what Jesus means to us, how he brought us to the point of our decision, how he has helped us ever since. Remember St Peter's counsel: '*Always* be ready to make your defence to anyone who demands from you an account of the hope that is in you' (1 Peter 3:15).

Suggested hymns
I, the Lord of sea and sky; O Jesus, I have promised; Thy hand,
O God, has guided; Will you come and follow me?

Second Sunday of Epiphany   *Second Service*
Everlasting Light   Ps. 96; Isa. 60:9–22; Heb. 6:17–7:10
*'The sun shall no longer be your light by day, nor for brightness shall
the moon give light to you by night; but the Lord will be your everlasting
light, and your God will be your glory.' Isaiah 60:19*

To be the Lord's light
For good measure, Isaiah says again, in v. 20, 'The Lord will be your
everlasting light'. We can read more about the eternity to which
Isaiah was looking in St John's 'updated' account in Revelation
(especially 21:23; 22:5). It is beyond our comprehension to imagine
permanent 'daylight' stronger than the brightest sun, in the proportion that gold is superior to bronze, or bronze to wood (Isaiah
60:17), but God would not promise if it was not to be (cf. John 14:2).

The Lord's light that now is
Until our Transition, we have a veiled light – yet it is still God's
light, shining out of and through our lives, from the Holy Spirit
within us. Strong enough to lighten every person in the world (cf.
John 1:9), it can nevertheless be hidden indefinitely, if we choose
not to use it. We can, in fact, be so successful in smothering this
precious light that even our nearest and dearest receive no benefit
from it. Such smothering is simply sinful – but it can be done. We
don't even need to listen to Satan: merely by doing nothing, we
can so hide the Spirit's light that no one would guess we were
Christians. By that time, we'd be non-Christians anyway.

Our responsibility
When we consider that Satan has no power at all over the Holy
Spirit, our responsibility to spread rather than shade the Spirit's
light is all the greater. No one compels us to 'shine as lights in
the world to the glory of God our Father', as one of the Baptism
Service prayers used to say. The Spirit is the greatest yet often the
most under-used power pack in the world, his light and energy

needing to be kick-started by a combination of our faith and God's grace – and the latter is always on offer. One day we shall need to give account as to how we have worked with our Holy Spirit – or we may have to listen while he himself gives the evidence. There is still time to stack up a good case for the defence!

A blessed light
'Lord, make me a blessing to someone today!' is a good prayer to start any day – and it means our Holy Spirit has a willing partner to work with. There are countless ways in which God can use us as blessings, spreading his light and making the world a brighter place for others. It was Charles Dickens who once said that no life is wasted which has made life easier for someone else. St Paul had had the same idea, two thousand years before, when he wrote: 'Bear one another's burdens, and in this way you will fulfil the law of Christ' (Galatians 6:2). Lightening the load of another spreads God's light ever further. It can work in the opposite direction, too. Let us always remember to accept help and light from others in the Name of Jesus, with gratitude and grace – even though 'It is more blessed to give than to receive' (Acts 20:35)!

Living in the light
To step into a house that is polished and 'squeaky clean' can be uncomfortable, as we contrast it with the impedimenta stashed behind our curtains at home, or the bits hurriedly flicked under a rug as we hurried to answer the doorbell, or the windows we meant to clean yesterday, or . . . Perhaps, as the thought of everlasting light, in a new life where there may not be any carpets to sweep things under – perhaps as this thought takes hold and becomes ever stronger in our minds, we can resolve not to brush things under the carpets in the present life, literally or figuratively, but to prepare actively, positively to live as openly as we can in God's light.

Suggested hymns
Fill thou my life, O Lord my God; Lead, kindly Light; Light's abode, celestial Salem; Ye holy angels bright

Third Sunday of Epiphany   26 January
Principal Service   **A Blessed Invitation**

Gen. 14:17–20; Ps. 128; Rev. 19:6–10; John 2:1–11

'And the angel said to me, "Write this: Blessed are those who are invited to the marriage supper of the Lamb." And he said to me, "These are true words of God."' Revelation 19:9

God's revealed blessings
St John of Patmos records seven blessings in Revelation (1:3; 14:13; 16:15; 19:9; 20:6; 22:7, 14). In today's reading he emphasizes the validity of the blessing: these are words of God that carry veracity; we disbelieve them at our peril. Some readers of the Bible are tempted to be selective in accepting its truths. Are we really to believe God would be untrue to himself? If we believe the Bible is like no other book, and that its writers were divinely inspired, we are veering into the area of compromise if we question its veracity. John of Patmos did not set out to be obscure when he wrote about his visions – yet Revelation is perhaps the most difficult book in the Bible to understand. But the people for whom he wrote would have had the key to his symbolism, and would find it easier to interpret than do we at a distance of two millennia.

Persecution
Towards the end of Domitian's rule (AD 81–96), the cult of emperor worship was stringently enforced, capital punishment or exile being the price for non-compliance. Presumably John had refused to compromise his faith, and had been banished to Patmos to work in the stone quarries. Perhaps due to age or infirmity his guards allowed him some time off on 'the Lord's day' (Revelation 1:10), and he had retired to a cave or a quiet spot, to be alone with God.

The Lamb's guest list
'Blessed are those who are invited', for all its comfort, also sounds a warning: the heavenly banquet is by invitation only. There will inevitably be some who will not be asked: perhaps because they have rejected Christ, perhaps because they never knew him. 'Invited' also implies choice; even those who receive an invitation are not compelled to accept – inexplicable though a refusal of such an honour may be. As in the banquet of Jesus' parable (Matthew

45

22:1ff.), there could well be refusals – and an extension of the original guest list.

Celebration
God has never been in the business of 'all work and no play'; the Sabbath was a time for worship and recuperation; Jesus' first miracle took place at a wedding feast (John 2:1ff.); and now John is given a vision of the celebration planned in heaven. When we get there, we may be surprised at the exuberance of God's future planning. Are we psyching ourselves up for it now? There is no biblical justification for the notion that eternity will be spent in lying on beds of flowery ease – but thank God that so much points towards a busy time, but also with time for celebration!

Anticipation
Can we not realize that God is, in effect, saying: 'I'm giving you these glimpses of glory, to whet your spiritual appetite. I want you to thrill with anticipation at the thought of spending eternity with me!' Just as an earthly parent delights in seeing trustful anticipation in a child's eagerness to open a present, so God wants us to run our race with eagerness – for the JOY he has prepared for us. Let us look at the wonderful world he has made – and have complete confidence that no detail of eternity will have been left to chance. Do we order our present lives with such meticulous care? No, but at least we still have time to try a little harder, before the Great Transition.

> For when you call, O Lord, we know
> You'll always give us grace
> To answer willingly, and so
> Fill our allotted place.
> A trust we have, dear Lord, to prove,
> A gospel love to frame,
> A soul to save, a life to live,
> Eternity to claim.

Suggested hymns
Deck thyself, my soul, with gladness; I come with joy to meet my Lord; Lord Jesus Christ, invited guest and Saviour; We come as guests invited

Third Sunday of Epiphany *Second Service*
Godly Zeal Ps. 33; Jer. 3:21–4:2; Titus 2:1–8, 11–14

'. . . Jesus Christ. He it is who gave himself for us that he might redeem us from all iniquity and purify for himself a people of his own who are zealous for good deeds.' Titus 2:14

For us
Does the truth of this impact? As Jesus hung on the cross, we were on his mind. For the good that we leave undone, and the bad that we still do, by rights we should be hanging on that cross now. But because our plight touched the loving heart of God he sacrificed himself in our place, wiping our slate clean. After every confession we can get up and get on with living, because of what Love has given. In an ideal world, this thought would stop us in our tracks whenever Satan trundled some strife along – but we are far from being perfect, and, come the temptation, how often do we remember too late?

Good intention
'Zeal' is not a word in common parlance, more's the pity. As we produce more labour-saving devices we persuade ourselves we have more free time – so we end up in all sorts of physical, mental and spiritual contortions in our efforts to fill that 'extra' time. It is a zeal of sorts, but wouldn't life be less complicated if we were single-minded in our zeal for God? Well, let's be fair, we *are*, some of the time. But the world and its business claims the lion's share. Nowhere is this better seen than when Christians go on a retreat, even for one day. The security of routine is supposedly at a distance, yet one finds it at every turn. 'I am going to pray!' seems a ready-made invitation for worries and wandering thoughts to crowd out communion with God. 'I am going to read the Bible!' – the daily business is still there, competing for attention. 'I'm going for a walk, to meditate!' – still the daily timetable impacts. 'I am keeping this vow of silence for so many hours!' – but thoughts will not be silent. At the end of the day, we have either planned our business schedule for the rest of the week – or, more rarely, have just begun to glimpse the true meaning of communion with God. Concentrating the mind is one of the most difficult exercises we can undertake.

The mind of Christ
But it can be done. St Paul proved it can be done – but by the
time such focussed attention became the norm in his life
(1 Corinthians 2:16), he had served an apprenticeship of zealous
dedication and sacrifice. Recollection (as the old religious used to
call God-focus) doesn't come cheaply. We have to work at it. For
each of us, the focussing comes in different ways: we may (to
take the worst scenario first) receive a drastic medical diagnosis,
and resolve to make the most of our remaining time – for God.
We may become aware of our mortality by losing someone close
to us, and in realization that their harvest has been gathered
in, resolve to set about ensuring a good harvest of our own. We
may experience a merciful deliverance from misfortune of one
sort or another, and in gratitude resolve to give ourselves completely to God. We may see God working powerfully in another's
life, and decide to change something in our own life that is presently relegating God to second place. Or we may simply come
again to Calvary, kneel at the cross, and re-dedicate our lives to
Christ.

Whichever way God invites us to come closer to him, let's
respond with zeal – or not at all. God is not looking for 'half-and-
halfers' (cf. Revelation 3:15f.).

Suggested hymns
Fight the good fight; In the cross of Christ I glory; New every
morning is the love; Oh, the love of my Lord is the essence

Presentation of Christ in the Temple
(Candlemas)   2 February   *Principal Service*
Festival of Light   Mal. 3:1–5; Ps. 24:[1–6]7–10;
Heb. 2:14–18; Luke 2:22–40
*'When they had finished everything required by the law of the Lord, they
returned to Galilee, to their own town of Nazareth.' Luke 2:39*

After all that
After the splendour of the temple, the amazing meeting with
Simeon and Anna, the astounding words that in her Baby Mary

had 'a light for revelation to the Gentiles, and for glory to [the] people Israel' (Luke 2:32) . . . *after all that*, Mary and Joseph took the Child back home. Just as, on Christmas night, the shepherds, after the visitation from the angel host, after worshipping the Child in the manger . . . the shepherds had returned to their fields and their sheep. Just as, years later, after being transfigured in glory on the mountain, Jesus led his disciples back to the daily routine of the mission team. Just as, after the wonderful resurrection and glorious ascension of Christ, the disciples (as Jesus had directed) returned to Jerusalem to await the Paraclete.

No matter how long we have been on Cloud Nine, we, too, must return to the daily business of living.

An ancient festival
The origins of observing Candlemas are lost in history. Certainly by the sixth century it was well established. In the Eastern Orthodox Church it's generally called 'The Presentation of Christ in the Temple', while Western Catholics prefer 'The Purification of the Virgin', and Protestants have combined the titles (both taken from the *Nunc Dimittis*), though across the Christian world 'Candlemas' is becoming the best known.

Candlelight
In many churches today two bundles of candles will be blessed and lit: long, thick candles which will be used at services for the coming year, and small candles held by worshippers as the Litany of Candlemas is said or sung. The winter days may still be short, cold and dark, but the candles symbolize the Light of the World – a Light that, when our wax candles are extinguished, can still burn in our hearts, for us and for others.

A new start
In the vastness of the temple that day a couple stood quietly, while an old man took a Child in his arms and blessed him. Folk would be passing backwards and forwards, with barely a glance at the homely scene. Yet the little group marked a great turning point in history – Simeon, old and near the end of his life, represented an age that was also passing, an age when innocent animals were offered for the sins of the people. Jesus, the Child with all of history behind him as well as all of life to come, stood at the start of the new dispensation: a Light for a world emerging from

49

darkness; an upcoming Sacrifice – himself – not just for the sins of the Jews, but of the world.

Few though we are
And today we stand in that long, long line of those who have seen and bear witness to (in fact, who are part of) that Light of Candlemas; the Light that was to say plainly: 'YOU [too] are the light of the world' (Matthew 5:14). Like those at the centre of that Presentation in the Temple, we may be few in number, and are probably overlooked by much of the rest of the world. But we shall return home from worship today richer than when we came in, for we have been in the presence of the 'Light to lighten the Gentiles'. We may take the Candlemas Litany home; we may pray it every day, even several times a day; we may let its beautiful words roll around in our minds, and gain great benefit from them.

But unless we translate that benefit into actually sharing the Light of Christ's Candlemas with others, most of the benefit will be lost.

Suggested hymns
As pants the hart for cooling streams; I sing the Lord God's praises (*Celebration Hymnal*); The Light of Christ is come into the world; Ye servants of the Lord

Presentation of Christ in the Temple
Second Service   **Sign of Light**   Pss 122, 132; Hagg. 2:1–9; John 2:18–22
'The Jews then said to him, "What sign can you show us for doing this?"' John 2:18

Sign of Candlemas
The Jews had pretty well concentrated their expectations of the Messiah between close parameters: so close that they didn't recognize him when he came. Hopefully, we shall be able to identify his sign at Candlemas: the Light for the world, in a little candle flame. But how do we identify Jesus at other times? By the sparkle in someone's eye? By good news of one sort or another? By an answer to prayer? Each of us, if pressed, would probably come

up with a different answer. For example, William Holman Hunt, in a painting now recognized the world over, illustrated Revelation 3:20, where Jesus, lantern in hand, knocks at the door of a human heart which can only be opened to him from within. Christ came to earth, and for much of his ministry spent time knocking on heart-doors that remained closed to him and to all he was offering. Have things changed very much, in two thousand years?

After Candlemas?
Many Christians after today will forget the little candles they have held. Just a few will remember, will perhaps take home a Candlemas Litany. But how far will the Light of Candlemas go, in a world that in so many ways is still starved of the Light of Christ? Candlemas marks a turning point in the year. Many churches will have kept their Christmas cribs in place until today. But Candlemas draws a line under the Christmas season, and from today we look towards Easter. Yet before that great celebration comes Great Lent – Lent with its challenge, its special services, its ashing and Complines, its Stations and vigils. Individually and corporately, we shall all seek to draw closer to God.

Light out of darkness
Back there in Jerusalem, while most folk didn't notice, two people – Simeon and Anna – were so close to God and his will that they responded when Mary and Joseph brought in the Child Jesus. The general darkness of misapprehension of the Messiah was lightened by the faithful few. And today, if we look for it, the Light of Christ shines out at times from unlikely quarters, in unexpected ways. We have recently observed the Week of Prayer for Christian Unity – and we have God's word that his Light shines out brighter, the more Christians are united. Yet after that annual Week of Prayer, the ecumenical gatherings tend to tail off; we return to our churches and familiar circles, our traditional ways of working, worshipping and witnessing. And, yes, after Candlemas, our candles will be blown out, and most of the Litanies carefully stashed away, until next year. Can we, this time, be thoroughly uneconomical, and give all our Litanies away, for worshippers to take home and use in prayer?

A low profile

Fair enough, even after their amazing time in the temple that day, Mary and Joseph collected their things together and took Jesus back home to Nazareth. For the next thirty years or so, the little family kept what might be called today 'a low profile'. We, too, can keep a low profile – just so long as we are completely sure that's what God is wanting.

Suggested hymns

Jesus, stand among us; Lead, kindly Light; Thy way, not mine, O Lord; Ye who own the faith of Jesus

Fourth Sunday before Lent (Proper 1)
9 February   *Principal Service*
Divine Undertaking   Isa. 40:21–31; Ps. 147:1–11, 20c; 1 Cor. 9:16–23; Mark 1:29–39

'[Jesus] answered, "Let us go on to the neighbouring towns, so that I may proclaim the message there also; for that is what I came out to do."'
Mark 1:38

Without deviation

Folk call it 'being mobile', when what really is happening is that they are flitting from one pursuit to another without giving any their serious attention for long. No one could have been more open to challenge and opportunity than Jesus – but he differentiated between what came from God and what the Devil was trundling along. God's will is set between sufficiently wide parameters to give us an equally fulfilling and exciting life – but if we want to deviate and attend to the temptations of Satan, we can do it. God is not after automatons for eternity (how *dull* that would be!), but those who have chosen his way above the Devil's.

Eyes on the goal

Jesus, knowing the trauma of Calvary lay ahead, still kept his sights set on the further goal (Hebrews 12:2); and the fact that 'the joy that was set before him' more than compensated for Calvary, should inspire us with thrilling confidence in eternity. God can work mightily with those inspired to take delight in doing (and keeping to) his will, here on the proving ground.

Power unlimited

Had we owned the unlimited power that belonged to Jesus, would we have settled for an itinerant ministry covering such a small area of the ancient Middle East? Wouldn't we have had worldwide evangelistic yearnings? Would we have restricted our mission team to a small, nondescript 'standing committee' of rough-hewn, unlettered preachers? How do our criteria today shape up to those employed by Jesus? Perhaps God is trying to tell us that, after all, he does know best!

It was not that Jesus was a workaholic; he would accept invitations to dinner and other celebrations – so long as these did not conflict with his mission. He would cross racial and cultural boundaries, give women a status rare in first-century society, show a complete disregard for poverty or wealth – all in the pursuance of God's will; and all with absolute power to do otherwise. The sheer thoroughgoingness of his choice takes one's spiritual breath away.

Time and motion?

Were we to run a God-centred time and motion study on our lives, with similar criteria, what would we need to jettison? The sport that conflicts with Sunday worship? The engagement that takes us into a grey area of compromise? The practice condoned by modern society, yet at variance with Holy Writ? The letter we wanted to write – before our friend died? The words that slipped out before our temper cooled? Once Jesus has brought such a thought to our mind, he will nudge and prod, ever so gently, until we've done something about it. Giving Jesus such opportunity for manoeuvre in our lives also means that we are in a position to see God's will before Satan's. The Devil can only move in on us as far as God permits: that's why Satan is so frustrated. While God's will is timeless, the Devil's time is limited, and running out fast (Revelation 12:12). We can meet every sixty seconds' worth of time with the calm assurance that Jesus showed in his ministry, if we carry before us this great truth: in God's keeping we are on the winning side, 'being protected by the power of God through faith for a salvation ready to be revealed in the last time' (1 Peter 1:5).

Fourth Sunday before Lent   *Second Service*
God's Stars   Ps. 5; Num. 13:1–2, 27–33; Phil. 2:12–28

*'Do all things without murmuring and arguing, so that you may be
blameless and innocent, children of God without blemish in the midst of
a crooked and perverse generation, in which you shine like stars in the
world.' Philippians 2:14, 15*

Full-time duty
The stars don't stop shining when the sun rises. God's daylight
only outshines them. Similarly, we are to shine as brightly as we
can for as much as we can – but we need also to acknowledge
God's greater light, which at any time can and will eclipse our
lesser lights. If we light up ourselves, and turn the spotlight on to
our best points, does God get the glory? We all have fine attributes
– for God made us in his likeness – and it's very pleasant when
others see these before we point them out! But let's give God the
credit for them. 'You have a wonderful memory!' 'Thank you, yes,
God's been so generous with me!' 'How you've come through
such an ordeal is absolutely marvellous!' 'Thank you, but it's all
due to God!' If we practise turning all the compliments over to
the Lord, it will become a blessed habit. It's his light, not ours.

Crooked and perverse
What changes? Well, not much in this world. History's wheel
continues to revolve around the pattern of laws being given,
broken, repented of, re-instituted. We see it throughout the Old
Testament, and down to the present day. 'Lord, send a revival,
and let it begin with me!' has many voices, many languages. Perhaps we have even said it (or can begin to say it) ourselves.

Too much light?
What should we do with a Revival on our hands? Open up redundant churches? Print more service books? Hit Satan harder with
newborn vigour? How should we cope with all the extra light?

Wouldn't we all love to have these problems! Then let's get serious with God, and 'argue it out' (Isaiah 1:18). It can come, if we are willing to let God work out in us what he's already worked in (Philippians 2:12) – yes, probably in 'fear and trembling'. Surely this sin-darkened world can never have too much light: it's not our problem to overload the candle power – but it *is* our problem if we withhold what God has given us to give.

Spiritual stamina
To go on the offensive for Jesus takes stamina: the sort that took him into the temple court to whip the entrepreneurs, topple their *bureaux de change* and release their pigeons; or that led him to face up to the hypocritical grandees and call them names; or that could round on his best friends when they stepped out of line. Jesus never curried favour, never flattered, never compromised. Nor did he ever hurry or linger; at times he seemed to delay (as in the case of the raising of Lazarus), but this was only in order to work a greater miracle. His light outshone all others, because it was simply pure (1 John 1:5).

Each star shines as brightly as it can, with the intensity God gave it. Almost certainly, we are not shining as brightly as we could. This may be far removed from what we find convenient, yet the differences may be all that's standing between us and Revival.

Suggested hymns
Eternal Ruler of the ceaseless round; God's Spirit is in my heart; O Lord of every shining constellation; Shine, Jesus, shine!

Third Sunday before Lent (Proper 2)
(Septuagesima)   16 February
Principal Service   **Spiritual Athleticism**
2 Ki. 5:1–14; Ps. 30; 1 Cor. 9:24–27; Mark 1:40–45

'So I do not run aimlessly, nor do I box as though beating the air; but I punish my body and enslave it, so that after proclaiming to others I myself should not be disqualified.' 1 Corinthians 9:26, 27

Energy for God

Most of us are very selective in the energy we use: of necessity, some has to be expended in our daily work, or we should starve. If God's work *is* our daily work, done in his name and for his glory, that is fine. But how do we use what is left – of 'our time and our talents, our loftiest powers' (Charles Wesley)? Are we wasting any of our God-given energies on peripheral, even dangerous, pursuits? If we are uncertain, we cannot do better than study our Lord's own example. He went nowhere that God would not go, said nothing outside of God's will, ate and drank nothing that could compromise his mission.

Were Jesus here today, should we find him attending questionable films or bawdy entertainment – watching or listening to programmes that broke the Ten Commandments? Would we hear imprecations escaping his lips, or the *double entendre* that so often taints conversation? Would we catch him accepting food sold by those who sponsor alcohol, tobacco or the use of harmful chemicals – or whose profits are built on the exploitation of child labour, or the destruction of rain forests?

Shadow-boxing doesn't work

Shadow-boxing gives the other chap time and space to plan the winning punch. On a spiritual level, it's playing into Satan's hands. 'So, don't do it!' counsels St Paul (v. 26). His missionary work had taught him to get his blow in first – against immorality, pagan cults and magic of one sort or another. And, in his bold 'Appeal to Caesar' (Acts 25:11), he had pre-empted the Jews' machinations, opened the door for an extended ministry into Europe, and consolidated Christianity at the heart of the Empire. We may see injustice, and lie low hoping either that it will go away, or that someone else will do something about it. We may hear of the growth of a pagan cult, and decide not to speak out against it, in case we are accused of racial or religious bias. Let us remember that Jesus was the most religiously biased man who ever lived: biased totally, unreservedly, unselfconsciously, uncompromisingly, absolutely courageously and unselfishly – for God. And today, as never before, the Church (and the world) stands in need of those who, spiritually speaking, will enter the ring and go the full distance – for God. Doesn't the prospect of beating the living daylights out of Satan appeal? Then it should!

Punishing the body

St Paul knew what it was to work for God, 'whether the time is favourable or unfavourable' (2 Timothy 4:2) – when he felt good, and when his body felt like death warmed up. And he is so fervent on this point, his language is strong: the body needs to be flogged into submission to God's will, just as a slave (at least in his day) was often beaten into submission. Paul is not being squeamish here! We have become adept at pampering our bodies: warmth and good food are alluring, and hard physical exercise and training are more often undertaken as an antidote to overindulgence than as part of the normal Christian life.

Great Lent is not far ahead now. Perhaps we can initiate some physical/spiritual training – or augment what is already in our daily commitment. The 'Church Militant here in earth' needs top-flight troops – and now.

Suggested hymns
Captains of the saintly band; Conquering kings their titles take; Fight the good fight; Soldiers of Christ, arise

Third Sunday before Lent   *Second Service*
The Learning Curve   Ps. 6; Num. 20:2–13; Phil. 3:7–21

'I want to know Christ and the power of his resurrection and the sharing of his sufferings by becoming like him in his death, if somehow I may attain the resurrection from the dead.' Philippians 3:10–11

Not yet there

And Paul goes on to assure his readers that he is not yet at such a high point of knowledge. We can surely stand alongside him – for we, too, are still on the spiritual learning curve. The essence of the Christian challenge is its constant call to higher, greater, nobler understanding and fulfilment. Jesus went to Calvary and met death with all he had set out to do accomplished. God would not have *allowed* the Passion one second before it was due. We do not have (or we don't recognize) the same authority over our lives that Jesus had; we certainly do not have the capacity to see what is to come, as he could see; but Paul is encouraging us, by his own struggles, to work and prepare as well as we can for the point at which our learning curve ends, at death.

Shared suffering
Whatever form our sufferings take, we know that Jesus has already experienced them, and has taken away the sting of permanence that formerly applied. And, as his own sufferings (on our behalf) culminated in resurrection, we can have confidence in a similar outcome. The time to worry is not when Angst is screwing us up, but when everything's set fair (cf. Luke 6:26). If anyone could speak from experience of many forms of suffering, it was Paul (cf. 2 Corinthians 11:23ff.). Our troubles are not likely to exceed his.

Till death

> *Take up thy cross . . .*
> *Nor seek till death to lay it down.*
>
> C.W. Everest, 1814–1877

If at any time we need to look back in our lives, to learn some lesson from the past or to review our progress, we shall in all probability see the signs and remnants of past suffering. But we should never be able to see our particular cross: that should be constantly on our shoulders until the time of death. If it is lying somewhere back there along our path, it means in effect that we are currently making no progress. The Christian way is not a battle, but a campaign – and unless we have our cross with us we are no longer in the fight. Paul is a realist: he understands that his suffering is a means of spiritual progression, and so, with Christ always taking the strain, the heavy end of the Angst, he can bear it – until death.

Resurrection power
The power that got Jesus out of the sepulchre was sufficient to resurrect every Christian who wins the campaign on earth, every man, woman and child who 'will not be harmed by the second death' (Revelation 2:11; cf. 21:8). It's a power that will elevate us (in an as yet unknown way beyond the scope of physics) into eternity. It is as though God is saying: 'I am giving you glimpses of eternity in my word. I want you to thrill with anticipation about

it. Don't carry on living here as though eternity has nothing to do with you!'

Beyond thought?
As, with Paul, we contemplate such power, it may well tease the imagination beyond thought. Almost certainly, it will underline for us the frailty of that 'sealed' sepulchre of Good Friday evening. It should also clarify for us the instability, impermanence and inadequacy of the so-called 'power' of evil. We are, with Jesus, on the winning side. And the celebration after victory is already lined up and waiting.

Suggested hymns
Christian, seek not yet repose; How firm a foundation; Jesus shall reign, where'er the sun; Stand up, stand up for Jesus

Second Sunday before Lent (Sexagesima)
23 February   *Principal Service*
Head of the Church   Prov. 8:1, 22–31;
Ps. 104:24–35; Col. 1:15–20; John 1:1–14
'He is the head of the body, the church; he is the beginning, the firstborn from the dead, so that he might come to have first place in everything.'
Colossians 1:18

First place
First place in everything? In the complicated, fast-paced, sophisticated world of 2003? Yes, Jesus still claims the first place: in the world, the Church, our lives and our hearts. Anything less is compromise. If there is anything at which the world of today excels, it is compromise; we have honed it to a fine art. The challenge in today's text is: run a spiritual audit on your church, your life, your heart. If you discover any compromise there, get rid of it. Strong stuff! Can we do it? Have we the courage and the will to do it? Dare we *not* do it?

Media exposure
Media exposure has experienced something of an explosion in recent years; politicians and prominent (as well as some not so

prominent) people from many walks of life – Christians included – have been 'brought down' from their pedestals by a press who has found that exposés are what Joe Public will pay to read about or watch. Consciences are salved by claiming that washing dirty linen in public is all for the nation's good. Well, let us hope and pray that standards will rise – and more quickly than the media can force. In that case, the exposures may have been worthwhile.

The wheel of history

History's wheel, since the time of the earliest giving of laws, has moved in a predictable circle. Laws are drawn up, then gradually standards slip until the deterioration of morals forces a reform; new laws are given, and once more the imperceptible slide begins, until the next reform – and so it goes on. Christians are inevitably travelling in history's wheel – but we have the power of Christ within us, to keep us from sliding; the power to reform before reform is imperative; the power, each day, to check the slide before it becomes a helter-skelter to destruction; the power to say 'Yes' and 'No' in the *right* places. We can exercise this power or not; the choice is ours.

The Church Militant

Christ is the head of the Church Militant here in earth, as well as the Church Triumphant in heaven. But the earthly militancy of the Church is so often not confined to outward fighting against sin, but also to in-fighting – between denominations, over traditions, and much else. If only we paused more frequently to consider the picture we are presenting to the rest of the world, the Church might work harder for unity that she does at present.

Then they'll know we are Christians by our love . . .

Peter Scholtes

is not always the message that the Church puts out. Christ is, sadly, divided. Is the division inevitable, merely because it has been so since the earliest days of the Church? (cf., e.g., 1 Corinthians 11:18; Revelation 2:14f.). If, as individuals, we resolve to give Christ 'first place in everything' (Colossians 1:18), we can make a difference. If we are careful to put Christ first in whatever we read, eat, watch, say or write, we can surely make a difference.

Yes, we can. If only we will.

Suggested hymns
Christ is our cornerstone; Head of the Church Triumphant; King
of glory, King of peace; The Church's one foundation

Second Sunday before Lent   *Second Service*
Tormenting Satan   Ps. 65; Gen. 2:4b–25; Luke 8:22–35

*'When he saw Jesus, he fell down before him and shouted at the top of
his voice, "What have you to do with me, Jesus, Son of the Most High
God? I beg you, do not torment me."'* Luke 8:28

Exorcism
Why this protest from Satan? Because Jesus had ordered evil to
come out of the demon-possessed. When the crunch comes, and
Satan finds himself before Jesus, he squeals. Surely we can take
heart from this – yet so often we see only the *person* giving us
strife, and not the evil motivating from within. We fight the carrier,
not the perpetrator, the mouthpiece, not the heart and root of the
evil. Still less do we claim the power that Jesus has handed down
to us (e.g. Mark 16:17), and order the Devil to go somewhere else.
Or perhaps we believe Jesus didn't mean us, when he gave this
power to his followers? The acceptance of the Great Commission
(Mark 16:15) had not been taken on board by the theologians who
told William Carey, in the eighteenth century, that he was being
presumptuous in wanting to go to India as a preacher. Thank God,
Carey persevered, and became 'the Father of Modern Missions'.
Yet today, when thousands of minority languages and dialects are
still waiting for any portion of the Bible, other concerns – trade,
commerce, space investment and leisure – have secured the focus
of many instead.

Recognizing Christ
While many of his own people failed to recognize Jesus, Satan
had no such problem. And today the old Devil can still be streets
ahead of us in identifying Jesus in a situation. We need to be
aware of this challenge: that is why the difference between our
mere knowledge *about* Christ, and our really *knowing* Christ, is so
crucial. Satan knows as much, and arguably more; but he does
not know Christ as Saviour and Lord; he cannot tap into the power

of Christ, since he has no Holy Spirit indwelling and empowering him. Can we not keep this great truth always before us, that while we can rely on *Christ's* power, Satan has to make do with his own! If we only realized this more often, we should do and dare greater things; there are still many mountains to be moved, many 'impossible' things to be attempted for God, in the power and strength of Christ. Why don't we give Satan a harder run for his money?

Subservience of Satan
When faced with Jesus, Satan brought the demoniac to his knees, to beg. This demonstrates so clearly the great gap between the opposing strengths of these two spiritual powers. In the presence of Jesus, Satan will crawl and grovel and whine. Who in his right mind would want to tangle with such a coward? Paul tells Timothy: 'God did not give us a spirit of cowardice, but rather a spirit of power and of love and of self-discipline' [AV: 'a sound mind'] (2 Timothy 1:7).

> *Jesus, the Name high over all,*
> *In hell, or earth, or sky;*
> *Angels and men before it fall,*
> *And devils fear and fly . . .*
> *We have no other argument,*
> *We want no other plea;*
> *It is enough that Jesus died,*
> *And that he died for me.*
>
> Charles Wesley

We can choose to ignore Satan. That merely gives him a breathing space. Or we can pitch against him with the white-hot intensity shown by our Lord and preachers of the ilk of Paul – for every soul that conquers before the first death will not have to face the second. We have Christ's own word for it (Revelation 2:11; 20:15; 21:8).

Suggested hymns
At the Name of Jesus; In the Cross of Christ I glory; Jesus, the Name high over all; We sing the praise of him who died

Sunday next before Lent (Quinquagesima)
2 March   *Principal Service*   Divine Heights
2 Ki. 2:1–12; Ps. 50:1–6; 2 Cor. 4:3–6; Mark 9:2–9

'As they were coming down the mountain, he ordered them to tell no one about what they had seen, until after the Son of Man had risen from the dead.' Mark 9:9

Mission impossible?
How would we have felt, in such a situation, having just come through an awe-inspiring transfiguration experience, and then being ordered to keep quiet about it until something even more incredible and seemingly impossible had happened? Why, God, do you work in such strange ways?

We may think life is complicated, at the human level – and so it is. But in our systems and examinations, our bureaucracy and government, we are dealing with statistics and levels set by our peers. As soon as God intervenes at a higher, divine level, we can be knocked out of kilter. Often it is tragedy, particularly death, that brings us up short; but there are also times (such as the disciples in our gospel reading had experienced on the mountain) when the glory of God also stops us in our tracks. We may call it 'a window into heaven', 'a wonderful sunrise/set', 'a miraculous birth' (perhaps against all odds), 'a wonderful deliverance'. We may even persuade ourselves that we have had a hand in it. But whatever the situation, there is (however briefly) impacted on us the realization that *Someone* is working at a higher level in our lives.

Prolonging the bliss
We may feel that this Higher Power is working against us: in fact, each of us at some point in our life has surely cried, in varying degrees of anguish: 'Oh, God, WHY? But, like Peter and the others on the mount, God also gives us times of glory. And, like Peter & Co., we think (if we don't actually say it): 'Lord, please extend this bliss a bit longer!' We may read these transfiguration verses often, and in spirit briefly enjoy that wonderful experience; but the times when God deals with us personally are in his timing, at his command. We cannot engineer them. Their very unexpectedness is all part of the mystery.

Working into God

Some of the old monks believed that if they gazed long enough and hard enough at a crucifix, the wounds of Jesus would appear on their own bodies. Well, in a very few cases (notably St Francis, St Veronica Giuliani and Padre Pio) the stigmata did appear – not because these saintly souls willed them, but as an entirely unexpected (and quite embarrassing) phenomenon.

Today we carry the wounds of Christ: in the crosses we bear, the trials we encounter, the sorrows, anguish and struggles that are integral parts of the Christian's way to God. Yet we also have our transfiguration experiences, our times of divine uplift, which are sent to encourage us to keep on keeping on. They are surely glimpses into the next stage of life: it is as though God is saying: 'See what I have in store for you! The victory will be worth all the effort! The best is yet to be!'

Investment for the future

Like the disciples, we probably don't realize the value of the experience until later – perhaps much later. Especially if, like them, we are very soon afterwards brought back to reality with a bump. But there is a difference: daily life itself may seem the same when we return to it – but we are not. We have met up with the super-life, the super-dimension. Having been in the presence of God, we re-connect with normality as super-energized, re-invigorated, Spirit-filled Christians. This revived state is a secret between ourselves and God. We can keep it so, if we choose, and the rest of the world will not notice anything different, and will never know where we have been. Or, as God gives us opportunity we can share what we have learned, and so extend the investment our Lord has made.

The world is seriously deprived of good news.

Suggested hymns

In days of old on Sinai; 'Tis good, Lord, to be here; When all thy mercies, O my God; Ye watchers and ye holy ones

Sunday next before Lent *Second Service*
It's True! Ps. 2[99]; 1 Ki. 19:1–16; 2 Peter 1:16–21

'For we did not follow cleverly devised myths when we made known to you the power and coming of our Lord Jesus Christ, but we had been eyewitnesses of his majesty.' 2 Peter 1:16

Personal testimony

That the author of 2 Peter was not writing specifically to Jews may be inferred from his reference to the myth of Ahikar (2 Peter 2:22), and also by this verse. 'Cleverly devised myths' were rampant in the first-century pagan communities: Egyptian and Greek mystery cults and practices would meet the early Christian missionaries at every turn. We know that St Paul, on reaching Athens, took advantage of the device used by the Greeks to worship the nameless, unknown god, by declaring to them his real identity: 'The God who made the world.' . . . 'This I proclaim to you' (Acts 17:23, 24). Similarly, our author today declares: 'We made known to you . . . Jesus.' There is no cleverness, no deviation, no dark hidden *gnosis*; the writer, with the value of personal testimony on his side, can afford to be simple. Two thousand years later, is our own personal testimony of Christ equally simple, or do we complicate our message by well-meaning obfuscation that perplexes rather than points our friends to Christ?

Knowing Jesus

Even the Devil knows about Jesus – but it takes a Christian to *know* him. Our book knowledge, in so far as it comes through the word of God, is fine; but it is our personal testimony of the daily working of Christ, the experiencing of Christ in our lives, that gives our witness the true depth of sincerity, and allows us to say: 'This is the truth; Jesus means this . . . has done this . . . for me; and what he has done for me, he can do for you.'

Beware!

There are even more 'cleverly devised myths' around today than in the first century: the occult has many forms, which spell destruction to the soul who takes them up. No less than the author of Ephesians, Christians today struggle 'not against enemies of blood and flesh, but against the rulers, against the authorities, against the cosmic powers of this present darkness, against the spiritual forces of evil in the heavenly places' (Ephesians 6:12). Satan is a devil of many parts, but his cunningly devised myths have one common denominator: exclusivity, the knowledge that those outside do not and cannot have. By contrast, the gospel of Jesus is one of openness and light; what had been hidden is now to be revealed; what had been whispered is now to be shouted from the housetops; what had begun in Galilee is now to be taken worldwide. The commission has been in operation for two thousand years, and is to run until it has been accomplished (Matthew 24:14; Mark 13:10). Exclusive only in the truth that Jesus is the only way to the Father (John 14:6), the gospel's inclusivity spans the world (Mark 16:15). He is the King. Our author today bears personal witness to his majesty.

Settling for less

It has always been tempting to take the easier way of Satan, the cleverly devised myth that promises esoteric benefits. But by the time the initiate has worked through the stages of 'perfecting', it comes as a dreadful anticlimax to reach the much acclaimed pinnacle, only to find oneself shrouded in a miasma of unfulfilled, vague hints of what may be to come if one relies on one's efforts or imagination. Such is the Devil's emptiness, that by this time the candidate has been so hoodwinked that to back out of the cult will either mean losing face, or will destroy his prospect of material advancement.

> *From the Devil's deviations,*
> *From the power of darkest myth,*
> *From the knowledge that destroys,*
> *Good Lord, deliver us.*

Suggested hymns

Guide me, O thou great Redeemer; Put your hand in the hand of the Man of Galilee; This is the Truth sent from above; Thou art the Way

Ash Wednesday   5 March   *Principal Service*

For God's Eyes Only   Josh. 2:1–2, 12–17 or
Isa. 58:1–12; Ps. 51:1–17; 2 Cor. 5:20b–6:10;
Matthew 6:1–6, 16–21 or John 8:1–11

*'[Jesus said] "Beware of practising your piety before others in order to
be seen by them; for then you have no reward from your Father in
heaven."' Matthew 6:1*

A great challenge

Are giving, praying and fasting not the hallmarks of religion? No,
says Jesus, keep them as a secret between you and God. The rest
of the world does not need to know. The things to share with others
are the fruits of the Spirit: love, joy, peace, patience, kindness,
generosity, faithfulness, gentleness and self-control (Galatians 5:22,
23). We cannot stop the rich giving ostentatiously; we may even
have taken part in large publicized prayer marathons, or supported those who have felt constrained to lose weight in aid of a
good cause. Are these things bad *per se*? If we take the words of
Jesus at face value, publicity of this kind is not what God is looking
for. In an age where PR impacts on virtually every facet of life,
this presents the Christian with a great challenge.

Between ourselves and God

'Humility,' said Dr Billy Graham once, 'is not just thinking lowly
of oneself; it's not thinking of oneself at all.' Giving with a fanfare
of trumpets may do the Church some good, and no doubt will
boost our 'feel-good factor' into the bargain; but, says Jesus, this
good is not God's *best*. The rich, ostentatious givers were not
praised as much as the widow who brought all she had and gave
it quietly (Mark 12:41ff.).

The Pharisee who swaggered into the temple and made the
rafters ring with his pride did not find favour with God, while
the tax collector who made far less noise got the ear of the
Almighty (Luke 18:9ff.). And those who fasted as a PR exercise
(in our gospel reading) were not on the same wavelength as, for
example, St Paul, who aligned his fasting with such rigours as
sleeplessness, inanition, cold and nakedness (2 Corinthians 11:27).
PR exercises are not the stuff of which true saints are made.

As others see us

The challenge of the gospel is to present Jesus, not ourselves, to the world – and, since we can't do this from the remote isolation of a desert island, or behind the locked doors and solid walls of seclusion, it needs to be in our normal, daily life. The disciples, though they would have given much to be allowed to remain wrapped in glory on the transfiguration mount, were led back to terra firma by their Lord. And even though Jesus knew what a fraught ministry his friends would have after he had left them and ascended, he still prayed: 'I am not asking you to take them out of the world, but I ask you to protect them from the evil one' (John 17:15). On the occasions like this when Jesus prayed openly, it was for his friends' benefit, not his own.

It can be hard to receive scorn, criticism and judgement from a world that believes we are mean, unchristian and pampering ourselves, if our giving, praying and fasting is carried out in accordance with the 'Jesus method'. But when we reach the Pearly Gates, it will be God's judgement that matters. The world's evaluation will not come into the equation.

No reward?

Turning religion into an ego-boosting exercise does not merely merit lukewarm response from God, but no reward at all. On one occasion Jesus warned his friends about those who may look pious and act piously: 'Not everyone who says to me, 'Lord, Lord', will enter the kingdom of heaven, but only one who does the will of my Father in heaven' (Matthew 7:21).

On this first day of Lent, may we examine not only the Christianity we let the world see, but also (and much more importantly) that which is a secret between ourselves and God.

Suggested hymns

Forty days and forty nights; Lord, teach us how to pray aright; Not my brother, nor my sister; Prayer is the soul's sincere desire

Ash Wednesday   *Second Service*
The Other Son   Ps. 102; Isa. 1:10–18; Luke 15:11–32

'"For all these years I have been working like a slave for you ..." Then the father said to him, "Son, you are always with me, and all that is mine is yours."' Luke 15:29, 31

Not the prodigal!
Don't we invariably home in on the son who sowed his wild oats, repented, returned and was welcomed back into the father's arms? But, on this first day of Great Lent, let's take time to consider the other fellow: the dull, boring one who had not pulled up any trees, nor painted the town red ... Hadn't he been taken for granted? Well, he thought he had.

Perhaps he had entertained notions of having a knees-up once in a while, but apparently he'd never got around to doing it – until, that is, all the stops were being pulled out for the reprobate. And then he saw red!

Where are we?
We are there somewhere – in the father, or one or other of the boys; perhaps a bit of us is in each one. Who hasn't jogged along in a comfortable rut, until someone else wins a fortune, or goes on a fabulous holiday, or updates the car, computer or caravan? The shock jerks us into thinking: 'If not, why not? Why can't I?'

Jesus teaches that WE ARE NOT TO MIND.

That is the simple message. In ancient times, God couched it rather more formally: 'Thou shalt not covet' (Exodus 20:17; AV). Whether it's good fortune, wealth, beauty, preference, physical qualities – whatever, we are not to wish for what anyone else has got, is doing, or is receiving. When Peter wanted to mind someone else's business, he was lovingly but firmly rebuked by Jesus (John 21:22).

And so it was with the father in our reading. Lovingly but firmly he assured his aggrieved son that he was cherished, his loyalty and devotion were certainly not taken for granted, and – as the elder son – he stood to inherit everything. The father could not be blamed if the son had not previously asked for a party.

Does God know?

But this does prompt the question. If either out of shyness or doubt we don't ask God for what we want (or think we need, or believe is our due), we should not blame him if he does not give it to us. 'Ask, and it will be given to you,' Jesus tells us (Matthew 7:1). Inference: if you don't ask, you needn't expect to receive.

The father in the parable was no thought reader. He couldn't have known all that was in the elder son's mind, as day by day the lad went about his work. But God does know our thoughts – yet still he requires us to put in a formal request. Why? One answer may be that once we have gone to the trouble of doing that, he knows we are really serious about the matter.

The supreme encourager

It's known as encouragement – God's way, not the world's. The world's method is to persuade us to get what we want, and let others go hang. God's way is to give us space to love and to be loved; to work, and not to look for comparable recompence, but to accept the magnificently unfair odds in which God deals; to mind our own business and bear our own cross, not being triumphant if we think we are doing better than someone else, or being aggrieved if the boot is on the other foot.

It means not being critical of others, whatever they may have, or do, or say. We are on business, to present Jesus to the world. That should be a full-time job, with no opportunity left for meddling in other folks' business or picking holes in their lives – but caring for them in love, rejoicing when they do well, and encouraging them when they are down.

We shall not measure up to these ideals all the time – but let's see how far we can get during Lent, for a start.

Suggested hymns

Be thou my vision; Christian, seek not yet repose; O Jesus, I have promised; Stand up, stand up for Jesus

First Sunday of Lent   9 March
Principal Service   **Desert Warfare**   Gen. 9:8–17;
Ps. 25:1–10; 1 Pet. 3:18–22; Mark 1:9–15

'And the Spirit immediately drove [Jesus] out into the wilderness. He was in the wilderness for forty days, tempted by Satan; and he was with the wild beasts; and the angels waited on him.' Mark 1:12, 13

The first stage
This was the first stage of a war that was to end in victory on Easter morning. Jesus and Satan meet and clash on the physical plane: first, on the body's need for food, then on the question of prestige, and finally one-to-one: the elevation of devil worship (cf. Matthew 3; Luke 3). Pandering to the body opens the door to worldly recognition, which in turn prepares one for compromise with Satanism (which currently operates under a variety of names including the occult, mysticism, astrology, magic and witchcraft).

The 'wild beasts' ensured the physical privacy of Jesus; he faced Satan's temptations without human support of family or friends – but God's angels were there to give him all the spiritual support at heaven's command.

Compelled by love
Of the three synoptic accounts of the temptation, only Mark's (probably the earliest) has the Spirit *driving* Jesus into the wilderness. Did he have a choice? Not really, for he had put his hand to the plough, and for the joy set before him he would not turn back. Can the Spirit act similarly with us? Certainly he can. Are there not times when, looking back, we think: 'How did I come to go there, to do that, to say that . . . ?' And if we are honest it is borne upon us that *we* did not go, do or say whatever it was, of our own volition. Perhaps, in fact, God acts in such a way because if he didn't, we might never get around to doing it! But when we have lost the capacity to acknowledge the Spirit's moving in our lives, we need to get serious with God, and back on track quickly.

On Calvary, Jesus was battling with Satan on a stage where we shall never be called upon to be; he was fighting to save the world from eternal damnation. We can walk the Via Dolorosa with him, but we cannot experience the full trauma. By contrast, we can empathize with his wilderness temptations to a much greater degree. Who has not felt the need for food outweighing more important considerations? Or been tempted to bask in the lime-light, just a little? Or scanned a horoscope, or watched a pro-gramme where the occult was being portrayed as 'a bit of harmless fun'? There is no sin in running up against such temptations; they are part and parcel of everyday life. The sin is not remembering in time to send them packing, with a piece (or two) of God's armour from his holy word. Jesus put it to good use every time he was tempted.

Every time. Message received?

Angelic backup
God is no respecter of persons. So do we think he would provide angelic reinforcements for Jesus and not for us? They are here NOW, legions of angels. Unseen, unheard (most of the time), they go to work on our behalf – and we probably don't recognize more than a tiny fraction of the dangers they avert, or the temptations from which they shield us.

Divine example
The magnanimity and humility that God showed in accepting the necessity of experiencing temptation for us, leaves us floundering; it's beyond human comprehension. Take a look at the world, outer space and the planets, stars and constellations, and try to under-stand that the Lord of All humbled himself – for us.

But we can surely believe that he was showing us that it is so possible to defeat Satan that those whom Jesus has invested with his Spirit can do it as well. God knows we can. And so does Satan – but, being a liar and the father of lies, he'll try to persuade us otherwise.

Let's resolve, this Lent, to take a leaf out of Jesus' book, and to knock Satan down with God's word in the manner that Jesus did. Decisively. Deliberately. Definitively.

We can. Yes, we really can. It's much more positive than merely giving up chocolate.

Suggested hymns
Christian, seek not yet repose; Fight the good fight; Filled with the Spirit's power; Lord, in this thy mercy's day

First Sunday of Lent *Second Service*
Obeying God Ps. 119:17–32; Gen. 2:15–17; 3:1–7;
Rom. 5:12–19 or Luke 13:31–35

*'For just as by the one man's disobedience the many were made sinners,
so by the one man's obedience the many will be made righteous.' Romans
5:19*

Obedient to death
The sheer obedience of Jesus is shattering. He did not come to do
his own will, but the will of the Father who had sent him. And
he was obedient to death, even death on a cross. Yet he was no
namby-pamby, incapable of thinking for himself. He could stand
up to Herod ('that fox'), to the Pharisees and Sadducees – and,
most significantly, to Satan. He could castigate his own disciples
when they were slow to respond, or showed a lack of faith. But
in it all, he never lost sight of his mission.

It's of no avail to protest that our world is harder to live in than
that of first-century Palestine. We are not, thank God, sitting under
an army of occupation. We have neither poverty nor sickness to the
extent that the ancient world suffered from them. We are not struggling against an established religion unsympathetic to our own.

But we, like the early disciples and Jesus, have to contend with
animosity, apathy, indifference, idolatry, luxury and too much
leisure. The underlying problems are the same, once one has
peeled off the wrappings of modernity.

Obedient to Life
Life with a capital L. This is the message of Paul in Romans 5.
One man, Adam, had messed things up. One Man, Jesus, restored
the eternal equilibrium. The cost of Calvary was not just astro-
nomical: it was much, much higher. Its selflessness takes one's
breath away. But we are not to drift into a daze of wonderment,
blissful and satisfying though that may be – for the challenge of
Christ's obedience meets us squarely between the eyes:

> *This I have done for you;*
> *What are you doing for me?*

We need not waste valuable energy in trying to count the
number of souls we have pointed to Jesus. Have we been obedient

in the exercising of our ministry? When we have received the prompting of God, have we been obedient to it?

Perhaps there is something God is trying to tell us just now. Perhaps he has been attempting to get our full attention for some time. Are we going to be obedient to his nudging? Or are we going to pretend to be busy with something else?

Looking back, we may identify a point in our lives where perhaps we made a decision that has since proved wrong – or, at any rate, second-best. If God has recalled the moment for us, it may be that he is giving us another chance to be obedient.

The innocent suffer, the guilty are saved
Such was the seriousness of Adam's sin, it made mankind guilty; otherwise innocent, men and women were 'infected' with sin. The ghastliness of this is appalling – and the Devil presided over the mess with satanic satisfaction.

On the other hand, when Jesus came to cancel out that sin by his own vicarious death, the otherwise guilty down to the End of Time were saved. Through no merit or virtue of our own, we were cleansed from a sin that we had been guilty of through no direct crime of our own.

The most expensive free gift!
Salvation may be free, but discipleship is expensive. In accepting the first, we take on the obligations of the second. Only a few make it. The rest settle for the easy way and tread the broad highway to hell. There's a lot more elbow room on the road to heaven – and it's uphill all the way – but glory's there at the other end.

Suggested hymns
Children of the heavenly King; God is working his purpose out; Inspired by love and anger; Lead us, heavenly Father, lead us

Second Sunday of Lent 16 March

Principal Service **My Followers** Gen. 17:1–7, 15–16;
Ps. 22:23–31; Rom 4:13–25; Mark 8:31–38

'[*Jesus*] *called the crowd with his disciples and said to them, "If any want to become my followers, let them deny themselves and take up their cross and follow me."* ' *Mark 8:34*

Following after Jesus

The Lord who in his life showed complete obedience to his Father, calls for a similar obedience from us. We hear people talking about 'taking control of their lives'; go-getters, they are, and sometimes don't mind how many others they walk over, while they're taking control. This is not the way of Jesus. We are to follow, while he leads. He is to be in the driving seat, all the way to heaven. If we have any other ideas, we are not bearing the weight of our cross, but have shifted it on to someone else – or have simply grounded it and walked away.

Not roses all the way

The 'name it and claim it' lobby, who see the Christian life as a bed of roses on earth and an even rosier future Hereafter, don't preach sermons on our text today. They see the true Christian way as happy, healthy and hugely prosperous – and if these benefits don't manifest themselves in a person's life, the explanation is often that prayer has not been sufficiently earnest, or there is unforgiven sin, or an inadequately earnest desire for the good things. But this is not justified by the teaching of Jesus. Yes, he does say: 'Ask, and it will be given you' (Matthew 7:7); but if we don't ask for the right things, we cannot expect them; and it's surely wrong to ask for an easy ride. Our Lord is not so sadistic as to make our lives unadulterated misery, but his own obedience to God's will involved pain as well as joy, tears as well as triumphs. He did not suffer more than anyone before or since just so that we could ride to heaven on flowery beds of ease. He suffered to give us a passport to eternity that, after the struggle on earth, heaven could be reached without us having to take in hell on the way.

Our vade mecum in the Beatitudes
If the Beatitudes are to be negated by an easy life on earth, Jesus was wasting his time in teaching them.

Blessed are the poor in spirit . . .
. . . those who mourn . . .
. . . the meek . . .
. . . those who hunger and thirst after righteousness . . .
. . . those who are persecuted . . .

Our 'cross' is in the experiencing of these, and in the power of the Spirit converting the experience into something beautiful for God.

Some of the saints of old went further, in their desire for a richer experience of suffering, and inflicted self-mortification in a variety of ways, from sleeping on beds of nails, to wearing hair shirts, cutting off their noses, or walking barefoot in the snow. Their motives may have been of the best – but Jesus did not teach such extremes. We can surely bear a sufficiently heavy cross in today's world without adding to the gospel teaching any excesses of our own making. To 'deny ourselves' is not to punish the body – which is a temple of the Holy Spirit – but to mould our will in line with the will of God.

The little voice inside
It is all too easy to become less proficient, less sensitive, in attending to the promptings of the Spirit's little voice inside. If we miss his early warning, and allow a temptation to take hold, our spiritual hearing becomes progressively worse. Lent is a good time to devote more attention to the dynamic power pack inside us. What is he trying to say? When did we last deliberately make an effort, in our busy schedules, to listen to him?

Listening out for the Holy Spirit is one of the best ways of denying ourselves and taking up our cross. But, be warned: the Holy Spirit can surprise us by what he says, how he acts, and who he causes us to meet!

Suggested hymns
In the Cross of Christ I glory; Led by the Spirit's power; Spirit of the living God, fall afresh on me; Take up thy cross, the Saviour said

Second Sunday of Lent   *Second Service*
No Place Like Home   Ps. 135; Gen. 12:1–9;
Heb. 11:1–3, 8–16

'They confessed that they were strangers and foreigners on the earth, for people who speak in this way make it clear that they are seeking a homeland.' Hebrews 11:13, 14

A-journeying

> *This world is not my home,*
> *I'm just a-journeying through;*
> *My treasure is laid up*
> *Somewhere beyond the blue.*
> *My Saviour beckons me,*
> *From heaven's open door,*
> *And I can't feel at home*
> *In this world any more.*
>
> > *G.R. Timms*

Jesus had no settled home, and he called his followers to leave theirs. Through the centuries since, some have denied themselves a home and become 'strangers and foreigners', tramping the world for Christ. But most of us like to put down roots, plant our little gardens, join the local church, the golf club, the Association of this, and the Fellowship of that . . . Well, it would be an unsettled and unsettling world, if everyone was on the move, wouldn't it?

Yet if we were all on the move for Christ, world evangelization would move into a higher gear.

The Homeland

How often are our thoughts centered on our final destination, our eternal Homeland? For most of the time we organize and plan for this present life, as though we were going to live here for ever. Death, when it comes, is seen as being 'too soon', an interruption of our long-range schemes, instead of the culmination of our preparations for eternity. We bend our energies into amassing a decent, if not generous, bank balance. We spend valuable time in assessing the best long-term provisions for retirement. When will we realize that it does not matter how much or how little we leave, so long as we can leave it without regret when the call comes to go to the Homeland?

Breaking new ground

Once Paul had been converted the compulsion was on him to preach, and as the urge to travel further afield took hold, he wrote to the Christians in Rome: 'I make it my ambition to proclaim the good news, not where Christ has already been named, so that I do not build on someone else's foundation' (Romans 15:20). Yet his ministry combined the best of both forms, for he spent three years in Ephesus (Acts 20:31), and at least two years in the capital when eventually his Appeal to Caesar engineered a passage to Rome (Acts 28:30). After every conversion, there needs to be follow-up discipling; the first is no more important than the second, but each complements the other. A mammoth crusade can see hundreds coming to Christ – but if the subsequent discipling and teaching falls short, many of the newly converted will drift away.

On the home ground

Today's reading is a challenge to every church community, large or small, as we look at the way new members are sought, encouraged and discipled; how far outreach has developed from our church; and how flexible we are in our approach to spreading the gospel among the converted and non-converted alike.

Are we a church that points members to what we can give them here – or how we can prepare them for their eternal Homeland? How is our involvement with other churches? What do we do together? If this world is not our home, what does that say about our parochialism?

Sometimes taking a look beyond the churchyard boundaries puts the parish into a new perspective. We may even wonder what our Lord would say about it, if he were to walk into Evensong with us today.

Suggested hymns

A Man there lived in Galilee; Lord, her watch thy Church is keeping; Tell out, my soul, the greatness of the Lord; There is a land of pure delight

Third Sunday of Lent 23 March
Principal Service **The New Order** Ex. 20:1–17;
Ps. 19; 1 Cor. 1:18–25; John 2:13–22

'The Jews then said, "This temple has been under construction for forty-six years, and will you raise it up in three days?"' John 2:20

According to custom
Quite possibly, in the extensive re-building of Herod's magnificent temple extra provision had been made to facilitate the burgeoning enterprise that Jesus had just convincingly attacked: the selling of animals for sacrifice, and the *bureaux de change* that enabled various currencies to be converted into legal temple tender. These practices had acquired the patina of respectability. Sacrifices and tribute were part and parcel of temple life, if not (strictly speaking) of temple worship. That an increasing number of folk made a good living out of the business was only to be expected in such an enterprise. They needed space and facilities – why not all under one roof? So ran the argument, and the result was that a large part of the temple resembled a market-place more than a place of prayer. Yet, taken as a whole, it all contributed to the worship of God – didn't it?

NO! thundered Jesus, and went to work with his whip on the money-changers' tables and the piles of cages with little doves.

Lure of tradition
It can be tempting to invest tradition with justification simply because it has existed for so long. Jesus was attacking more than the extension of lawful provision into entrepreneurial gain. He was heralding the new order, in which animal sacrifice would play no part; and in which the temple, for all its magnificence, would be transformed into the lives of many people who in their bodies would 'en-temple' the Holy Spirit.

Can we blame the temple hierarchs for not comprehending all this?

The Church today
Theology may tell us that the Church today exists in the hearts of believers, that the Holy Spirit is 'en-templed' there, rather than in stones and mortar. But we worship for the most part in these man-made temples, and a significant proportion of our resources

is directed towards their maintenance – much as it was in first-century Palestine. Most of us feel comfortable worshipping every Sunday in the context of stained glass and candles. And our church buildings send out the message that Christ has a visible presence in our city, town or village. Certainly, if Jesus came today he would find many of our churches being used for more than the Sunday services: the bookstalls, coffee rooms, Junior Church areas and even conference and committee, restaurant and theatre complexes, would be shown to him as being necessary parts of modern church life.

And would he agree?

Mission – at home and abroad
This is mission on the home front, and it is vital. But the challenge is that mission has no bounds, and in the divine scheme of things history has shown that the home mission grows in proportion to its extended mission. That is the challenge of our gospel reading today: the question implicitly posed by the Christ who so explicitly made his point in the temple court on that day so long ago. This is the 'sign' – and we do well to ponder it.

> '[Jesus said], "the kingdom of God is not coming with things that can be observed ... For in fact the kingdom of God is among you."' Luke 17:20, 21

Suggested hymns
From Greenland's icy mountains; Inspired by love and anger; The Church of God a kingdom is; The Church's one foundation

Third Sunday of Lent *Second Service*
Knowing Christ Pss 11, 12; Ex. 5:1–6:1; Phil. 3:4b–14 or Matthew 10:16–22
'I want to know Christ and the power of his resurrection ... because Christ Jesus has made me his own.' Philippians 3:10, 12

Our chief aim
If we were asked what our main desire in life is, how many of us would stand with Paul and declare: 'I want to know Christ'? Yet

in baptism and confirmation we have implicitly made this our chief aim: to glorify God, as Christians. We cannot do that if we do not know Christ. A modern version of the Prayer of St Patrick goes:

> *May the strength of God guide me this day,*
> *and may his power preserve me.*
> *May the wisdom of God instruct me;*
> *the eye of God watch over me;*
> *the ear of God hear me;*
> *the word of God give sweetness to my speech;*
> *the hand of God defend me;*
> *and may I follow the way of God.*
> *Christ be with me, Christ before me;*
> *Christ be after me, Christ within me;*
> *Christ beneath me, Christ above me;*
> *Christ at my right hand, Christ at my left;*
> *Christ in the car, Christ in the train;*
> *Christ in the bus, Christ in the plane;*
> *Christ in the heart of everyone who thinks of me,*
> *Christ in the mouth of everyone who speaks to me,*
> *Christ in every eye that sees me,*
> *Christ in every ear that hears me.*

Two's company

'And remember, I am with you always,' Jesus promised (Matthew 28:20). We are in his company all the time. If we could only remember this more often, surely we should be much more careful about what we ate, drank, looked at or read; where we went and what we got up to. 'Can I bring Jesus into this situation?' Well, he is here anyway, so we'd do well to check each situation for Christian compatibility. And not only is he here with us, he has already experienced every situation we can ever have; there is no set of circumstances he cannot deal with. Let us remember that, on those occasions when we try to be unique and to tell ourselves that no one has been treated so badly or that no one has been here before.

Knowing Christ takes a lifetime, but as soon as we are ready for the fulness of this knowledge, we shall be translated to the next stage. Knowing Christ begins with a sense of the love that led him to Calvary; it expands in the power of the force that raised him from the dead; and it really takes off when he accompanies us in our sharing of the good news with others. Two's company – and more is the Church.

Satan knows about him, too

Knowing Jesus is as far above knowing about him, as Mount Everest is higher than a molehill. Even Satan knows about him – more, in fact, than we do, for he was in heaven with Jesus before he got too big for his boots and fell from grace. But Satan cannot *know* Jesus; he cannot fellowship with him or experience him as Saviour. This makes all the difference between the Devil and us. In the worst of times and in the best, may we never lose track of this great truth, that Satan cannot come between us and Jesus at this point.

Knowing about Jesus is learning what he has done for others. Knowing him is realizing what he has done for us – and his ongoing involvement in our lives. The most important work we can do is to share him with others. We can give others a list of theological books which may be of some help; we can tell them how God is operating in different countries and continents; but when we look them in the eye with Christian love and tell them straight what Jesus has done for us, we are really and truly making him known.

Suggested hymns

Firmly I believe and truly; I'm not ashamed to own my Lord; Jesus, I my cross have taken; Put thou thy trust in God

Fourth Sunday of Lent (Mothering Sunday)
30 March *Principal Service* **Christ's Peace**
Ex. 2:1–10 or Sam. 1:20–28; Ps. 34:11–20 or Ps. 127:1–4; 2 Cor. 1:3–7 or Col. 3:12–17; Luke 2:33–35 or John 19:25–27

'And let the peace of Christ rule in your hearts, to which indeed you were called in the one body. And be thankful.' Colossians 3:15

Thank you, Lord
To the Triune God of the 'Three mothers' we bring our thanks today:

> *For our own mothers,*
> *For Mary, Mother of our Lord,*
> *and for Mother-Church.*

In this triple gift of motherhood, God has been magnificently generous. The old saying 'God could not come himself, so he made mothers', is an indication of the value of motherhood; mothers are born, not made. And God underlined their value, when he gave Mary to his Son, when the love for her God prompted her to give her *Fiat*, to take that great step into the unknown future, when she told Gabriel: 'Let it be with me according to your word' (Luke 1:38).

Thank you, Lord, also, for Mother-Church, and the support we get from her, and the love we give to her, as we pray on this Mothering Sunday for grace not to take Mother-Church for granted.

The Church on earth
We may think the outlook would be brighter if every seat in our churches was filled every Sunday. We may look at the divisions which still operate in the Church – though, thank God, for all their complexity these divisions are not as great as they were even a generation ago. But Jesus has said, that, come what may, *his* Church – *our* Church – will always carry on. 'The gates of Hades will not prevail against it' (Matthew 16:18). The Church has, and is, what God has given it and made it, to go on into eternity. It's as though God is telling us, we all *need* a Mother in our walk with him.

Mother's always here!
Do we ever take Mother-Church for granted? God willing, *we* don't, but many do – many who darken her doors only at times of matching, hatching and despatching, take it for granted that when they need her, Mother will be there and waiting. We can reflect today on a time when – thankfully only temporarily – Mother was *not* available. In the twelfth century, a brilliant young scholar, Lotario di' Conti, was elected Pope, taking the name

Innocent III. He firmly believed that the Bishop of Rome should rule not only the Church but the world. It was not long before Innocent and King John of England disagreed over the appointment of Stephen Langton as Archbishop of Canterbury. On 24 March 1208, Innocent, bridling at John's refusal to allow Langton entry to England, placed the country under an interdict: all services stopped, churches were locked, the bell towers fell silent, churchyards were closed for burials, and the celebration of the Mass was forbidden. As well as withholding Mother-Church from her 'children', Innocent released England from loyalty to John, and advised France to sail across the Channel and invade us.

Predictably, John capitulated, but the experience gave people an insight not only into the workings of the papacy, but also the problems when Mother-Church was not giving her children the support that we, in our day, have known from birth.

As Jesus hung on the cross, he was paying the price for our membership in his Church, our passport for eternity – far, far beyond the highest figure we can imagine. He had us on his mind. Yes, we are an integral part of the Church for which he died – the Church that he knows can withstand all the trouble that Satan can dream up against her – the Church that can light up, turn around, revive and re-invigorate the world of today.

Suggested hymns
For Mary, Mother of the Lord; Jesus, good above all other; Maiden, yet a Mother (*Celebration Hymnal*); The Church of God a kingdom is

Fourth Sunday of Lent *Second Service*
At the Right Time   Pss 13, 14; Ex. 6:2–13; Rom. 5:1–11
'For while we were still weak, at the right time Christ died for the ungodly . . . God proves his love for us in that while we still were sinners Christ died for us.' Romans 5:6, 8

God's timing
God's timing is perfect. That should not surprise us, for God made time; he is the perfect Master of time, and only he can operate

both within and outside of time. One day (for want of a timeless expression!) we shall be without time – and we probably shall not even miss it.

Perhaps some thought that had Christ come to minister on earth at another time, he would have been more quickly recognized, and might have attracted more support. On the face of it, first-century Palestine was in an awful state; the Jews were writhing daily under an army of occupation; only the time-servers among them had any love for the Romans. Pilate had already earned the people's wrath by bringing in the standards of Rome under cover of darkness (and had had to lower them as soon as daylight brought a Jewish furore), and by ordering a bloodbath among Galilean insurrectionists. Everyone was living on a knife edge, in expectation that riots and unrest could provoke a repeat performance at any time. Why, then, did Jesus not come to make his point in an age when people could concentrate more on what he had to say? The answer must be that it was time in the eyes of God, to come when he came.

We know best?
Yet, geared as we are in today's world, to pigeonholing time into neat compartments – our schedules, Filofaxes and computers monitoring, timetabling every minute – we try to tell God exactly when we'd like him to do this, or to arrange that. And we are quickly aggrieved when (by our reckoning) he responds too early, too late, or seemingly not at all.

Why, God, why? Weren't you listening? Don't you care? I've lost that contract. I haven't any money. I've missed that opportunity . . . Oh, isn't it all God's fault! (Well, if we don't actually berate the Lord out loud, we come awfully close to thinking such grievances.)

No wrong time
If only we stopped to consider the consistency of God. He is always, unerringly true to himself. It's his nature, he cannot be otherwise. He is all light, and no darkness; all good, and no evil. Therefore, he is completely positive in his operation of time. For him, there cannot be a wrong time for doing anything. The ministry of Jesus could have taken place at whatever time God chose. We can rest assured that in this case, as with everything else, God got it right – while we were yet sinners, but before we had gone beyond the point of no return.

The right time for us
The sacrifice of Calvary was, therefore, at the right time for us.
Our birth came also at the right time; we have not been called to
live in the sixteenth, eighteenth, or any century but the present.
The situations and circumstances of today are those which the
Lord wishes us to experience. We have been brought into being
for Christian work, worship and witness, *in our time*. Uniquely,
we are crafted to meet the challenge of today. Instead of criticizing
our times, can we not bend all our energies towards meeting the
challenge tailor-made by God for us?

> Lord, you have made me for a purpose: not yesterday or
> tomorrow, but today. Help me to focus on you *at this time* –
> before it slips into yesterday and is gone for ever.

Suggested hymns
A few more years shall roll; At even, ere the sun was set; Days
and moments quickly flying; My times are in thy hands

Fifth Sunday of Lent (Passion Sunday)
6 April *Principal Service* Exit Satan
Jer. 31:31–34; Ps. 51:1–12 or Ps. 119:9–16; Heb. 5:5–10;
John 12:20–33

*'Jesus answered, "This voice has come for your sake, not for mine. Now
is the judgement of this world; now the ruler of this world will be driven
out."' John 12:30, 31*

Writing on the wall
The writing was on the wall for Satan – but we are so familiar
with these words of Jesus that it is difficult now to quantify how
courageous of him it was to speak so openly. The inference was,
to those of his criticizers who were within earshot: 'I know you
are looking for an excuse to apprehend me. Go ahead, take me on
this one, if you can!' Sometimes we are not as bold for Christ as
we could be, and yet we have much less to lose.
  All authority in heaven and on earth was given to Jesus
(Matthew 28:18), and after Calvary he powered down through hell
and out the other end, taking the keys of death and of hell with

him (Revelation 1:18). One way or another, Satan could not help seeing the writing on the wall.

It's a lie!
Yet for as long as he can, Satan will try to persuade us that he still has a kingdom, he still has some authority on earth. It's a lie – from the worst liar in the business, though he manages to convince millions of folk. We are in the 'Church *Militant* here in earth' (BCP Holy Communion Service), because Satan is still capable of causing trouble, dispossessed though he is. But although we sometimes make heavy weather of the fight, in our reading today Jesus is assuring us that the battle has already been won. The winning blow was struck at Calvary – once, only once, and once for all.

Yet, as we heard, God needs to go to some trouble to get this truth across. Not too often in modern times do we identify a *Bath Qol* ('daughter of the voice', a voice from heaven): usually we say it's thundering. Perhaps we need a little less commonsense and a lot more faith . . .

Bad news travels fast
At times Satan seems to have the multimedia operation in his pocket, as bad news grabs the headlines and holds on to them. But much that is good can make the news, if Christians see it happens. Jesus gave us all the encouragement necessary; if we fail to use it, we are virtually relegating his sacrifice to the historical past, and are elevating Satan to a position to which he has no right. 'A cheerful heart is a good medicine' (Proverbs 17:22). If God does not thunder the good news of Jesus in a *Bath Qol* today, is it not because he believes his folk on earth should thunder it for him? Christ has no voice but ours, no hands but ours, no feet but ours. If we don't bombard the universe with the truth, Satan will plug the gap with lies and junk of his own.

The world was judged on the day of Calvary. It was found to be suffering from disbelief, apathy, animosity and heresy – but in none of these areas was it assessed as being terminally ill. God reckoned it to be worth saving. So the crucifixion sacrifice of the Lord went ahead.

If the realization of this does not inspire us to do our utmost to spread the good news, nothing will.

Every time the Christian gospel is shared, Satan takes a knock.

Remember, he is mortally wounded already. One day, his limit of endurance will be reached: the sand in his glass is already running out.

'The devil has come down to you with great wrath, because he knows that his time is short!' Revelation 12:12

Suggested hymns
Great is thy faithfulness; I will sing the wondrous story; Oft in danger, oft in woe; Through all the changing scenes of life

Fifth Sunday of Lent *Second Service*
The Stronger by Far Ps. 34; Ex. 7:8–24; Romans 5:12–21

'But the free gift is not like the trespass. For if the many died through the one man's trespass, much more surely have the grace of God and the free gift in the grace of the one man, Jesus Christ, abounded for the many.' Romans 5:15

Adam – and Jesus
Adam had brought sin and death upon the whole human race, by the thoughtless indiscretion of a moment. Jesus gave freedom from inherited sin, and the prospect of eternal life to a burgeoning human race, by a deliberate act of vicarious love: the greater price, the greater effect, by far. Adam disobeyed God for one brief, unholy moment. Jesus showed a love and obedience throughout a life that by human standards was short, yet which did more good for humanity than any before or since. Adam's fall cost nothing, except in consequential heartache, but was expensive for the human race. The sacrifice of Jesus cost more than anyone can imagine – yet its benefits have been made freely available to all who have faith to believe.

Accepting with grace
We need the grace given only by God, so that we can accept the gift of Jesus' sacrifice, for we did not earn it, we were not worthy of it. Only because God so loved the world that he wanted to involve mankind in his ongoing purposes, were we saved from

eternity in hell. Here on the proving ground, as the purposes of God unfold minute by minute, we are being prepared for an extension of time, talents and powers that only God can know. We can only accept that eternity will somehow justify the price paid at Calvary, because God never wastes time. And the importance of Calvary is underlined in the eternal visibility of the wounds inflicted there: wounds that in an eternity where pain and sorrow play no part, will somehow have their sting removed.

Light for the world
The light of Christ, shining from a cross that in itself betokened darkness and death, continues to spread across the world, pushing back into annihilation the darkness of Adam's sin. We may reverently ponder how our Lord thrills with loving satisfaction, every time a pinprick of Christian advance sends back to heaven a ray of light. Does Jesus consider the spread of his gospel is keeping up with his schedule – or are we ahead, or behind, in the work? Here are his people, shining as lights in the world – but how much of a difference are we making? Are we indeed showing by our enthusiasm for mission that we value the price of Calvary above everything else? God has invested heavily in lighting up the world: how diligently are we working to give him a good return for his expenditure?

Good news for all
If we thought that the world still had no secrets to be revealed, the new languages and dialects that are currently being discovered would disabuse us of that notion. As more Bible translations are being made, more are being required. Were it not for the fact that our Lord has given us the commission to evangelize the world (and thus it must be possible, with and through his grace), the complexities and scale of the Indian and Chinese dialects, for instance, would be daunting.

We all need encouragement at times, and recalling how our Lord has faith that we can accomplish whatever he calls us to do, is surely the best encouragement anyone can ever have.

It's the same encouragement that saw a Galilean fisherman to the bishop's chair at Rome; a London parlourmaid to the rescue of a hundred Chinese children; and a North Carolina farmer's boy to lead the greatest Christian crusades of the twentieth century. May we, in our turn, be encouragers of those whom God causes us to meet – as we share the news that one Man's sacrifice is still sufficient for all.

Suggested hymns
Cross of Jesus, cross of sorrows; In the cross of Christ I glory; Once, only once, and once for all; The sands of time are sinking

Palm Sunday 13 April *Principal Service*
Liturgy of the Passion Advance Planning
Isa. 50:4–9a; Ps. 31:9–16; Phil. 2:5–11; Mark 14:1–15:47 or 15:1–39[40–47]

'[Jesus said], "Go into the city, and a man carrying a jar of water will meet you; follow him . . . He will show you a large room upstairs, furnished and ready . . ."' Mark 14:13, 15

It's all prepared
Jesus' preparations for the Last Supper had been made with meticulous care – just as he had arranged the provision of a donkey for his ride into Jerusalem (Mark 11:2) – just as he had arranged the provision of the temple tax, on the day he and his disciples visited Capernaum (Matthew 17:27). We can learn much from these examples:
1) It is natural for us to ask questions. God has given us the ability to ask, and he is not fazed when we do.
2) He knows in advance what we shall ask, and what we need to know.
3) Most importantly, even before we ask, he has the answer ready to give us. He may not give it to us when we want it, or expect it – but he has it for the time he knows we need it. His purposes involve us, and he has gone ahead to make it possible for us to do what he intends we should do.

The palms and the passion
Beginning with the Palm Sunday ride of Jesus into Jerusalem, the series of events of Holy Week have a sense of mystery, even of unreality.

Why did Jesus commandeer a little donkey and make such a public entry into Jerusalem?

Why did he defy the growing hostility of the clergy of the day, and teach openly in the temple?

Why did he turn the Passover meal (which had stood unchanged from the time of the Exodus, some fifteen centuries or so before) into a eucharist?

Why did he allow the betrayal, arrest and crucifixion, when at any time he could have employed *force majeure* and turned events the other way?

Why, why, why?

Simply because he had turned everything on to God, and had voluntarily, deliberately agreed to let God occupy the driving seat. 'Not what I want, but what you want' (Mark 14:36).

Jesus came up to every situation in the frame of mind which said: 'Father, *you* have brought me to this place – now *you* take me on into it, through it, and out the other end, as *you* want, not as I may want.'

Our way forward

And this can be our way forward, too. When we can come up to a situation in that way, no matter how awful it is, the weight of it is lighter because we've been given the grace to offload the responsibility on to God. But far too often, with a superabundance of martyrdom and self-confidence, we decide we can carry the load ourselves – for all the world as if the problem was either not important enough for God to take a hand in it, or that it was too difficult even for God to handle!

The Jerusalem crowds

The crowds thronging the temple, the Gabbatha, the Via Dolorosa, Calvary ... were so intent on looking backwards, so diligent in observing the old law, so locked on to the old covenant, the old dispensation, that they could not see the Lord moving as God among them. They were so enslaved by the past that they were not asking God 'Why?' any more.

We, too, can get so caught up with history that we lose the perspective of the ongoing purposes of God today.

God works from the past, in the present, for the future – and his future is so long, it makes the past and present combined a mere moment of time by comparison. Everything God leads us into is a preparation for the future: his future, our future. Pray God that we may see the Passion in the light of this truth.

Suggested hymns
All glory, laud and honour; Lord, through this Holy Week of our salvation; Ride on, ride on in majesty; When I survey the wondrous cross

Palm Sunday *Second Service* Unholy Fear
Ps. 69:1–18; Isa. 5:1–7; Mark 12:1–12

'When they realized that he had told this parable against them, they wanted to arrest him, but they feared the crowd. So they left him and went away.' Mark 12:12

The wrong approach
These 'chief priests, scribes and elders' (Mark 11:27) did not fear the prospect of arresting Jesus and manoeuvring his crucifixion. Instead, like cowards, they were afraid that unless protected by guards (as would be the case, come Thursday night, in Gethsemane, Mark 14:43ff.), they were inviting assault from the crowds if they moved in on Jesus too soon.

The 'eleventh commandment'
If one runs a time and motion study on the gospels, one discovers that the most frequently given command of Jesus is not 'love your neighbour', or even 'love God' – but 'do not fear; don't be afraid'. Fear is bad at any time. Don't tangle with it! is Jesus' message.

Most of us manage to get through life without committing murder. Many of us try to avoid lying and stealing. But most of us break this 'eleventh commandment' every day. For some reason we decide that giving way to fear is not a sin. But if we are fearful at all, we have lost faith. And that is serious. When Jesus caught the disciples panicking in a storm on Galilee, he did not chide them gently for having let go some of their faith. He criticized them sharply: 'Why are you afraid? Have you still *no faith*?' (Mark 4:40). Accept fear into your life, and faith flies out of the window. In our reading the grandees who feared the people had allowed fear to cloud their judgement. It does. And in addition it can paralyze our bodies, whiten our hair, and stop our hearts. Fear is bad news.

Pilate's fear
Come Friday, we shall re-live the scenes of injustice and cruelty. We shall see a procurator, frustrated and out of his depth, letting a guilty man go free and committing an innocent man to the cross, because of an implied threat from the Jewish hierarchy to inform Caesar that Pilate was acknowledging the kingship of Jesus. Pilate proved that he was not man enough to stand up to such a threat.

In true focus
If we are focused on fear, we are not looking to God. There is no fear in God. So, when we are fearful, we are in effect focusing on Satan. So long as he can induce us to fear, the Devil knows he can muscle in, because our faith guard has slipped.

Centuries before Jesus, the psalmist had got his mind focused on God: 'The Lord is on my side; I will not fear' he sang (Psalm 118:6; AV). If only we would remember our divine backup, we'd save ourselves a lot of Angst.

Perhaps Jesus wondered why he had to repeat this 'eleventh commandment' so frequently, to men in whose hands he would soon be leaving his mission.

But then the miracle happened.

The disciples agonized through the arrest, trial and crucifixion of Jesus, in paroxysms of fear. Even Easter Day found them huddled behind locked doors 'for fear of the Jews' (John 20:19). Yet this is *the last time* we hear of them being afraid. As soon as the realization of the resurrection hit home, they became new people. Even the ascension of Jesus didn't unsettle them. While one may have expected them to be devastated by the departure of their Best Friend, instead we find them returning to Jerusalem 'with great joy' (Luke 24:53).

Can we not take a leaf out of their book? Isn't our resurrected Lord sufficient to keep us focused, faithful and unfearing?

Suggested hymns
Courage, brother, do not stumble; Fill thou my life, O Lord my God; Give me the faith that can remove; O, for a heart to praise my God

Monday of Holy Week   14 April
Compounding the Sin   Isa. 42:1–9; Ps. 36:5–11;
Heb. 9:11–15; John 12:1–11

'So the chief priests planned to put Lazarus to death as well, since it was on account of him that many of the Jews were deserting and were believing in Jesus.' John 12:10, 11

Satan's stranglehold

When the Devil believes he has got his man, he turns up the pressure – which is often his undoing, as what may have been tolerated or even gone undetected, develops into mega crime. While the chief priests' anger had been directed against one man – who was relatively unknown in and around Jerusalem – as soon as they turned against one who was presumably well established, a householder and integral part of the community, they could expect local opinion to turn against them. Now we don't know for certain that this happened; but, reading between the lines of the Passion accounts in the gospels, it seems pretty likely that it did: the 'case' against Lazarus was quietly dropped before it had really begun; and, perhaps partly as a knee-jerk reaction, the chief priests' venom against Jesus hotted up to white heat, as they resolved to use Judas' defection to rush through the arrest and trial of Jesus 'under cover' (as it were) of the turmoil that the Passover celebrations always brought to Jerusalem.

Wheels within wheels

Still it happens today, in pretty much the same way. Terrorists choose a time when attenttion is deflected elsewhere, to plant their bombs or launch their attacks. Innocent people are targeted to provide a smoke screen for other activities – then, sometimes, as quickly dropped as was the threat to kill Lazarus, with no thought on the part of the perpetrators of the anguish and uncertainty which tortures the ex-victim and his family for ages.

That is Satan's *modus operandi* – fostering fear and suspicion among the innocent, while squeezing the guilty in all directions until they have lost all sense of what is right or wrong.

In a word

'Fear' in a word sums up the Devil's armoury. So it is no wonder that the command Jesus voiced more than any other, according to the gospels, was 'Do not fear'. Fear opens the door to Satan – and the old Devil only needs a toehold to thrust that door wide open. Everyone working against Jesus as the dreadful drama of the Passion was played out, was a captive to fear: the chief priests, Judas, Herod, Pilate – all feared for their positions, prestige and power.

The tragedy was that most of them could not, if pressed, even have been able to quantify their fear – for there was so much that they did not know about the nature of the innocent Christ who confronted them. Today, little has altered. Whatever the nature of our fears, can we truthfully quantify them? So much of all fear is nameless and shapeless; that is the nature of the Devil's best weapon, and the quality that gives fear its terrible, cutting, killing edge. Could we but realize it at the time, much of what we fear not only *will* not happen, but *cannot* happen. But Satan is the last person to come out into the open and tell us this.

The only way
The only way out of the problem is to *obey* Jesus when he says, 'Do not fear', instead of seeing his words as merely a nice suggestion. 'Yes, Lord, I *will* not fear,' may need to be our prayer a hundred (or more) times a day.

It may seem impossible to break free of the stranglehold of fear – but this is the only way. In this, our 'Holy Week of salvation', may we pray it will be true.

Suggested hymns
Give me joy in my heart; Lord, through this Holy Week of our salvation; My song is Love unknown; O Jesus, I have promised

Tuesday of Holy Week   15 April
The Hour Has Come   Isa. 49:1–7; Ps. 71:1–14;
1 Cor. 1:18–31; John 12:20–36

'Jesus answered them, "The hour has come for the Son of Man to be glorified . . . Now is my soul troubled. And what should I say – 'Father, save me from this hour?' No, it is for this reason that I have come to this hour."' John 12:23, 27

For this reason
If we are in the will of God, as was Jesus, we can declare: 'It is for this reason' that we are in such and such a situation. It may not be to our liking, but God's liking and ours do not always run in tandem. There was not much for Jesus to 'like' about his hour; but in God's will it was his, and therefore he would see it through. We, who so often (implicitly, if not explicitly) pray for easier lives, have much to learn from this courageous acquiescence of Jesus. The flowers may seem to be blooming more luxuriantly in our neighbour's garden than in our own; but this is the 'hour' God has called us into. We may find a blessing if we choose another way – but the richest blessing will be reserved for 'the hour' we see through without imposing our own will. Jesus could have extended his ministry for a few more years, journeyed further afield – could have argued that his disciples were not yet ready to be left to carry on on their own . . . the crucifixion could have taken place in ten, twenty, even thirty years' time . . . but his hour had come at *this* time, for a reason.

Nothing to chance
God leaves nothing to chance. Look how he prepared for the ride into Jerusalem, and for the Last Supper. And so he had drawn the strands together, to be woven into the Passion: a murderer to be released as a sign that justice had flown out of the window; a puppet king who would ally himself with Pilate in a common misunderstanding; a frustrated procurator who would have Jesus crucified under a legal, regal *titulus*; a couple of influential believers, in Joseph and Nicodemus, who would honour the body of Jesus with the respect due to a king . . . and see how he had prepared the way for Mary and the others on Easter morning, by having the great stone rolled away!
St Augustine once said:

> Work as if everything depended on you;
> Pray as if everything depended on God.

We are often significantly more proficient in doing the first, at the expense of the second. And unquestionably we are more ready to ask why God has brought us to an 'hour' that is not to our liking, than to thank him when that 'hour' is one exactly in line with our wishes. What divine stores of patience the Almighty must have!

And how merciful he is in not telling us how near we come to running him short!

A long week
This is the longest week of the Church's year, and we still have far to go 'along the sacred way' with our Lord. But today can we reflect especially on his single-mindedness to effect the world's salvation, *at any cost*. Even when taken 'to the wire' in Gethsemane, he will recognize his 'hour' and the reason for it. Our lesser trials and temptations surely fall into a more understandable perspective in the light of Jesus' Passion. Charles Haddon Spurgeon used to say how often he had to go back to the cross, and begin all over again as a pardoned sinner, when his circumstances went awry. We all need to go back, time and again: there is no safer place for the Christian than at the cross. It is the one place where Satan dare not linger.

In the world
The difficult part comes when we leave the cross, when we return to the world that is always waiting beyond the Safety Zone. It was just so for the earliest disciples – and this was the reason that Jesus made his open prayer to the Father: 'I am not asking you to take them out of the world, but I ask you to protect them from the evil one. They do not belong to the world, just as I do not belong to the world' (John 17:15, 16). However the Devil may try to identify us with the world, we have Jesus' word that we are different, we do not belong here; our proper home is elsewhere.

So, back off, Satan. We, like Jesus, are only passing through.

Suggested hymns
Beneath the cross of Jesus; Christian, seek not yet repose; In the cross of Christ I glory; Lord, through this Holy Week of our salvation

Wednesday of Holy Week   16 April
Fair Warning   Isa. 50:4–9a; Ps. 70; Heb. 12:1–3;
John 13:21–32

*'After saying this Jesus was troubled in spirit, and declared: "Very truly,
I tell you, one of you will betray me." . . . [Judas] went out. And it was
night.' John 13:21, 30*

The betrayer
Jesus warned him. Even at that stage, Judas could have accepted
the warning and returned to the fold. He could have quietly
resolved not to do the awful deed – and only Jesus would have
known. He could have stood up there and then, and openly confessed his wicked intention, and contrition – and everyone would
have known (but would probably have understood and even
forgiven).

But he didn't.

He made the decision, even though Jesus knew, and left the
room. And it was night: darkness in his soul, and round about
him.

Oh, we would never have done likewise, would we? But how
can we be so sure? How can anyone be certain of how they would
act, what they would say, in a situation which as yet they have
not experienced?

The inevitable
Judas had been given one last chance. As soon as he had blown
it, part of the tension he had left in the room evaporated, as our
Lord recognized that now the inevitable would happen. We, too,
can plead for a remission, but then the crisis proves unstoppable
– and there is a strange relief. The anguish and sadness may still
be there, but the onus of pleading, the effect of trying to alter
events, has been taken from us. King David found that, when his
child died (2 Samuel 12:20ff.); and Hezekiah, once he knew his
remaining time would see the country at peace (2 Kings 20:19).
It's as though God is saying: 'Enough is enough; I am doing this
my way. I know exactly how much you can take.'

At such times, the wonder is that anyone can doubt that there
is a Lord, and that he is in the driving seat.

We are free to choose

Although he knew what was in Judas' mind, Jesus did not make it impossible for him to sin. Nor did he plead with him to reconsider. Nor did he try to hide from the other disciples what was happening. If they had been wide awake, they would have seen and known. For centuries, it had been prophesied that the betrayal would take place – but Judas had not been named. Right up to the end, he could have chosen to act otherwise. The betrayal would still have taken place – if not by him, then by someone else.

By the same token, someone is going to be the evangelist to point the greatest number of people to Jesus. No two evangelists share the gospel with exactly the same folk. Who will be the most diligent? Who will bring in the largest sheaves?

Someone is also going to be the Christian who will most successfully and consistently kick the habit of being afraid. Again, who will this be? Each of us has the chance to change this world for God, if we choose.

After a war, a disaster, an epidemic, one hears on all sides: 'This must never be allowed to happen again!' After Holy Week came Easter with its convincing message that there could not be another crucifixion of the Son of God. Quite true. But, as Sergei Bulgakov, the Russian theologian, once said: 'As long as there is evil in the world, the Lamb is *still being slain*.' The Pilates of our age are still making ghastly decisions; the Peters are still ashamed of standing up for Jesus – and the Judases are still betraying him.

What will it take, to ensure that the Lamb is not still being slain?

A lot more than the Church at present is doing.

Suggested hymns

Lord, it belongs not to my care; Lord, through this Holy Week of our salvation; Said Judas to Mary; Take up thy cross, the Saviour said

Maundy Thursday   17 April
A New Commandment   Ex. 12:1–4[5–10], 11–14;
Ps. 116:1–2, 12–19; 1 Cor. 11:23–26;
John 13:1–17, 31b–35

'[Jesus said], "I give you a new commandment, that you love one another. Just as I have loved you, you also should love one another."' John 13:34

The way of the Church
The timing is significant. Jesus has been speaking of Judas and the betrayal. In the new Church, the operative word *must be* (it is a command) LOVE. Others must be able to see the love that Jesus' followers have, not only for him but for each other. And the content is crucial. The perfidy of Judas will not jeopardize the formation of the Church; but the rest of the disciples must know that the example Jesus has set them *must be* followed: the foot-washing, the patience, the dedication, the courage, the will to see the best in others. Love must rule.

Jesus is looking ahead, and foreseeing how the betrayal, arrest, crucifixion – and also the resurrection and ascension – will impact on his friends. We ourselves know how trauma, tension, change can affect our relations with friends and family. The future of the Church would soon rest in the hands of these eleven men. If any strife developed between them, the entire project would be threatened.

Love – and strife
Love and strife cannot co-exist in a person's life. They are mutually incompatible. If we are in strife with someone, we cannot love him. If we love him, then strife does not move into the equation. Of the two, love, being the stronger, stands the best chance of winning. For the Christian, the chances are improved still further, for the Lord is on our side (Psalm 118:6).

The Church today
The 'new commandment' is ever as crucial today. Where there is strife in the Church, growth and development are inhibited. Outsiders are quick to see dissension and disunity, and those in the Church – even if not directly involved – are still tainted with the aura of strife, as members together of the Body of Christ.

'Is Christ divided?' once asked St Paul (1 Corinthians 1:13; AV). The answer – if the Church is in strife at all – must be 'yes'. The question is that serious.

The example of Jesus
Our Lord had shown his disciples how to love, how to bear each others' burdens, how to suffer patiently the many little strifes that surface in the course of a normal day. The strife itself is not sinful; it is only when we become part of it and take it to ourselves, that

the trouble starts. Strife, if it can be seen as temptation, is then more easily avoided; but strife is more subtle than temptation, and one is often in the middle of it before it's been identified. The smallest irritation or friction can grow into mega strife, and once established can ruin relationships for far longer than the mere memory of the initial rift persists.

'As I have loved you' – with a compassion that sees to the heart of a person, yet still loves; sees the devious machinations, and continues to show patience and unconditional, caring concern; sees a broken world, yet loves it enough to die for it. This is love, as God understands it and demonstrates it. This is new love.

May this love shine in us, and through us today, as we draw so close to the Passion of True Love. As we remember that Judas, even after three years of close association with this love, could betray it, let us pray that we may have grace not to go the Judas way.

Suggested hymns
A new commandment I give unto you; Bind us together, Lord; Love Divine, all loves excelling; We are one in the Spirit

Good Friday 18 April *Principal Service*
'What Have You Done?' Isa. 52:13–53:12; Ps. 22; Heb. 10:16–25 or 4:14–16; Heb. 5:7–9; John 18:1–19:42
'Pilate replied, "I am not a Jew, am I? Your own nation and the chief priests have handed you over to me. What have you done?"' John 18:35

Silent under questioning
Jesus could have replied: 'I have preached the good news, healed the sick, cast out demons, raised the dead . . .' But he remained silent. Yet as Christ the King, he wore the purple robe and crown of thorns. As Christ the King, people raised their eyes to him on Pilate's judgement pavement. As Christ the King, he would be lifted on the cross at Calvary.

Divine, yet human, kingship

What has Jesus done, as King, in our lives? What are we praying that he will do? If we are not expecting him to do anything, then we must be prepared for just that.

> *King of my life, I crown thee now,*
> *Thine shalt the glory be;*
> *Lest I forget thy thorn-crowned brow,*
> *Lead me to Calvary.*
> *Lest I forget Gethsemane,*
> *Lest I forget thine agony,*
> *Lest I forget thy love for me,*
> *Lead me to Calvary.*
>
> Jenny Evelyn Hussey

Yet still round the world – or perhaps as close to us as next door – there are those who cannot accept the cross, who cannot come to Calvary, leave their old selves there and take up the new life that Christ's crucifixion bought.

Without Calvary, we have no King.

Without a King, we cannot inherit a kingdom.

Calvary made it possible

As the Christ King's disciples, it is our work to share the gospel with as many as we can, sharing, widening, extending the inheritance that Calvary made possible. We do the telling. God does the convincing. It's a combined operation.

Pilate asked Jesus: 'Are you the King of the Jews?' (v. 33), to which Jesus replied: 'Do you ask this on your own, or did others tell you about me?' (v. 34). Others may tell us of Jesus – may share with us their experiences of his love and guidance; but each has to come to Christ by himself. Others may intercede for us; that is part of the strength of the Body of Christ; but the actual bonding with Christ is our responsibility. Remember when Jesus asked the disciples who people were saying he was, and followed this up by the key question: 'But who do you say that I am?' (Matthew 16:15). And on that post-resurrection morning by Galilee, Jesus affirmed his faith in Peter's loyalty; but when Peter, carried away by the moment, tried to discover what was to be John's mission, Jesus roundly told him to mind his own business (John 21:22). So here, in our text today, Jesus is implicitly telling Pilate not to accept spoonfed information, but to think and act for himself.

A Roman perplexed
But Pilate is out of his depth. He is also conscious of the precariousness of his own position. He will bow to the strongest voice – but the irony is, the strongest voice is not the loudest. And so Pilate makes the worst error of judgement in history.

Knowing what was in Pilate's mind, and anticipating the verdict, Jesus nevertheless gave the procurator a splendid chance to save his honour. If Pilate had chosen to do what was right, God could have worked mightily through him. The sacrifice of Jesus would still have taken place – for that was how the world was to be saved – but it would have involved someone other than Pilate. The Roman's freedom of choice had not been withdrawn. He had no one but himself to blame.

Jesus is asking
Today, Jesus is asking us to take time to sort out our reasons for following our King:

What do we expect of him?
What does he require of us?

There is no danger that he will disappoint us. Pray God, we shall not fall short of his expectations.

Suggested hymns
Forgive them, O my Father; His are the thousand sparkling rills; It is finished! Blessed Jesus; O, come and mourn with me awhile

Good Friday   *Second Service*
The End of the Day   Pss 130, 143; Gen. 22:1–18;
John 19:38–42 or Col. 1:18–23
'And so, because it was the Jewish day of Preparation, and the tomb was nearby, they laid Jesus there.' John 19:42

The tension is over
After the drama, pathos, anguish of the day, the tension is over as the stone is rolled ponderously across the mouth of the sepulchre. Yet, despite two intervening millennia, the commemoration of the greatest sacrifice of all time still leaves the mind a mass of whirling thoughts.

We may wonder why mankind had got into such a state as to make Calvary necessary – and wonder still more why today's world can in many areas still take so little notice: why life today for many has been going on as normal. How it must grieve the Lord who went through such agony to lift humanity above the normal and mundane!

Our mission
The world needs Christians and our message, quite as much today as it did on that first Good Friday. There are times when we may feel like square pegs in round, dark holes. It may be that a certain dark hole needs the friction that a square peg can give. It may be that we ourselves, in the mercy of God, need our corners smoothing off. Even if the hole has been of our own making, if God is still there with us we can turn the experience into something not only beautiful for us, but probably also for others; such is the extent of our responsibility. Pilate could have saved many more beside himself. But he chose otherwise.

Using the power of Christ
The power that Christ has given us – that broke free of its restrictions on Good Friday, to energize the world – is what we need to use to complete our mission: not at our last, trembling gasp, but in triumphant strength, as Jesus did (Luke 23:46). John tells us clearly: 'I pray that all may go well with you and that you may be in good health, just as it is well with your soul' (3 John 2). And Paul counselled his young protégé Timothy: 'God did not give us a spirit of cowardice, but rather a spirit of power and of love and of self-discipline (2 Timothy 1:7) – that is, a mind centred on the power that comes from God – a mind that is not so naïve as to accept without question whatever drifts across its vision, but one that recognizes God in its life.

The Good Friday mystery

There are those who are so determined to come up with a 'rational' explanation for the inexplicable that they try to argue God out of daily life altogether – just as many will have been treating today as merely a holiday rather than a 'holy' day. They have not tried to understand the mystery of Good Friday – so it will be kept hidden from them, unless we who are under our Lord's orders to proclaim the gospel, get up, get out and proclaim it.

Commemorating the sacrifice of Good Friday is our privilege. Sharing it, is our duty. The two are complementary.

Working it out

John tells us (1 John 4:4) that the power that is in us – the Holy Spirit, our constantly running dynamo – is greater than anything outside us; so we go out into ministry with the advantage on our side from the start. Let us accept this truth, and apply it to every situation into which God brings us. The crowds who wanted Jesus to heal their sick kept close company with him. We should do the same, feeding our inner Spirit with his word, claiming our right – won for us on Good Friday – as inheritors of the kingdom with Christ, to the promises that comprise our covenant with him. Because they are freely available, too often we make heavy weather of accepting them and applying them.

Today, because we *know* that the stone cannot long seal the tomb, we have a hope that the disciples did not have on that first Good Friday. But let us share it: Christ did not only die – and rise – for us alone.

Suggested hymns

Be thou my vision; Low in the grave he lay; My God, I love thee, not because; When I survey the wondrous cross

Easter Eve *(not the Easter Vigil)*   19 April
'I Will Rise Again'   Job 14:1–14 or Lam. 3:1–9, 19–24; Ps. 31:1–4, 15–16; 1 Pet. 4:1–8; Matthew 27:57–66 or John 19:38–42

'The next day, that is, after the day of Preparation, the chief priests and the Pharisees gathered before Pilate and said, "Sir, we remember what

that impostor said while he was still alive, 'After three days I will rise again.'"' Matthew 27:62, 63

[*The following reflections for Easter Eve may be used also as corporate meditations or as a litany*]

These chief priests and Pharisees had remembered Jesus' promise to rise; it is this same promise that sustains us as we reflect on his Passion – sustains and uplifts us even on this solemn Easter Eve, for it came so wonderfully true.

While the rest of Jerusalem, the rest of the world, goes about its business, you are resting in the tomb, Lord. Yesterday, you fell with weakness under the weight of the cross, exhausted by the load of our sins.
Lord, we love you

We look to you so often, as Sovereign Lord, as God, who is stronger than we ever are.

We look to your power, that holds us up when we feel frail.
Lord, we love you

We think of the strength that burst in life out of the sepulchre.

But that was only after you had borne our sin – had taken it to hell and left it with the Devil who had caused it.
Lord, we love you

You had carried our sin to Calvary. We also must walk the way of suffering with you, if we are truly to understand why it had to be.

The love that brought you to the ground, under the cruel weight of the cross of our sin, is the same love that keeps us close to you; close to your tomb on this Easter Eve; close at times when we are tempted to choose an easier way.
Lord, we love you

Even with the help of Simon of Cyrene, Lord, your cross became heavier as our sins continued to weigh upon you. Your blood flowed faster, more and more, to wash those sins away.
Lord, we love you

Lord, our little world seems so important to us – there are times when so much crowds in, that we lose sight of you.

We don't remember how you suffered in your Passion.

We don't remember, when lots of little, busy things take our attention.

Jesus, help us to focus on your weakness – which, terrible though it was, is still stronger than our power.

Lord, we love you

We cannot grasp, Lord, how many people's sins you took to Calvary.

We cannot grasp how God could wear a form like ours, and take our place of guilt.

You had more than the cross to carry, Lord. For the whole world, you carried murder, adultery, forgery, theft, and every possible sin.

We cannot grasp it, Lord – but help us to remember.

Lord, we love you

Where are you, Lord? Where have you gone?

You lived. You died. For us.

And now – it's all over?

No, Lord, for you – for us – *some thing* is only just beginning.

We don't know what it is, Lord. It's called 'the Future' – and we cannot see it, or feel it, or understand it. No one has yet lived it, to come and tell us all about it. The tomb lies silent, Lord – but it will not be tenanted when the stone is rolled away. Not even the *form* of God who walked the earth will be there.

You cannot die, Lord.

You go on for ever living in our hearts – because there is no cross there. Only you.

The cross – you left it, Lord, behind, at Calvary. *Amen.*

Suggested hymns
Be still, for the presence of the Lord; Be still, my soul, the Lord is on thy side; O, the love of my Lord is the essence; The day thou gavest, Lord, is ended

Easter Vigil   19–20 April   Go and Tell

Ex. 14:10–31; 15:20–21; Canticle: Ex. 15:1b–13, 17–18, and a minimum of two further OT readings from: Gen. 1:1–2:4a; Gen. 7:1–5, 11–18; 8:6–18; 9:8–13; Gen. 22:1–18; Isa. 55:1–11; Canticle: Isa. 12:2–6; Ps. 136:1–9, 23–26; Ps. 46; Ps. 16; Baruch 3:9–15, 32–4:4 or Prov. 8:1–8, 19–21; 9:4b-6; Ps. 19; Pss 42, 43; Ps. 143; Ps. 98; Ezek. 36:24–28; Ezek. 37:1–14; Zeph. 3:14–20; Rom. 6:3–11; Mark 16:1–9; Ps. 114

'But go, tell his disciples and Peter that he is going ahead of you to Galilee; there you will see him, just as he told you.' Mark 16:7

Do something about it!

This morning, we emerge from the long, dark tunnel of Lent. Lent, which has taught us how to die, gives way today to Easter in which Jesus is showing us how to live – not only how to live in eternity, but in the here and now. When he rose, that first Easter, he didn't tell his friends to sit around and have a party. He wanted them to respond dynamically to the news he had been to so much trouble to bring them. He said to Mary: 'Go and tell.' The angel said: 'Go and tell.' Five times in the Easter accounts we have it recorded: 'Go and tell.'

Don't cry. Don't even touch me. Don't hang around this grave-yard. It's a place for the dead, and not the living.

'I'm ALIVE!' Jesus is still saying. 'GO AND TELL!'

So much else

But how can Christians get so excited about Easter, when the world is in such a state? Someone probably asked exactly the same question of the disciples – for their country was in an awful state. It had the Roman army of occupation sitting on it, much to the frustration and chagrin of all good Jews. Pontius Pilate, according to the gospels, had caused a bloodbath among insurrectionists in Galilee once, and he could do it again if trouble flared. No disciple of Jesus was safe in the seething cauldron that was Jerusalem. Yet into this tense, volatile situation, came a few ex-fishermen from Galilee, with news so amazing that practically no one would believe it.

We should not be surprised that today a significant proportion of the population prefers to stay outside our churches. Easter is the time of year that Satan hates most. It was at this time that the Devil received his fatal blow, and he's been licking the wound ever since, in agony, bitterness and frustration.

His death throes may be taking longer than we'd like; but time IS running out for him. Yet while he can, he will do all the mischief possible.

Our short cut
But not even Satan can dampen the Christian's Easter joy, as we celebrate Christ's victory that has given us not only our passport to eternity, but a short cut to heaven. Because Jesus, at some time between dying on the cross and rising three days later, sorted out hell, we can go straight to eternity with God, without having to take in the underworld on the way.

Don't stop!
'Go and tell!' is the message of our risen, Easter Lord. And may we be given grace not to stop going, not to stop telling, until we have met and told as many folk as we can.

Jesus has risen as the answer to the whole world and its problems; not just to part of the world, nor just to some of its problems. If we believe otherwise, we are saying, in effect: 'Lord, your sacrifice was not enough; we've managed to come up with something bigger than you can handle!'

Be like Jesus!
In commanding us to 'Go and tell', Jesus is only asking us to put into practice what he did throughout his earthly ministry. Whether he was among friends or enemies, in calm or in a disturbance, newly awake or tired out, Jesus had one aim: to tell the truth, and tell it loud.

'Go and tell!' The message of the Easter Christ is not passive, but active; not inert, but dynamic. It's a message he calls us, this very morning, to take to the world: 'Christ is risen! Alleluia!'

Suggested hymns
Alleluia, alleluia, hearts to heaven and voices raise; Jesus Christ is risen today; Now the green blade riseth; The Day of Resurrection

Easter Day   20 April   *Principal Service*
Where Is He?   Acts 10:34–43 or Isa. 25:6–9;
Ps. 118:1–2, 14–24; 1 Cor. 15:1–11 or Acts 10:34–43;
John 20:1–18 or Mark 16:1–8

'So [Mary] ran and went to Simon Peter and the other disciple, the one whom Jesus loved, and said to them, "They have taken the Lord out of the tomb, and we do not know where they have laid him."' John 20:2

Not daring to hope
Some years ago, a certain meteorologist made the now famous mistake of forecasting as only a gentle breeze what materialized into a devastating hurricane. Since when forecasters in general have tended to err on the gloomy side – and don't folk feel good when the weather turns out better than they had expected!

We see a variation on this pessimism, as Mary, finding the tomb open, immediately takes the negative view that Jesus' body has been moved, instead of daring to believe what he had already foretold.

The day that had begun with freedom from death, hell and the tomb, was to prove a long day for Jesus, as he sought to convince his closest friends that he had risen. But the convincing had to be done, for on their belief hung the fate of the Church.

On our belief today still hangs the fate of the Church. In the measure that God has entrusted us with faith to spread the good news, evangelism will be expected of us. It is lovely to worship among the flowers and candles of celebration, and to enjoy the familiar Bible readings and joyous hymns of Easter; but the risen Christ is still commanding: 'Go and tell!'

Consistency
On Easter Day, when we celebrate God's most wonderful act of all time, it is good to recall St Paul's counsel to Timothy: 'All scripture is inspired by God and is useful for teaching, for reproof, for correction, and for training in righteousness, so that everyone who belongs to God may be proficient, equipped for every good work' (2 Timothy 3:16, 17).

If we are to be consistent in our faith – if we believe God is the same, yesterday, today and for ever – we must believe that his power is consistent, undiminished, as it was in the tomb, as it is in our services, and in our lives today. The alternative would be that God is inconsistent, that he changes, that he no longer deals in the miraculous, the supernatural, the exciting, the unexpected and amazing.

When we took up the Christian challenge, we were in essence giving God the freedom to amaze us, to excite us, to do and say the unexpected to us, according to the purposes and plans he has had for each of us as individuals since before the time we were born.

The Church provides no 'let out' clauses, whereby we can forego this experience of the divine working. So, while 'we profess and call ourselves Christians' (BCP), we are, *with Christ*, in that blessed but high risk situation, of being at any time surprised, excited, stimulated, amazed by God. He has said: 'I know the plans I have for you – plans to prosper you and not to harm you; plans to give you a hope and a future' (Jeremiah 29:11; NIV).

So we need not be afraid. We must not be afraid, to accept the challenge as well as the joy of Easter. We are simply to trust and believe, as we put our hand into his who knows the future. He may make his surprises known in really startling ways – or he may come as quietly as he came to his closest friends on Easter Day, with the simple question: 'Have you anything here to eat?' (Luke 24:41). Do you remember how he said, 'Give the child something to eat,' after he had raised Jairus' daughter from the dead? As the tensions of Holy Week evaporate into Easter joy today, may we *laugh* with our risen Lord, who knows how to be human as well as divine!

Suggested hymns
Christ the Lord is risen today; Jesus lives! thy terrors now; The Lord is risen indeed; The strife is o'er, the battle done

Easter Day   *Second Service*   He Has Risen!
Pss 114, 117; Ezek. 37:1–14; Luke 24:13–35
'That same hour they got up and returned to Jerusalem; and they found the eleven and their companions gathered together. They were saying, "The Lord has risen indeed, and he has appeared to Simon!" ' Luke 24:33, 34

The simplest of acts

The empty tomb, the appearance of Jesus to Mary earlier in the day, even the long expository sermon on the road to Emmaus – all these, together with belated recollections of Jesus' promise that he would rise, had not opened the disciples' eyes. The turning point came when Jesus took bread and gave thanks (v. 30).

In reverence as well as holy joy, we can only wonder at the impact made on the disciples by the realization of the identity of their fellow traveller – and the even greater impact of realizing that the Man eating bread with them should, by natural laws, be lying in the sepulchre! As the truth dawned, faith took over from the fear, doubt and worry that had paralyzed the minds of those disciples until then.

Just as he had done before

He took the bread, broke it and said grace – just as he had done when feeding the five thousand; just as he had done when feeding the four thousand; just as he had done, a few short days before, in the Upper Room on the night of his arrest.

Every day, we are interpreting and understanding new situations, with the memories and experiences of the past. Twice it says in the Book of Proverbs that old landmarks must not be removed (Proverbs 22:28; 23:10). Why do you think God went to the trouble of repeating such advice? We need the landmarks of the past in order to navigate the present. The future is in God's hands, he'll take care of that, but it is how we navigate through today that matters.

The disciples on the Emmaus road were floundering with their spiritual navigation. All the signs had pointed to *something* happening on the third day – but their Lord found them heading off to Emmaus without even waiting for the day to finish.

Not as we had hoped

We, too, can be knocked out of kilter by the unexpected. The disciples had not witnessed a mighty rising complete with fanfare of trumpets (or even a voice from heaven), and they'd been expected to believe what mere *women* had said! We try to tell God at times how to act – and we also get wrong footed; and we tell ourselves – just as the disciples were telling Jesus on that road – that God hasn't done what we thought he would do.

One-to-one

So Jesus explained everything, on a one-to-one (or one-to-two) basis. And so it still happens: we go to church; we listen while some part of the word is explained. We may get really interested – but how often do we accept that God has given us that word, and that God has brought us to church at that particular time; and that it's God who is saying, one-to-one: 'Look! this is for you, for your life, your situation, your problem, your progress, your benefit, right now!'

Faith to believe

No thunderclap, no earthquake – but the resurrection had happened. God had had the power to shake the world into believing, but he wanted it this way. God had planned and executed his great saving act with meticulous care and one hundred per cent devotion; and he is still looking for one hundred per cent disciples who take meticulous care about their work and their faith. He wants wholehearted commitment. One can give oneself to a cause, even die for it, out of austere, stoical determination – but God wants determined LOVE.

He wants eagerness, fervour, joy and enthusiasm. If we, as a church or as individuals, have forgotten how to be joyful about our faith, let us pray our risen Lord to re-awaken joy in us – for unless we have it we cannot share it.

Suggested hymns

Christ the Lord is risen today; Come, risen Lord, and deign to be our Guest; Good Christians all, rejoice and sing; On the resurrection morning

Second Sunday of Easter   27 April
Principal Service   **Joyful Encounter**   Acts 4:32–35; Ps. 133; 1 John 1:1–2:2; John 20:19–31

'Then the disciples rejoiced when they saw the Lord.' John 20:20b

The Easter miracle

These nine little words encapsulate the Easter miracle. It had taken the best part of a day, but now the truth has really dawned on the grieving, fearful disciples. Behind the locked doors, terror gives way to joy.

It has taken a seven-mile sermon, but now the two disciples who were joined by our Lord on the Emmaus road, have the added joy of seeing their companions realize the glorious truth. And, St Luke tells us, Jesus followed up the revelation by another sermon – his second of the evening (Luke 24:44).

Seeing Jesus

We may consider that the disciples were extraordinarily slow to believe the resurrection, but Jesus often goes unnoticed in the world of today. We take the credit for a miracle ourselves, or we blame someone else if anything goes wrong. We laud the advances in science, technology or the arts – but how often do we see a greater force, a divine hand, behind the words and actions? If God is not credited for moving in the lives of his people outside of Sunday services, we are restricting him beyond belief. Yes, it is as simple, yet serious, as that.

In the proportion that the joy of Easter overflows in our worship, it is intended to influence the world beyond our doors. The problems of parish shares, roof maintenance, provision of candles and supplies, can monopolize our agendas, until evangelistic outreach barely gets a mention. We, too, often lock our church doors from Sunday to Sunday, for fear of vandals, for fear of increased insurance premiums. Is this really how God wants his Church to operate? Dare we ask, Is it God or Satan in the driving seat?

This is the challenge of the locked doors to that upper room in Jerusalem. Jesus found them no barrier – but what was his message once he had circumvented those doors? 'As the Father has sent me, SO SEND I YOU!' (John 20:21). The time for locking doors and sitting tight was over; now the disciples must emerge from hiding and get moving with spreading the news.

The giving of the Spirit

Jesus immediately gave them the Holy Spirit, to be up and doing. Yet we learn from St Luke that another fifty days elapsed before an even greater push was needed to get those disciples energized enough to act: in a mega dramatic way at Pentecost, the Spirit was given again – this time, in a tempest, flames and a cacophony of tongues (Acts 2:1ff.).

Yet still the disciples were reluctant to leave Jerusalem – and it took an eruption of violence to thrust them out eventually to Pella; and then the mission really took off, as they ventured further and further with the gospel.

We should probably have done the same. Let's not pretend otherwise. But let us thank God for the patience, the love and the care he showed, in encouraging those early disciples. He wanted his gospel to spread so much that he was willing to take infinite trouble to ensure its success.

So in the Church today, he nurtures and cajoles us, encourages and inspires us, as we struggle against the pleasures and pains of a world that constantly tugs in the opposite direction.

This Easter, let us pray our risen Lord to help us arrange our priorities in line with his own.

Suggested hymns
Guide me, O thou great Redeemer; Put thou thy trust in God; Thine be the glory; Thy way, not mine, O Lord

Second Sunday of Easter *Second Service*
Amazing! Ps. 143:1–11; Isa. 26:1–9, 19; Luke 24:1–12
'But Peter got up and ran to the tomb; stooping and looking in, he saw the linen cloths by themselves, then he went home, amazed at what had happened.' Luke 24:12

God at his most surprising
This is God at his most surprising, doing what he has said he would do! Peter was not the first, or the last, to be taken off guard. We ask God for a miracle – or he gives us a vision, an inkling, an idea, a conviction – and then, perhaps sooner, perhaps later, it happens, and we are often either so surprised that we don't believe it, or we've become so immersed in something else that we don't recognize it. No truer words have yet been spoken, than those in Isaiah 55:8, 'My thoughts are not your thoughts, nor are your ways my ways, says the Lord.'

Off limits
It comes down to a question of limits. God doesn't have any limits, while we are bound by them: limits of time, space, gravity and a

thousand more. And we hedge ourselves round with as many limits as we can, as a form of protection – whether it's by locked doors, high walls, thick clothing, or a tight circle of friends. We keep off certain foods, stay well away from certain areas, speak only to certain people – not 'we' personally, but different members of society. And we're terribly ready to feel good when we see others limiting their lives more than we are doing ourselves.

It does us good to read the gospels, and to see how Jesus overrode the self-imposed limitations of those around him. He 'harvested' corn on the sabbath day (Mark 2:23); he conversed with undesirables, and folk of other races (Matthew 9:11; John 4:9); he touched lepers (Matthew 8:3); he caused a furore in the hallowed courts of the temple (Luke 19:45); he defied the religious grandees of the day (Matthew 23:13). And he went further: he produced a mountain of food from one boy's picnic lunch (John 6:9); he walked on water (Matthew 14:25); and – he rose from the dead (Mark 16:9).

Present – and future
Certainly some of these freedoms may not be experienced by us in this life; but many of them can be. Jesus challenges us in today's reading, in the empty tomb and discarded grave clothes, to examine the limitations we may have imposed unnecessarily on our lives. Can we profitably get rid of any of them? Are they inhibiting our *raison d'être*, which is to share the gospel? We can become so used to restrictions that they accumulate and strengthen imperceptibly until they become the 'normal' way of living. We do well to remember that what may be normal for us is probably not God's way. If we have built a protective crust of limitation around our lives, can we not get serious with God in prayer, and ask him to show us how we can live more dangerously for him? Dare we make such a request? Dare we not?

The one who would not dare
There was a man who was really enthused about the gospel. All he needed was the final word from Jesus, and his ministry would be up and running. 'What do I have to do, to clinch the matter, Lord?' he asked. And Jesus told him. Only one measure needed to be taken. Just one.

But the man simply couldn't do it. He was really cut up; it was *such a pity*, but he simply couldn't do it. St Matthew tells us:

'He went away grieving, for he had many possessions' (Matthew 19:22).

Suggested hymns
Give me joy in my heart; I heard the voice of Jesus say; Take up thy cross, the Saviour said; Will you come and follow me

Third Sunday of Easter   4 May
Principal Service   **See What Love**   Acts 3:12–19; Ps. 4; 1 John 3:1–7; Luke 24:36b–48
'See what love the Father has given us that we should be called children of God, and that is what we are.' 1 John 3:1

Our spiritual sight
George Matheson was a blind boy who became an ardent preacher. He wrote the beautiful hymn, 'O love, that wilt not let me go', in five inspired minutes, in the manse at Innellan, near Greenock on the Clyde, one June evening over a century ago. Each summer, groups of holiday makers crowd into the little church and sing his hymn under the chancel window depicting 'The Light of the World'. And, as if God is giving an extra blessing to Matheson's memory, the lantern in our Lord's hand in that so-familiar window seems to shine out brightly even on a misty day. Dr Matheson preached in the church at Innellan for eighteen years, without seeing the beautiful window, yet his hymn has lit up many lives.

Jesus tells us: 'Let your light shine before others, so that they may see your good works and give glory to your Father in heaven' (Matthew 5:16); and his message has been paraphrased in our text from St John. If we do not *perceive and receive* God's light of love, we are ill-equipped to share it with others.

God's love
God's love shone out at its brightest when he sent his Son into the world. He didn't need to do it. He didn't have to show such love. This beautiful world in which we live is just a tiny speck in the universe. Yet with galaxy after galaxy of stars and worlds and earths and planets, God so loved *this* one, that he put himself out to save us.

Two friends – US President Theodore Roosevelt and the author William Beebe – used to observe a quaint little ritual after they had dined of an evening. Going outside, they would locate a star in the left-hand corner of Pegasus, and recite together:

> 'That is the spiral galaxy of Andromeda.
> It is as large as our Milky Way.
> It is one of a hundred million galaxies . . .'

Then they would exchange smiles, and the President would say: 'Well, now, guess we both feel small enough. Let's call it a day.'

Yes, we are small – physically – in relation to the universe. Yet spiritually we are anything but small; spiritually, we have within us the mighty power that made the universe: the power that Jesus gave to his disciples after the resurrection, to go and evangelize the world (and who knows how much else, in eternity?). We cannot evaluate the power of the love that God has invested in us, implanted in us. We cannot put a length, breadth, height or depth to it. But it motivates us, in Christ's name, to do God's work, to go the extra mile, to turn the other cheek. It motivates us to get up and get on, even when Satan has sent us reeling for the umpteenth time.

Making the difference
There is one big difference between Christians and non-believers. We may fall short of perfection – but we keep on aiming for it. They fall short of it because they're not aiming for it. What *makes* the difference? Simply, the love of God – which we have right here in our hearts, and non-believers haven't. It's a love that is capable of making a success of living, in a world where success is so often measured in status, power and wealth. It's a love that knows it's totally undeserved – and thus can be freely shared. It's a love that is unconditional – because in the first place it cost the Giver so much. No one but God can – or ever will be able to – put a price on Calvary.

God's love enables us to see the world as he sees it. It empowers us to say, 'I am a sinner, but I'm saved by grace.' With humility, but *true pride*, we can claim to be sinners, yet 'children of God'. Alleluia!

Children of the heavenly King; O, Love that wilt not let me go;
O, the love of my Lord is the essence; Thee we adore, O hidden
Saviour

Third Sunday of Easter *Second Service*
Loveless and Persecuted Ps. 142; Deut. 7:7–13;
Rev. 2:1–11

*'To the angel of the church in Ephesus write . . . you have abandoned
the love you had at first.' Revelation 2:1, 4b*

The loveless church
Years before, Paul had warned the Ephesian church leaders to be
vigilant against spiritual predators (Acts 20:29, 31). Now, writing
from Patmos, probably in AD 95, John is inspired to castigate
them for over-scrupulosity. Their religious zeal has become more
important than loving concern for each other. The Ephesian Christians have been so fervent in fighting the battle that they have lost
the best part of it. What really matters is, God is love. Despite its
apparent strength and vigour, this little church is in danger of
losing its light – of ceasing to be a real church. Come back to God,
is the message: remember, repent, and do the things you did in
the first enthusiasm of believing. The Nicolaitans (v. 6) were false
teachers who claimed not to be destroying Christianity, but to be
modernizing it, rather like the insidious fifth column, destroying
it from within. At least the Ephesian Christians have rightly
divined this danger.

Did it work?
We hear of Paul's three-year ministry in Ephesus (Acts 20:31), and
thrill at the drama of the demonstration in the great theatre
(Acts 19) – but now the question is: did the Spirit's letter from
Patmos work? The Bible intriguingly keeps us in suspense; but
God has provided us the answer in another way. Writing twenty
years after John of Patmos, a letter has been preserved for us from
Ignatius (Bishop of Antioch), who pays tribute to the *charity* as
well as the discipline of the Ephesian Church.

Letter writing *does* pay!

'To the angel of the church in Smyrna write ... Be faithful until death, and I will give you the crown of life.' Revelation 2:8, 10b

The persecuted church

Founded in the twelfth century BC by the Greeks, with a major re-building under Alexander the Great, Smyrna had grown rich in trade, minting its own coins from the time of Augustus (first century BC). But in all this opulence, the Christians here had got their priorities right. This was enough to get the Devil really roused (v. 10). Persevering but persecuted, sums up this struggling little church (one of only two in these Seven Letters to earn unqualified praise).

The fact that Jesus returned to life proves that whatever Christians have to suffer for the cause of truth, it is not in vain (v. 8). These Smyrnian Christians may be materially poor (surrounded by material riches), but in their Lord's eyes they are rich (v. 9, cf. James 2:5). The Jews in Smyrna appear to be giving the Christians some Angst, as they did in the earliest days of the Church (Acts 13:44, 45; 14:16). Sixty years after John wrote, Polycarp (Bishop of Smyrna) was martyred, and it was recorded that when wood was being gathered to burn the saintly old man, 'the Jews were extremely zealous, as is their custom, in assisting at this', even though the execution took place on 'a great Sabbath day' (*The Martyrdom of Polycarp*).

The crown (v. 10b) is eternal life. In the Greek there is an article with 'life', but not with 'death': literally, 'Be faithful until death, and I will give you *the crown of the life.*' Troubles, deprivation, poverty. We tend to see these as failures of one kind or another. The modern world (as in first-century Smyrna) runs as fast as it can after fortune, plenty and wealth. But God requires life on a spiritual scale; and the loyalty and strength of the church in Smyrna will earn it 'the crown of the life' when the hurdle of death has been cleared.

We may reflect today upon whether our own church mirrors more nearly the church of Ephesus, or that of Smyrna. We, too, have our problems. We, like Ephesus and Smyrna, matter to God.

Suggested hymns
Spirit of God, as strong as the wind; The earth, O Lord, is one wide field; Thy Kingdom come, O God; The Saviour of men came to seek and to save

Fourth Sunday of Easter   11 May
Principal Service   **The Good Shepherd**
Acts 4:5–12; Ps. 23; 1 John 3:16–24; John 10:11–18

'[Jesus said], "I am the good shepherd. I know my own and my own know me."' John 10:14

Sheep of the fold
As sheep carry the mark of their shepherd, painted on their back and imprinted in their ear, so we Christians bear the mark of our good shepherd: the cross traced on our forehead at baptism, the imprint of the episcopal hand at confirmation – and the fruit of the Spirit shining out of our hearts: love, joy, peace, patience, kindness, generosity, faithfulness, gentleness and self-control (Galatians 5:22, 23).

But unless we actually 'tell it straight', unless we broadcast the *Name* of our shepherd, folk may be forgiven for not identifying us with the flock of Christ. Let's face it, *our* identification doesn't matter – but his does. And wherever the Name of Jesus is not mentioned, Satan muscles in to take over what is not his.

Christian Aid
At this time of the year Christian Aid posters go up, envelopes are pushed through letter boxes, parish magazine editors take a break from the local news, to focus our minds on the Church worldwide. It is borne in upon us, ever more clearly, just how much of the world still doesn't know the Name of Jesus, still isn't part of his fold. Families, villages, cities, countries still have not only a physical famine, but a famine of hope. Great work is being done to alleviate the physical deprivation – but the famine of hope need not be terminal. Every Christian has been given the power to turn it into a treasury of hope. The power is not ours: it's God's. We can take this power to the stricken areas; we can write books about it, and send them there. And we can pray. There is no Christian who cannot do at least one of these.

Downtown mission
To downtown New York, where Nicky Cruz was the feared head of one of the strongest, cruellest mafia type gangs, went David Wilkerson, with the Name of Jesus. The two men met, in a sordid back street, alive with peering eyes from alleyways and broken

windows. 'I'm going to kill you,' promised Nicky, pulling a gun. Wilkerson stood his ground, a bare three feet from the barrel. 'In the Name of Jesus, I'm telling you, Nicky, God loves you,' he said. 'And I love you. I love you alive; and if you kill me, I'll go to be with God, and we'll *both* still love you.' Nicky pulled the trigger – again, and again. But that crackshot gangster just couldn't hit his mark, even from one yard. Go now to any Christian bookshop and they'll find you the autobiography of Nicky Cruz – of how, in the love of the Good Shepherd, the one-time gang leader has become a full-time missionary for Christ.

Getting it out
Overcoming spiritual laryngitis takes a plus of determination. We don't (usually) mind folk seeing us come to church; but sometimes our throats seize up, our tongues twist into knots, when we are asked point-blank WHY we believe, and what Jesus is to us.

David Wilkerson was looking into the business end of Nicky Cruz's gun, when he had to explain his faith. We're not likely to be presented with quite such a fraught situation.

> *Jesus, let me tell someone of your*
> *love today, and someone else tomorrow.*
> *You are my Best Friend, my Good Shepherd.*
> *I want the world to know, and I have*
> *to start somewhere.*

There's a world out there, careening towards oblivion. It isn't God's fault. He is able. He would never have allowed a person to be born if he wasn't able to save that person. God's there, loving them. Satan's there, hating them. Between the two, is Jesus – Good Shepherd, Advocate, Mediator.

The only snag is, since the ascension, Jesus is over at God's right hand.

Guess who's supposed to be doing his work, right here?

Suggested hymns
Forth in thy name, O Lord, I go; Jesus, I my cross have taken; Loving Shepherd of thy sheep; Make me a channel of your peace

Fourth Sunday of Easter *Second Service*
The Two-edged Sword Ps. 81:8–16; Ex. 16:4–15;
Rev. 2:12–17

'To the angel of the church in Pergamum write, These are the words of him who has the sharp two-edged sword.' Revelation 2:12

The over-tolerant church

Ephesus (Revelation 2:1–7) had been criticized for its intolerance; now Pergamum for its over-tolerance. This city had the oldest temple dedicated to the worship of the Roman emperor: 'Pergamum ... where Satan's throne is ...' was also the centre for the worship of Asclepius, the god of healing. It has been described as 'the Lourdes of the ancient world'. The city was justly proud of its fine library of over 200,000 scrolls. Founded by Eumenes II, it rivalled that of Ptolemy Philadelphus of Alexandria who, fearing his pride and joy would be outshone, is said to have banned the export of papyrus to Pergamum (whereupon the resourceful people of Pergamum developed what we now know as parchment [from *pergamena*]).

Jesus gives the Christians here encouragement: come emperor worship, wealth, luxury, heathen cults – as Judge and Executioner, he will overcome those who oppose his followers (v. 12)! The sword of the Christians is double-edged: one to cut evil into little pieces, the other to pierce in love to the heart of a person with the truth of the gospel.

Hidden manna

In Moses' day, a pot of manna had been 'hidden' in the ark of the covenant – hidden in the *sanctus sanctorum* of the tabernacle (Exodus 16:14f.; Hebrews 9:3, 4), where only the high priest entered once each year, on the Day of Atonement. But, like Jesus before them, Christians get to enter not into a temple made with hands, but into heaven itself (Hebrews 9:12, 24). At their resurrection, corruption is exchanged for incorruption, mortality for immortality – a marvellous provision of God, symbolized by their being given the imperishable 'hidden manna'.

The white stone

What is this white stone (v. 17)? We don't know for certain, but several suggestions have been made:

1) Perhaps it symbolizes a happy (red-letter) day?
2) Or an amulet for good luck?
3) Or a rabbinic link with the manna?
4) Or a stone in the high priest's breastplate?
5) Or a reference to the *urim*, used in casting lots?
6) It could have been an allusion to the glistening array of temples, halls and statues in the architecturally magnificent Pergamum. John may have visualized the Christians after death triumphant with a brightness outshining these man-made buildings, being admitted in their brilliance to the Almighty's throne room.
7) Perhaps it was a ticket for 'bread and circuses'. In Roman times pebbles were sometimes used as tickets, to gain entry to important events. So the white stone may indicate something special for the conquering anointed Christian: a ticket to an honoured place in heaven at the marriage of the Lamb (Revelation 14:1; 19:7–9).
8) But the suggestion which seems to carry most weight is the stone of acquittal. In Roman courts, stones were used in passing judgement: a white stone for acquittal, a black one for condemnation (often to death). The Pergamum Christians would, given this, be judged favourably by Jesus, if they can in the meantime correct the infiltration of the heretics they appear to be tolerating: the Nicolaitans (whom the Ephesian Christians had seen through, v. 6), and those holding to the teaching of Balaam.

Balaam's subtlety
In the days of Moses, King Balak of Moab had hired Balaam, a non-Israelite prophet who knew something about God's ways, to curse Israel. God resisted Balaam, compelling him to pronounce blessings for the Israelites. Balaam pacified Balak's indignation by suggesting a more subtle attack: Let Moab's women seduce Israel's men into sexual sin and idolatrous worship of the false god Baal of Peor! The tactic worked.

But, like the Christians of Pergamum, we need to be on our guard against subtlety of this, and other kinds, today. The hidden manna and the white stone are not given indiscriminately, even though the Christian's Judge knows more about compassion than the ancient Romans.

Suggested hymns
I hunger and I thirst; Immortal, Invisible, God only wise; Judge
eternal, throned in splendour; Lord, enthroned in heavenly
splendour

Fifth Sunday of Easter   18 May
Principal Service   **Already**   Acts 8:26–40;
Ps. 22:25–31; 1 John 4:7–21; John 15:1–8

*'[Jesus said], "You have already been cleansed by the word that I have
spoken to you."' John 15:3*

Wasted energy
It is a waste of energy to ask for what we have already been given.
The Chinese preacher Watchman Nee used to say it was like being
asked to be put into a room that one was in already. And our
Lord himself showed impatience when Philip asked to be shown
the Father. 'Jesus said to him, "Have I been with you all this time,
Philip, and you still do not know me? Whoever has seen me, has
seen the Father. How can you say, Show us the Father?"' (John
14:9).

Some Christians sit and dream about how wonderful it would
be to bring other souls to Christ, to preach to great crowds, to go
about laying hands on the sick, to take the gospel here, there and
everywhere. To them, God is still saying: 'You have already been
cleansed [prepared] by the word that I have spoken [given] to
you.' We have the power, the word, the inspiration. All it needs
is our willingness to put it into practice.

The stimulus
Jesus, the Vine, is the stimulus, the growth, the energy, the
dynamic force making visible the living power of the invisible
God. We, as the branches, are either linked to him and thus part
of that growth, energy and potential, or . . . well, what are branches
when they're not growing as part of a vine? Merely useless bits
of wood, fit only for being burned to ashes on a fire. This is Jesus
at his most ecclesiastical: the True Vine in its entirety – that is,
Jesus, plus you, plus me, plus every other Christian in heaven and
earth – is the CHURCH.

125

The sap begins with Jesus, but, as it is given to the branches, these in turn put out new growth, extending, growing and developing. We have been given the capital. We must put it to good use.

God is still there!
But God, like the best vine-dressers, doesn't leave us to grow untended. After a while he prunes, trains and cleans us, just as a natural vine is cut back, tied in and given its twice-annual wash to remove harmful growth and bacteria.

Vine branches with little or no promise get short shrift; the Vine-dresser cuts them out, and they end up being shredded or burned. It seems hard, but to leave them on the vine would serve no useful purpose. And a lukewarm or unfaithful Christian suffers the fate of a recalcitrant or withered branch.

The Christian life is unthinkable, untenable and impossible without Christ. Jesus said, very clearly: 'He who is not with me, is against me.' We are either on his side, or on someone else's. Either attached as branches to his vine – or to someone else's.

God knows his material
God works to certain rules – rules which have governed our development since the days of creation. He knows our abilities; he knows our limitations; and he knows he will never ask of us anything we cannot deliver. Yet at times we make a poor show of understanding where his pruning and training is heading. We are very human, even though we have the divine Spark of Pure Life in us. We shall make mistakes. God knows our ways better than we know ourselves. He is not fazed when we act as though we have not understood his directions. He knows we need to be pruned a bit more here, a lot more there – and *then* we shall change the world for him!

A wise old preacher used to say each morning:

Lord, help me to remember that nothing is going to happen to me today, that you and I cannot handle together.

Why not? We're part of the same vine!

> *Thou true Vine, our Lord and Saviour,*
> *May we fruitful branches be,*

Ever drawing from thy fulness
Strength to serve and follow thee;
Vine of beauty, ever growing,
Till thy vineyard spans the earth,
Bearing fruit in every nation,
As new life is brought to birth.

Suggested hymns
Give me the faith that can remove; I, the Lord of sea and sky; Lord, it belongs not to my care; Thou true Vine, that heals the nations

Fifth Sunday of Easter   *Second Service*
Wake Up!   Ps. 96; Isa. 60:1–14; Rev. 3:1–13
'And to the angel of the church in Sardis write ... Wake up, and strengthen what remains.' Revelation 3:1, 2

The sleeping church
Sardis had been a wealthy city. Built on a hill, it was considered to be impregnable, yet it was captured five times. The complacency had also impregnated its Christians. Once the capital of the fabulously wealthy King Croesus, Sardis had known a superabundance of luxury, but had now fallen on hard times. Yet the church there was one of which everyone spoke well: a model of inoffensive Christianity. It was, however, incapable of distinguishing between the calm of well-being and the calm of death. The Sardian church was lifeless, in danger of being blotted out of the Book of Life (v. 5). No one can earn the right of an entry in this precious book – but everyone can forfeit it. The church in Sardis had become spiritually impoverished. For the first time in these Seven Letters, Jesus does not begin his message with a word of praise. This little church may have the reputation of being active and alive, but Jesus, with his sevenfold (i.e. complete) spiritual sight, can detect that it is spiritually dead. Apparently most of its members have sunk into an apathy similar to their condition before they became Christians (cf. Ephesians 2:1–3; Hebrews 5:11–44).

Jesus also reminds the congregation elders that he is the one who has 'the seven stars' (v. 1). He has the authority to direct the work of shepherding the church. These elders in Sardis need to remember the joy they first had when they learned the truth; they should recall the blessings they received then. But they have allowed spiritual activity to flag; their congregational lamp is flickering because of lack of works of faith.

Encouragement

After the strictures, a little encouragement (vv. 4, 5). A few members have remained true and alive. Make the most of this nucleus! A little leaven can lift a lot!

This is the loving Lord who is just and merciful, and who will not lose any opportunity to encourage even a flicker of faith. Those who stand firm against the prevailing current of apathy will be rewarded.

For it is important to note here in Sardis that neither persecution nor heresy is the problem. Instead, a combination of disinterest and misconduct is responsible for the church's parlous state. Just a few who have resisted the rot and have kept themselves pure, are seen by John as forming the embryo of a revival church. They have a lot going for them: a good name to the outside world, apparent freedom from imperial pressure, pagan cults or even discontented Jews. Nor does finance seem a problem.

Like a thief

The threat of Jesus to come like a thief in the night (v. 3) would remind the Sardians of the Persian (549 BC) and Seleucid (218 BC) attacks, which had caused such harm while the Sardians innocently slept. The Christians are in danger, but this little church is still precious to God, and has not gone beyond the point of no return; she can still heed the warning; and this letter underlines the rewards (vv. 4, 5).

The Book of Life

The size of this book – even though many may be called but few chosen – teases the mind out of all thought. Can we, perhaps, spend a little time today praying for those whose names we would commend to God for inclusion in this wonderful book?

> Lord, I care not for riches,
> Neither silver nor gold;
> I would make sure of heaven,
> I would enter the fold.
> In the Book of thy kingdom,

With its pages so fair,
Tell me, Jesus, Lord Jesus,
Is my name written there?

Lord, my sins they are many,
Like the sands of the sea;
But thy blood, O my Saviour,
Is sufficient for me.
Where no evil thing cometh
To despoil what is fair,
Where my loved ones are waiting,
Is my name written there?

M.A. Kidder

Suggested hymns
Glorious things of thee are spoken; I will sing the wondrous story;
Jerusalem the golden; When the roll is called up yonder

Sixth Sunday of Easter 25 May
Principal Service **No Strings Attached**
Acts 10:44–48; Ps. 98; 1 John 5:1–6; John 15:9–17
'[Jesus said] "I have said these things to you so that my joy may be in
you, and that your joy may be complete." ' John 15:11

Complete joy
Do we ever really experience complete joy, with no strings
attached, in this life? Only if we are rooted and grounded in
Christ. Otherwise it is a fleeting happiness, a partial satisfaction,
a qualified success, that brings a brief respite in the daily routine.
The joy in an examination success lasts only until one is studying hard for the next. The holiday all too soon comes to an end,
and extra work is waiting which has been accumulating while we
have been away. Birth is followed by death, pleasure by pain,
summer by winter ... So says the pessimist – and much of the
world.

But the Christian, as the eternal optimist, sees it in a different
way; success at work brings more fulfilment; hard work is the
prelude to a holiday; death is but the birth of a new life; pain does

not last for ever; and every winter is followed by God's beautiful summer.

Divine encouragement

So it is with Jesus. He has just been teaching his disciples about the True Vine; and the pruning, training and nurturing by the Divine Gardener is meant to encourage his friends. But to those outside his Church, the operations seem stringent. It was so all through his ministry. Teaching, preaching, healing miracles were all punctuated by his command: 'Don't fear, don't be afraid.' For the joy set before him was set on enduring the Passion. He tried to infuse something of this quality into the disciples for whom 'joy' meant something less.

What is joy?

If we, too, limit 'joy' to mean merely fleeting happiness, we shall miss out on much of Jesus' teaching. His joy lay in doing the will of his Father, whatever that entailed. It did not matter whether it made him happy (though on any reading of the gospels, it did); it didn't matter if it made everyone else happy (which it didn't). God's will can divide families, cut through carefully laid plans, disturb, distress – but any other way leads away from heaven and down the broad highway to hell.

When every sort of hardship comes against you, 'Rejoice, and be glad!' Jesus tells us, 'for your reward is great in heaven' (Matthew 5:12). How can we do this?

'Three times I was beaten with rods. Once I received a stoning . . .' St Paul enumerates his hardships (2 Corinthians 11: 24ff.). Yet he was rejoicing at being counted worthy to suffer for Christ. How could he do that?

Misunderstood

The world doesn't understand us when we take hardship on the chin. We're either mad, stoical or drugged, says the world – and, well satisfied with such a verdict, promptly loses interest. So we shall have to do more than that to get the point across. There is only one way: to follow the example of Jesus, as Paul, Peter and the others did: teaching, preaching, healing, casting out demons – yes, and raising the dead. This is exactly what is happening in many churches in the so-called 'Third World', where they don't clutter up religion with too many caveats of 'Will it work? What if it doesn't?' – but go right ahead, believing God will work through them as he has promised. And he does. And joy abounds.

The Church needs to be the place where people find teaching, healing and joy. As in the early days of Christianity, they will then keep coming back for more. Real joy is the most highly contagious thing yet invented. Let's pray we can spread this infection ever more widely!

Suggested hymns
Come, sing with holy gladness; I feel the winds of God today; Give me joy in my heart; Glad that I live am I

Sixth Sunday of Easter   *Second Service*
Neither Cold nor Hot   Ps. 45;
Song of Sol. 4:16–5:2; 8:6–7; Rev. 3:14–22

'To the angel of the church in Laodicea write ... "I know your works. You are neither cold nor hot. I wish that you were either cold or hot."'
Revelation 3:14, 15

Why lukewarm?
Lack of water, a major problem for Laodicea, had been overcome by channelling water down from hot springs some distance away. By the time it arrived in the city, it was lukewarm. Jesus may have had this in mind when he accused this over-complacent church of being neither hot nor cold.

At this time, Laodicea was a prosperous city, built on banking and commerce. The sale of a well-known eye salve added to its wealth, and it was also famous for a range of high quality garments produced locally from a fine black wool (cf. v. 18, where Jesus counsels the Laodicean Christians to come to him for white robes of life and purity, not of funereal black, and his ointment to allow them to see clearly his way, not the eye salve which is merely a physical medicine). These people can only see the material benefits that Laodicea provides. Despite their exercising (= discipline) – Laodicea's gymnasiums have been unearthed by archaeologists – they are 'wretched, pitiable, poor, blind and naked' (v. 17).

The danger of affluence

'Affluent' sums up Laodicea. Fiercely independent, the citizens had confidently rejected the offer of imperial aid for repairs, and had seen to their own rebuilding following a severe earthquake in AD 60.

So many advantages! But of the Seven Letters to the Churches, it is Laodicea which comes in for the worst strictures.

Where is your fervour and enthusiasm, Laodiceans? Can't you show excitement for the gospel – or even strong disapproval? Wealth has stultified Christian growth; theirs is the gold that is of poor quality and will not last. Those who drape themselves in black (and pay handsomely for the privilege), and smear their eyes with salve and their ears with medicament from the city's highly renowned medical foundation, should rather be wearing white in honour of the Name they bear. No medicine can open eyes to see God's truth, or ears to hear his voice.

Criticism on all counts! Can you imagine the congregation hearing this read out in church? In a few short lines, the wealth and status of Laodicea has been demolished virtually to nothing. Money, material, medicine – their three economic staples – castigated at a stroke.

We may reflect on how our staples help us to know God better. Or are they hindering our Christian witness?

The Light of the World

William Holman Hunt's famous painting *The Light of the World*, based on Revelation 3:20, brings the salvation Jesus offers into sharp focus. Hunt was 27 when his painting was first exhibited in 1854. Jesus is shown standing outside a door overgrown with brambles. There is no handle, no way in, unless the door is opened from inside. His right hand is raised to knock. In his left he holds a lantern, its beams illuminating the path. Yet already he half-turns to leave. If the person within does not respond quickly, he may depart, never to return.

Who knows when the Lord will stop knocking? Yet if he is given entry, he promises not merely to bring light to our lives, but to share those lives; not merely to embrace us and leave, but to sit down and eat with us (v. 20)! Can you imagine that? The Master of the Universe sharing such an honour with us! There he stands, among the brambles, and on the ground around his feet lie fallen apples and straggling weeds, reminding us of the Fall.

132

From his shoulders hangs a kingly robe, but on his head – thrown into even greater prominence by his glory – is still the crown of thorns.

If he knocks at our heart's door today, will we let him in?

Suggested hymns
Abide with me; I heard the voice of Jesus say; Knocking, knocking, who is there?; Lord Jesus Christ

Ascension Day   29 May   Carried Away
Acts 1:1–11 or Dan. 7:9–14; Ps. 47 or Ps. 93;
Eph. 1:15–23 or Acts 1:1–11; Luke 24:44–53

'While he was blessing them, he withdrew from them and was carried up into heaven. And they worshipped him, and returned to Jerusalem with great joy.' Luke 24:51, 52

Right teaching
A recent report from China, from a young man training for the ministry, highlighted a visit from a prominent cleric to the seminary; he had told the students not to be afraid to say that Jesus did not rise physically from the dead. The young man went on to write: 'Our teachers are very evangelical, and don't like the modern "liberal theology", so they tell us quietly to make no fuss, and just forget his teaching.'

In comparison with our own, the Church in China is very young, and is in real danger of being tossed about with 'liberal' teaching.

Many 'liberal' sermons are preached on Ascension Day, as we all struggle with the how's and why's. Somehow, many Christians with both feet firmly on the ground find difficulty in accepting that Jesus could override the laws of gravity. The same Christians may have no problem with the feeding of the five thousand, or the changing of water into wine, or even the raising of Lazarus – but the ascension is something else.

What do we make of it?
Do we duck the issue, and simply believe it happened, without delving too far into the logistics? Does it really matter how it happened? We can be sure of at least two truths: the ascension

needed to happen, and it did happen. But is it really so simple? Jesus had told his friends: 'If I do not go away, the Advocate will not come to you, but if I go I will send him to you' (John 16:7). So there was a divine necessity, a divine obligation, a divine imperative for the ascension. It would take place because it could take place. Our God is an awesome God.

Is it not incredible to doubt that a God who could create universe after universe, who could feed thousands of people out of one schoolboy's tuckbox, who could raise folk from the dead, could accept his own Son into glory in any one of a multitude of ways? God is not at a loss for the means or the ingenuity to carry out his purposes – and because he is streets ahead of us in inventiveness, he can leave us wondering, time and again: 'How did he do it?' Yet there are those – within the Church as well as outside it – who refuse to acknowledge that God is cleverer than they. One can be so 'liberal' as to strip God (in a manner of speaking) of all 'otherness'.

Amazing record
The account of the ascension is an amazing record that never loses its wonder, for all its familiarity. Remember that St Luke is not writing as a mystic, or a high falutin' theologian, but as a scientist, a practical, highly educated physician: not the type to dream on Cloud Nine.

The theologian J.C. Ryle used to say: 'Read the Bible fairly and honestly. Determine to take everything in its plain, obvious meaning, and regard all forced interpretations with great suspicion. As a general rule, whatever a verse of the Bible seems to mean, it does mean.'

Jesus returned to glory. And, since 'glory' is very definitely not part of our physical world here, then it follows that in some way he left this earth. He could hardly go downwards. Had he gone sideways, he would sooner or later have returned to Jerusalem. So there are not too many options left.

We can only begin to fathom the deep, deep love of a God who could leave glory – for us; who could die the most awful death of all – for us; and who could then defy all the known laws of chemistry, physics and biology – for us.

If Christ's ascension is to mean anything to us, our lives are going to be different from this day on. We have glimpsed glory today. We can choose to bask in it, to feel virtuous and at peace with the world. Or we can choose to share this glory, and to know that this very Lord of Glory is at peace with us.

Whatever we do, God will notice.

But if we choose to share the glory, the world may notice as well.

Suggested hymns
At the Name of Jesus; Crown him with many crowns; Hail the day that sees him rise; The head that once was crowned with thorns

Seventh Sunday of Easter (Sunday after Ascension Day) 1 June *Principal Service*
Making It Known Acts 1:15–17, 21–26; Ps. 1; 1 John 5:9–13; John 17:6–19

'[Jesus said] "I have made your name known to those whom you gave me from the world. They were yours, and you gave them to me, and they have kept your word."' John 17:6

Already God's own
The disciples belonged to God before Jesus ever called them – even Judas. While this knowledge should give us great encouragement, there is also the danger that being God's does not mean we can rest on our laurels and let him do all the work. Like Judas, we can let our precious inheritance slip away. God does not relieve us of the responsibility for our words and actions.

Jesus valued his friends: not only for what they were going to do, but for who they were. They had (more often than not) given him support, friendship and fellowship during his ministry; but as the time came for him to leave, he knew how vulnerable they were. If they could deny and desert him in his time of need, however were they to stand firm when he had gone?

Prayer and promise
So he prayed on their behalf to his Father, to look after them; and he promised to send the Holy Spirit to guard, guide, remind and reinforce them. What more could he do?

His concern for them must have deepened when, on Easter Day, it proved so difficult to convince them that he had risen. If we could only appreciate Christ's concern for us today, would we not step out into the daily battle with greater courage, and more determination than ever before to work and witness for him? It has been said that the greatest competitor to love for God is service for him: we can become so locked on to the practicalities of our religion, that we give less time to the reason for it.

His concern, our concern

Realizing Christ's concern for his people should give us an increasing concern and compassion for others. The story is told of a student who asked his rabbi: 'When would you say is the precise moment when day succeeds night? When it is possible to see an animal, and to tell whether it is a dog or a sheep?' 'No, it is not day then,' was the reply. 'When it is possible to see a tree, and to tell whether it is a fig or an olive?' 'No, it is not day then,' was again the reply. 'When *would* you say it was day?' asked the baffled student. 'It is day,' said the rabbi, 'when you can see the face of another, and can tell it is your brother or your sister. If you cannot tell that, it is still night.'

With God, it is never night, and he can even tell the hairs on our head, with a concern and compassion beyond our comprehension.

> *Except I am moved with compassion,*
> *How dwelleth thy Spirit in me?*
> *In word and in deed,*
> *Burning love is my need;*
> *I know I can find this in thee.*
>
> *Albert W. T. Orsborn*

The more we listen to the Holy Spirit's prompting, and act upon it, the more he will go to work on us. To be so 'taken over by the Spirit' is a high risk business, for we don't know when he'll decide we've reached our limit. He may well postpone such a decision, for he knows no limits; he is God!

Giving God the lead does not make for an easier life, but surely for a more exciting one. Time and again, we need to go back to the Book of Revelation and to learn from God's strictures on the lukewarm church in Laodicea (Revelation 3:14–22). Are we on fire for God, determined to use all the time he gives in his service? Charles Haddon Spurgeon used to say that unless the Church was at a white-hot heat for mission, God's will would not be accomplished.

It is our reason for living; our reason for seeing that other folk live instead of dying from lack of knowledge of salvation. If on the shoulders of the apostles rested the work of taking the gospel from Jerusalem, on the shoulders of today's Christians rests the even greater responsibility of completing worldwide evangelism.

Suggested hymns
A charge to keep I have; Father God, I wonder how; Father, I place into your hands; Thy hand, O God, has guided

Seventh Sunday of Easter *Second Service*
Today! Ps. 147:1–11; Isa. 61:1–11; Luke 4:14–21

'And [Jesus] rolled up the scroll, gave it back to the attendant, and sat down. The eyes of all in the synagogue were fixed on him. Then he began to say to them, "Today the scripture has been fulfilled in your hearing."'
Luke 4:20, 21

Declaration of intent
Whether the reading had been pre-set, or Jesus chose it himself, it was a declaration of intent. Thus the carpenter's Son, in his hometown synagogue, was giving formal notice of his message and mission. He had been welcomed at the service, but he was taking the chance of being misunderstood from now on. At no point in his ministry did he alter his message by way of accommodation or compromise. His listeners were free to accept it or reject it, but he would not modify it to suit their mood of the moment.

The gospel today can be so altered to meet a supposed need (or lack of need), until very little of its original impact remains. As those commissioned by Jesus to preach or teach or share, it is not our remit to tinker with his holy word. We must 'tell it straight', as God has given it, and allow God to be God. He will safeguard his honour; we must not compromise our own, but as faithful witnesses to the truth preach Christ crucified, risen and ascended – *every* Sunday.

Luke 4:16 is an important verse, because it infers that Mary and Joseph had brought up their Son to observe regular sabbath worship. Jesus did not just happen to drop by the synagogue that particular sabbath; it was his custom.

To worship God

His later ministry was to see him often at variance with the priests, particularly in the Jerusalem temple. He didn't like their methods, he objected to their ordering of temple matters – and he told them so, without mincing his words. But none of this was to prevent his attendance at the services.

We still find plenty to puzzle over, even to complain about, in the Church of 2003. But, like Jesus, most of us come every week not for the preacher, not even for the company or the singing. We come to praise God, to hear his word – and because Jesus gave us his own example of dedicated church attendance to follow.

Visible sign

The church building is the visible sign of a worshipping community. There are other signs, but this is the first one that people see on coming into the area.

The ancient Jews used to bind around their heads little pouches (phylacteries) in which were stuffed tightly folded key texts of scripture. For them, these were the visible reminders of God's word – in much the same way that we wear our crosses. But there is no real substitute for having the word of God in our hearts, as Jesus had it.

When the point goes home

The townsfolk of Nazareth had welcomed 'the local lad made good' – but when Jesus claimed personal fulfilment of the old prophecies, it proved too much for them to take. He was only the carpenter's Son, after all! Perhaps we hear things at church which conflict with our way of thinking. Do we bristle up and stay away the following week? Do we keep the matter to ourselves, and either pray about it until God sends us enlightenment, or worry until we've blown it out of all perspective? Do we discuss it with someone else? If our worship services don't move us to taking at least one of these options every so often, perhaps we need to ask if we have (spiritually speaking) nodded off to sleep!

When we have stopped asking about our faith, we have stopped growing in it (cf. 2 Peter 3:18).

Suggested hymns
Come, ye faithful, raise the anthem; Fill thou my life, O Lord my God; I, the Lord of sea and sky; To God be the glory

Pentecost (Whit Sunday)   8 June
Principal Service   **If I Go**   Acts 2:1–21 or
Ezek. 37:1–14; Ps. 104:24–34, 35b; Rom. 8:22–27 or
Acts 2:1–21; John 15:26–27; 16:4b–15

'[Jesus said], "Nevertheless, I tell you the truth: it is to your advantage that I go away, for if I do not go away, the Advocate will not come to you, but if I go, I will send him to you."' John 16:7

The spiritual battle
Life is complicated – generally so complicated that we find difficulty in focusing on more than one bit of it at a time: troubles, worries, preoccupations, plans, priorities, pains and pleasures are all vying with each other for our attention.

But for the Christian there is another, wider dimension. In the beginning, God created order out of chaos, light from darkness; patterns of life and living from the futility of randomness. Therefore, although we are constantly battling against Satan's chaos, darkness and randomness, we have God's order, light and life on our side. The Advocate sent by Jesus is the catalyst that links us to God and ignites us to react to him in his will.

God doesn't help us in this battle as Jesus helped his disciples – by physically standing between them and the powers of evil. With the care and attention he has used ever since the creation he has planned *beyond* that, by giving us the Advocate to help us from the inside out.

'I will send'
'If I go, I will send.' This is a cast-iron promise, from a God who does not deal in lies. Moreover, the Advocate will guide us into all truth, and will remind us of Jesus and his words, even if we

have forgotten them (John 14:26). It is a belt-and-braces job on the divine scale.

Ten days ago, we celebrated the ascension of Jesus. Today, we focus on the descension of the Advocate. He came in a way that caught everyone's attention in that windswept house, frightening the daylights out of many who were there. And there is no record of his ever having ascended back to glory. We can surely believe not only that he is still here, but that he will be with us for as long as it takes for God to get his purposes done in us. It is a risky belief – because it means that we have Someone on our side who can do *anything* in the fight against evil. It is no longer just *our* fight – it's *his* fight, too.

The enemy
Let's face it, we are nothing in ourselves against the Devil's 'principalities and powers'. Let's have no illusions on that. In the ordinary way, Satan outclasses and out-manoeuvres us on every count. If it was otherwise, Jesus wouldn't have gone to the trouble of sending us the Advocate. God doesn't ever waste time. Yet we can live for all the world as if we thought our Advocate needed a rest. It takes precious little effort to be mediocre. Satan *loves* mediocrity. It means we never rock the boat, we bend over backwards not to argue, not to show our head above the spiritual parapet. By contrast, those who are willing to make their lives count for God see a wrong and march in to do something about it. They detect evil, and winkle it out of its dingy corner into the cold, clear light of day, where it can be seen for what it is. And they suffer, because Satan takes umbrage at that sort of courage.

Here and now, we are commissioned by God to go ahead, firing on all cylinders, in the sure and certain knowledge that the Advocate given to us on that first Whit Sunday is not in the business of blowing a gasket. We cannot ask too much of him.

God has *ordered* our spiritual backup. Satan doesn't know the meaning of order. Read any newspaper, watch any news programme, and see the chaotic way in which the old Devil works, the randomness with which he chooses his victims. We need all the power of our Advocate to avoid being sucked into the vortex of Satan's evil enterprise.

Yet even Satan recognizes that we have power – power given to us in perpetuity from that first Whit Sunday onwards. Power that we can never out-use or over-use. Just the *thought* sends the

Devil into convulsions; our putting it into practice can make his life even harder.

Suggested hymns
Come down, O Love Divine; Breathe on me, Breath of God; Spirit of the living God; When God of old came down from heaven

Pentecost *Second Service* **This Jesus**
Ps. 139:1–12[13–18, 23–24]; Ezek. 36:22–28;
Acts 2:22–38

'Therefore let the entire house of Israel know with certainty that God has made him both Lord and Messiah, this Jesus whom you crucified.'
Acts 2:36

Lord and Messiah
Pentecost is one of the thirteen appointed days of the year when the Athanasian Creed (*Quicunque Vult*), according to the BCP, must take the place of the Apostles' Creed at Morning Prayer. Dating from the fourth century, many believe that it is still the best definition of the Trinity that has yet been written. Of its forty-two verses, only three do not include reference to God *the Son*, and the last fourteen verses deal entirely with him. The creed goes to great lengths to expand what we heard Peter preaching to the crowd at Pentecost – the climax of that sermon, as we have heard, being 'God has made him both Lord and Messiah'. And the *Quicunque* says we must 'believe rightly the Incarnation of our *Lord* Jesus Christ . . . for God and Man is one Christ.'

God the Son
As Christians, it's only natural we should focus more on God the Son than on the other two Persons of the Trinity. True, we pray (as God the Son commanded) to God the Father – and again (as God the Son directed) we acknowledge the indwelling of God the Holy Spirit. But it was, after all, God the Son who took our nature upon him, who confined his divinity to a human body, who died for our sins, and who rose again for our justification.

141

Lord

To call Jesus 'Lord' means to acknowledge his sovereignty and saving power. Peter has already said, 'Every one who calls on the name of the Lord shall be saved' (Acts 2:21). Remember when the disciples came to Jesus one day, complaining that a stranger was performing miracles in the Name of Jesus. It upset them, but Jesus was unperturbed (Mark 9:38f.). The Name of the Lord is powerful. It can, as Charles Wesley once wrote, 'make devils fear and fly', and it can bring down both angels and men.

St Paul, in his letter to the Romans, emphasizes the great power of Jesus' name: 'If you confess with your lips that Jesus is Lord and believe in your heart that God raised him from the dead, you will be saved' (Romans 10:9). The resurrection of Jesus confirmed and extended his Lordship, above every other title except one.

'God has made him both Lord and Messiah'

As Messiah, the Lord above all lords added suffering to sovereignty. Messiah (Christ, Anointed One) had been anointed as the innocent Lamb to suffer for the sins of the world. As the *Quicunque* says, 'God and Man is one Christ, who suffered for our salvation.' When Jesus, part-way through his earthly ministry, had asked his disciples who they believed he was, Peter had been inspired to say: 'You are the Messiah' (Matthew 16:16).

Messiah – looked for, expected by thousands of Jews for thousands of years, to come in glory and secure the future of his chosen people.

Messiah – who would come as Judge-and-Jury, to restore justice for mankind.

Messiah – for whom the Jews continued to look, long after the resurrection and ascension.

'God has made him both Lord and Messiah' – Peter's words at Pentecost, recorded for us by Luke the Gentile: Luke, who could stand back from the earlier Jewish beliefs and doctrines of Lordship and Messiahship, and who could simply accept the evidence of Jesus' ministry, resurrection and ascension, from an eyewitness.

And we can do the same. God has made this same Jesus, who meets us in the manger, the wilderness, astride a donkey, on a cross, *fully* alive in a resurrection body . . . this same Jesus is Lord of our life, and Christ of our soul. He must be *both* – or we only half-know him.

Come, thou holy Paraclete; Come, Holy Ghost, our souls inspire;
Jesus, stand among us; Veni, Creator Spiritus

Trinity Sunday   15 June   *Principal Service*
Undying Love   Isa. 6:1–8; Ps. 29; Rom. 8:12–17;
John 3:1–17

'[Jesus said], "For God so loved the world that he gave his only Son, so that everyone who believes in him may not perish but may have eternal life."' John 3:16

Living for eternity
You – and I – are going into eternity. There are days when things go wrong, or we feel bad, when eternity is the last thing that concentrates our minds. Instead, we feel hemmed in, pressed down, by cares and worry. And there are those days when every-thing runs on wheels – yet so often again we forget about eternity: this time, because life here is pretty good.

And there are other days – such as Trinity Sunday – when we hear this best known, best loved verse, and its comfort washes over us and we go gently to the seventh heaven . . . but sooner or later we have to return to the mundane and to get on with this life; just think what we've got to get through this week . . . and will there be time . . . ? Before one can blink twice, we're worrying all over again.

'Let us live for eternity,' counselled J.C. Ryle. 'Oh, that men would live as those who may one day die! Here we are, toiling and labouring, wearying ourselves about trifles, and running to and fro like ants on a heap, yet after a few years we shall all be gone.'

On the proving ground
It means consciously using our life here as a proving ground: learning to do best what we already do better (which is often what we like doing anyway), as a preparation for what is to come. A lady who had struggled to raise her six children as good Christians, on her death bed confessed to a friend: 'I've done what I could, but if only I could have my time over again, I'm sure I could do

more! I feel I've only just learned how to bring up children in the faith!' Well, bless her, perhaps God is letting her do exactly that, somewhere in eternity.

Limitless love
We cannot limit God, or eternity – and if we ever feel like imposing our restrictions on either (as if we really could – but we do try), let's remember that this wonderful earth, with all its wonderful people (including us), is a very tiny part of our universe; and that our universe is a very tiny part of all the other universes, out there in the vastness of space.

Yet God so loved the folk on this little planet earth that he went to great lengths to give us the chance of eternity – except that, since God does nothing by chance, we only have to believe in Jesus to ensure our place in eternity.

In an interview to mark the evangelist's eightieth birthday, Sir David Frost asked Dr Billy Graham: 'Billy, what do you think you'll be doing in eternity?' And Billy laughed. 'My friends tell me I'll be out of a job,' he said. ' 'Cos they reckon there won't be a need for any preachers in heaven – but there's all those other worlds out there. I believe in eternity that the Lord will have plenty of work lined up for all of us – including preachers!'

Improving our talent
We sing, in one of our morning hymns:

> *Improve thy talent with due care,*
> *For the great day thyself prepare.*
>
> Bishop T. Ken

Trinity Sunday isn't only for trying to understand how Three Persons can be One God, nor how those Three Persons inter-act. We cannot fully comprehend the Trinity – so let us accept it in faith. But we can 'improve our talent with due care', in preparation for eternity. We have a vested interest in eternity: we're heading straight for it, at the rate of sixty seconds a minute.

God is for us
But the Lord is on our side (Psalm 118:6; cf. Psalm 56).

God gives us a short testing now – and unending joy, love and peace in eternity. He prunes and trains first, for us to grow and blossom later. That's God's way: testing – then transformation, growth and delight. The world's way is pleasure now, and pay later. The world's way is to anaesthetize the person, then inflict the pain – and only when the anaesthetic wears off does the patient realize what he has let himself in for. God does not anaesthetize us. He requires us to meet what each day brings, in the full knowledge and awareness that he is on our side. That is protection enough. He wants us to meet Satan's onslaughts in full possession of the senses he has given us – and the greatest sense is the awareness of our Lord's proximity.

Suggested hymns
Eternal Ruler of the ceaseless round; Father of heaven, whose love profound; Holy, holy, holy, Lord God Almighty; Three in One, and One in Three

Trinity Sunday   *Second Service*
A Door Standing Open   Ps. 104:1–9;
Ezek. 1:4–10, 22–28a; Rev. 4:1–11

'After this I looked, and there in heaven a door stood open! And the first voice, which I had heard speaking to me like a trumpet, said, "Come up here, and I will show you what must take place after this."' Revelation 4:1

Revelations
It has been said that Revelation is the hardest book in the Bible to understand. It has also been said that it's the most important. It is timeless, dealing with past historic prophecy, present-day situations, and a future beyond time. And these are not conveniently set out one after the other. To study Revelation means to work hard. No other piece of writing covers such a wide field: the sheer scope of its twenty-two short chapters takes one's breath away. As the theologian G.B. Caird once remarked, 'it teases the imagination out of thought'. Of its 404 verses, 278 are reflections of the Old Testament, though nowhere does John quote the scriptures verbatim.

Patmos
John had been exiled to the bleak isle of Patmos, around AD 95.
Domitian had been emperor since 81, and his reign had not started
too badly, but had deteriorated when he sought to impose emperor
worship. Anyone refusing to acknowledge him as a god was tortured, killed or exiled. Those banished to Patmos were forced to
quarry stone, carrying it down to the beach, from where ships
ferried it across the Aegean to the mainland of Asia Minor. There
it was used to build more and more extravagant palaces, which
Domitian would never see, as within a year of John writing Revelation the emperor was assassinated.

Open doors
Revelation is a series of open doors, one of which we share in
today's reading: doors giving us glimpses of a world, a glory, a
busyness and drama far beyond our daily experiences. Jesus
appears to John with seven messages to be sent to seven church
congregations in Asia Minor (Revelation 2 and 3), and then the
heavenly visions begin – in the throne room of God.

Eight hundred years or so before, Isaiah had received a similar
vision – so dramatic, so noisy with spontaneous, fervent worship
and praise, that we're told the doorposts shook in their sockets
(Isaiah 6:1–8). There is no shortage of excitement in John's visions
either: flashes of lightning, thunder, and a round-the-clock concert
of praise from the royal musicians. If we ever imagine that heaven
will be serene and peaceful, with a superabundance of drowsy
stillness . . . we need to get serious with our Bible study.

When we read Revelation (and Isaiah, Daniel, Ezekiel and the
rest), God's message coming across again and again is: 'Look, I'm
giving you a peek into eternity. I want you to thrill at the thought
of what is in store for you. Get excited about it!'

A sevenfold blessing
There are seven blessings – seven beatitudes – in Revelation, and
in one of them God lays great emphasis on the veracity of what
has been given to us via St John: 'Blessed are those who are invited
to the marriage supper of the Lamb . . . These are the true words
of God' (Revelation 19:9). This is all of a piece with what Jesus
said: 'In my Father's house are many dwelling places. If it were
not so, would I have told you that I go to prepare a place for you?'
(John 14:2).

Does the prospect exhilarate, or leave us cold? Can we read Revelation and get fired up about it? Or do we ignore it as something either beyond our ken or as not applying to us? Mark Twain once said: 'Most people are bothered about those passages of scripture they don't understand. But I have always noticed that the passages that bother me most are the ones I do understand.'

Unless we're prepared to *work* at our Bible study, we may miss out on what God is trying to tell us. We need to remember that God is love, and he is not trying to make his word obscure – but he does intend that we should use the minds he has given us to the full.

Trinity Sunday and its readings are intended to stretch us – but even more to encourage us to be stretched even further, all the way to eternity! And if we can pray: 'Lord, open up to us your word,' we really have to *want* him to do it.

Suggested hymns
Firmly I believe and truly; I bind unto myself today; Three in One, and One in Three; Thy way, not mine, O Lord

Corpus Christi 19 June (Day of Thanksgiving for the Institution of the Holy Eucharist) **Just Abiding** Gen. 14:18–20; Ps. 116:12–19; 1 Cor. 11:23–26; John 6:51–58

'[Jesus said] "Those who eat my flesh and drink my blood abide in me, and I in them."' John 6:56

The sacrament of communion

It can be easy for those of us who have been coming to the communion rail for a long time, to take at least some of the eucharist for granted – certainly it is difficult really to imagine what the sacrament of communion must look like and mean, to those outside the Church.

Even when we read these verses from John 6, we can let them drift over us in gentle familiarity. After all, we are 'into' the eucharist, and its mystical meaning, aren't we? These are well-known verses, describing a familiar doctrine, which the Church has incor-

147

porated into a service which is observed more regularly than most, if not all, other services.

A holy day
Today was once kept as a major festival – a general holy day, with processions and jollifications after the main eucharist of the day. But mention *Corpus Christi* to many folk now, and one receives a blank stare, as they wonder vaguely if it's something to do with Christmas.

Back in the fifteenth century, St Bernadine of Siena declared: 'If of these two things you can only do one – either hear the Mass or hear the sermon – you should let the Mass go, rather than the sermon. There is less peril for your soul in not hearing Mass than in not hearing the sermon.'

The sermons in the fifteenth century must have left little to be desired! But Bernadine's words can profitably be applied today. To enquiring or new members of a congregation, the word of God is arguably more helpful and meaningful than the communion. This may sound harsh, but in taking the Bread and Wine a person is feeding his own soul; in sharing the gospel, he is also feeding someone else's soul. 'The words that I have spoken to you,' said Jesus, 'are spirit and life' (John 6:63). We need to take the gospel to people as a means of leading them towards communion – rather than from the outset trying to feed them with communion in a liturgy which is largely alien to them.

What do we do with Jesus' life?
How is the Church shaping up to the multi-pronged commission of Jesus? 'Go and baptize in the Name of the Father and of the Son and of the Holy Spirit,' he said (Matthew 28:19). What percentage of our young population is baptized? 'Unless you eat the flesh of the Son of Man and drink his blood,' said Jesus, 'you have no life in you' (John 6:53). So we do. Many millions out there don't.

But we come to the eucharist – if not daily or weekly, then as often as we can. So we have life in us: Jesus' life – in a mystical, desperately poorly understood way. His Body and Blood. What do we do with it?

It is supplemented by our intake (hearing, seeing, memorizing) of his words ('they are spirit and life,' said (John 6:63)). So, what do we do with these words?

We can amalgamate these two questions into one: 'What do we do with the LIFE that is in us?'

Endless possibilities
The possibilities are endless. We can go knocking on people's doors. 'Oh, but wouldn't that antagonize people?' This is a desperately sad response, but it happens. Look back two thousand years, and it was happening then. Jesus antagonized the entrepreneurs in the temple when he overturned their tables, sent their money spinning, and set their little pigeons free. He antagonized his own folk in hometown Nazareth, because they thought he wasn't acting like a carpenter's son ought to do. He antagonized the chief priests because he preached the truth, and they were on another wavelength. Jesus ran athwart many of the people he met, and he knew things wouldn't be much different for those who took up the challenge of his gospel. May we never be proud of belonging to a church that's afraid of antagonizing anyone – because this so often means it's not going flat-out to encourage anyone either.

Let's take these words of spirit and life – words that have no sell-by date; words that can bring out the best in folk designed by God for eternity. Tell them again, and again, until you have no breath left – and by that time your mission will have been accomplished.

Suggested hymns
Author of Life Divine; O thou, who at thy eucharist did pray; Once, only once, and once for all; We hail thy Presence glorious

First Sunday after Trinity (Proper 7)
22 June *Principal Service* **Still No Faith?**
1 Sam. 17:[1a, 4–11, 19–23]32–49; Ps. 9:9–20 or
1 Sam. 17:57–18:5, 10–16; Ps. 133; 2 Cor. 6:1–13;
Mark 4:35–41

'[Jesus] said to them, "Why are you afraid? Have you still no faith?"'
Mark 4:40

Cause to fear
Didn't the disciples have cause to fear, with the storm transferring the lake into their boat at a rate of knots? Wasn't it the most natural thing in the world to panic? But they had forgotten that their Passenger was Lord of the whole earth. They'd also not realized that when God tells a man to do something, the two of them will see it through. Jesus had told them to sail across to the other shore. There was nothing on earth could stop them getting there, if only they kept to his word.

Bad news
Sometimes folk try to tell us that a bit of fear is all right; it gets the action going, and things are accomplished more quickly. But it also takes the colour out of our hair and can stop our heart. According to Jesus, fear is bad news. If fear is taken on board, faith takes a header into the water. We can either have fear, we can take note of the trouble and danger around, and let it get hold of us. Or we can have faith in the power of God to be greater than anything on earth, and we can come through any crisis in that power. But, says Jesus, we cannot have it both ways. If we are afraid of anything, our faith is *kaput*. If we are operating in faith, then we are not letting fear get the upper hand (or even a hold at all).

Fear can never get the better of God. But this side of the grave we are still mostly human. We have the Holy Spirit, and the more we avail ourselves of his power, the less freedom of manoeuvre there is for the Devil to come at us with fear. But, let go the awareness of the Holy Spirit, and fear gets a toehold, then a foothold – and if we are not careful, full-blown panic sets in.

Operating in faith
God requires us to keep spiritually awake, to steer clear of the world's cocktail of fear. Unless we are in full possession of our spiritual, God-given faculties, we're going to make a poor fist of operating in faith.

Take the example of St Paul. There was a man who had known fear, and how to replace it with faith – even in areas where he was a lone voice in the midst of pagan apathy, fear and Angst. Today we don't have to go as far or as fast as Paul went; there are places in our neighbourhood where not only indifference and apathy hold sway, but where anti-Christian forces are active, influencing many lives. We have *all the time in the world* to show our faith to the world – to show just what Christians who operate without fear can do, in the strength of the Lord. We may not be in a little boat on Galilee – but we're crossing the lake of life. There are storms within, as well as without – spiritual dangers, outnumbering the physical ones. But, as on Galilee, our Lord has promised to see us to the other side. 'In my Father's house are many dwelling places. If it were not so, would I have told you that I go to prepare a place for you?' (John 14:2).

There is no way Jesus would go to so much trouble if he didn't intend us to take up residence in that heavenly accommodation. So, because Jesus lives, we can face tomorrow. Because the Holy Spirit lives, in us, we can face today. Come hell, or even high water.

> *For he's promised to be there for us, for ever,*
> *Just a breath, a sigh, a tearful prayer away,*
> *Bringing peace and love, restoring us for service,*
> *If only we will let him have his way.*
>
> *My Jesus, Lord, I come to you in weakness,*
> *Give me your grace to fight my whole life long.*
> *I come to you in sorrow, give me joy, Lord;*
> *I come to you in sickness, make me strong.*
>
> *Help me to pray, and not to do things my way,*
> *To ask, and seek, and knock upon your door;*
> *For you have promised help, Lord, and I need it;*
> *Give me the faith to pray and praise you more.*

Suggested hymns
Fierce raged the tempest; Give me the faith that can remove; Peace, perfect peace, in this dark world of sin; Strengthen for service, Lord

First Sunday after Trinity   *Second Service*
The Full Number   Ps. 49; Jer. 10:1–16; Rom. 11:25–36
'I want you to understand this mystery: a hardening has come upon part of Israel, until the full number of the Gentiles has come in.' Romans 11:25

A personal message
Romans differs from Paul's other writings in that it isn't as intimate, answering queries raised by earlier visits, or reprimanding known converts for letting their faith weaken. Paul hasn't yet been to Rome; he's writing to a largely unknown community (though in chapter 16 it's nice to see quite a list of relatives and friends apparently shared with his secretary, Tertius), but he is very keen to meet these Roman Christians, of whom he's heard so much. Yet Romans is in a way more personal than his other letters, for Paul slips in a lot of autobiographical details, doubts, fears, failings, to reassure his new friends that he is not immune from the trials and temptations they face. He wanted them to encourage his readers. And in today's excerpt, he seeks to encourage both Jews and Gentiles: God's plans include them all.

Because the Roman Christians have progressed beyond initial conversion, Romans is more liberally laced with strong meat than with the babies' milk he reserved for the newly baptized (1 Corinthians 3:2). It means that Paul, as well as being encouraging, can be challengingly frank: the Jews have messed up their religion, but there is still hope. The Gentiles had drifted for a long time in darkness, but now the light has come, is being offered to them, and is being accepted. It's a variation on the theme 'one sows, another reaps', but both participate in the harvest.

Not a solo operation
Paul's view of Gentile involvement in salvation had been heightened by his own experience of mission. After his Damascus road conversion, he had received encouragement from Ananias, Barnabas, and later the other apostles. He had also not forgotten how slow some had been to accept him. He had preached to cult-besotted crowds in Ephesus, and to sophisticated, polytheistic worshippers at Athens. He has been praying and interceding for these Roman Christians, and now he outlines how their eternal inheritance has come about, and how they can play their part in God's purposes.

Valuing others
Paul has come a long way from the fanatically minded Saul who persecuted the Christian Church, and stood watching in approval as Stephen was stoned to death. His aim is to unite people – across barriers of race, creed, culture and sex. How much do we involve

others in our family, work and church? Or are we in danger of taking the feel-good factor of independence too far? If two Christians agree together in prayer, said Jesus, great things can be done (Matthew 18:19). Think of the example he gave: God himself accepting the companionship of fishermen, tax collectors and the like, whose rough language and dim-wittedness could have driven many to distraction. The ability to make others feel valued is a gift. Thank God, it has been made available to us by the Holy Spirit.

Hanging on to prayer

Paul had known worry, danger and opposition, and the immorality and resistance to God in many regions he visited could have plunged him into despair; but he kept his prayer life working, and drew strength from the God who still gives more grace as the going gets tough. Sometimes God seems magnificently unfair. We have the idea that we are waiting for him, when really he is waiting for our response. Paul knew what it was to 'get the message'. When he and Barnabas were barracked by the Jews in Pisidian Antioch, they boldly replied: 'It was necessary that the word of God should be spoken first to you. Since you reject it and judge yourselves to be unworthy of eternal life, we are now turning to the Gentiles' (Acts 13:46). Male, female, Jew, Gentile – God's 'favouritism' is governed only by our response. What a blessing it does not have to be earned!

Paul outlines to his unseen friends in Rome how they can live a new life in Christ, because the Lord has gone ahead and taken away the power of the world to harm us (cf. Romans 5:12–6:14). Of course he still gives us the option of struggling along with as many burdens as we want to carry . . .

Suggested hymns

In Christ there is no east or west; Jesus shall reign where'er the sun; The earth, O Lord, is one wide field; Thy Kingdom come, O God

Second Sunday after Trinity (Proper 8, or SS Peter and Paul, q.v.)   29 June   *Principal Service*   **Do Not Fear!**   2 Sam. 1:1, 17–27; Ps. 130; 2 Cor. 8:7–15; Mark 5:21–43

'But overhearing what they said, Jesus said to the leader of the synagogue, "Do not fear, only believe."'   Mark 5:36

Don't be afraid

When we have stopped ignoring this command, or thinking it applies to someone else, or seeing it merely as a mild suggestion, we'll be obeying God. That's the long and the short of it. We've probably got fearing to a fine art: every day the media line up to coach us into a doctorate in fear. But Jesus says, simply, NO! Don't give in to fear! In the natural, that is an impossible command. It's human nature to be fearful. But God deals in the impossible – and, as Christians, we are not on our own: we are his. Without fear, we need to step out from our *selves*, with the power of Christ.

This command is the one Jesus gives in the gospels more than any other. He meant us to take it seriously, because fear is the Devil's Number One weapon, and the Devil has become mega proficient in employing it.

Every time circumstances press, tell Satan: 'The Lord is on my side. I will not fear' (Psalm 118:6, cf. Psalm 56). Every time panic rises, someone we were counting on lets us down, the bills mount up, the postman brings no cheer ... declare firmly: 'The Lord is on my side. I will not fear.'

God knows us

If God had not made us – our inside as well as the side we show to the world – we might have some reason for thinking he has not caught up with our situation. But he not only appreciates exactly what we are going through, he also knows how he is going to bring us out of the trouble. So he can afford to move at his decided pace, which may well seem far slower than the rate at which we'd like him to move. If we could see as far as he can, surely we should not fear; but can we not take comfort from the fact that he knows the future is hidden – so he is not asking us to endure more than he knows we can cope with. The thought that God estimates our stamina higher than we do ourselves, should give us a spiritual uplift – but if we have taken a nosedive into fear, resurfacing can seem a big challenge.

A man's anguish
Jairus, in the normal course of events, might have been as wary of Jesus as were many of his ilk, but anxiety for his child had humbled his spirit. Yet anguish had tightened his nerves to such a degree that, at the seemingly unnecessary delay while Jesus healed another person, his fear came out into the open. Jesus could see beyond the crisis, to the raising of the little girl. He could picture already the father's joy; and he did his best to reassure him in the meantime. Similarly, even while fear may be throttling us, God is still saying: 'Don't be afraid. This is nothing that I cannot handle.' If we were only as resilient in holding on to faith as we are to hugging fear ever closer, the Devil would have to work much harder than he does.

No quick fix
There's no easy method to kick the habit of fear, though perhaps if we recognized it more clearly as an addiction, we might go to work on it more thoroughly. It may be that a hundred times a day it will be necessary to take and re-take our stand against it. We may experience withdrawal symptoms of panic, dereliction and doubt. God is still there, still commanding: 'Do not fear.' And when we come through the trauma, and life is good again . . . before long, another fear will roll up, and the anguish will begin again. Will it be as bad, the next time round?

It all depends on how much of the fear we decide to take on board.

Suggested hymns
Fight the good fight; God moves in a mysterious way; How firm a foundation; Through all the changing scenes of life

Second Sunday after Trinity   *Second Service*
Out of Debt   Ps. [52]53; Jer. 11:1–14; Rom. 13:1–10
'Pay to all what is due to them – taxes to whom taxes are due, revenue to whom revenue is due, respect to whom respect is due, honour to whom honour is due. Owe no one anything, except to love one another; for the one who loves another has fulfilled the law.' Romans 13:7, 8

Debt of love

A woman once showed the precious debt of love with awe-inspiring devotion and dedication. Married to Patricius, a pagan, she prayed for his conversion for sixteen years, and for Augustine her son for twenty-two years. Her name was Monica, her son became the famous saint and Bishop of Hippo (AD 354–430). Think of the loss to the Christian Church, had Monica run out of spiritual steam! It is a great privilege to be a prayer warrior, holding up others to God, interceding for them, paying back some of the debt we owe to our Lord. No one has ever evaluated the price of prayer, nor its power, for both are inestimable.

Earthly dues

Earthly dues and demands are unavoidable; despite flood, fire, strikes, tempests, they always make it into our letter-boxes. And more often than not, we pay them, because life is then easier than if we don't. Jesus paid his dues, but he did not let the worry of them affect his ministry. On one occasion, he sent Peter to get the tribute money out of the mouth of a fish (Matthew 17:27). On another day, he borrowed a penny from someone to illustrate a parable (Mark 12:15). He employed a treasurer in his mission team, yet though he knew Judas was helping himself to the funds, he did not reprimand him (John 12:6, cf. 13:29). It was an attitude to money that seems incomprehensible to many people today, who have made money their god.

> *Money, in truth, is one of the most unsatisfying*
> *of possessions. It takes away some cares, no doubt; but it*
> *brings with it quite as many cares as it takes away.*
> *There is trouble in the getting of it.*
> *There is anxiety in the keeping of it.*
> *There are temptations in the use of it.*
> *There is guilt in the abuse of it.*
> *There is sorrow in the losing of it.*
> *There is perplexity in the disposing of it.*
> *Two-thirds of all the strifes, quarrels*
> *and law suits in the world, arise from one*
> *simple cause – money!*
>
> J.C. Ryle

How can we be free?

How can we know the freedom from money that gave Jesus the time, strength and attention to devote himself to God's work? Only by keeping our eyes on God, and asking what he would have us do, in any situation. He is the Master Banker; if we pray him to oversee our finances, we have to be prepared to follow his guidance. Driving along the M1 motorway, one passes several sites of telecommunication aerials, lit up brilliantly at night. The antennae are positioned to catch and transmit signals over a wide area. Similarly, we can train our spiritual awareness to receive more incoming signals – from God, from our neighbours next door, from further afield. We can fine-tune these spiritual air channels so that even when God speaks in a still, small voice, we can hear. When he fleetingly brings a situation, opportunity, need, solution, individual or community to mind, may we take notice and pray, and ask for guidance in any action he wishes us to take – showing an earnestness to pay our debt, transaction after transaction.

If we concentrate on the incoming messages, God will take care our debt is paid through the outgoing action.

For *love* is positively the best canceller of debt.

Suggested hymns
A debtor to mercy alone; A Sovereign Protector I have; Fill thou my life, O Lord my God; Love is his way

Third Sunday after Trinity (Proper 9)   6 July
Principal Service   **Sufficient Grace**   2 Sam. 5:1–5, 9–10; Ps. 48; 2 Cor. 12:2–10; Mark 6:1–13

'*A thorn was given to me . . . Three times I appealed to the Lord about this, that it would leave me, but he said to me, "My grace is sufficient for you."*' 2 Corinthians 12:7, 8, 9

Messenger of Satan

Whatever form this 'thorn in the flesh' took, it inconvenienced Paul in his ministry. Three times he tested whether God was prepared to take it away. After the third apparently abortive prayer, Paul

157

obviously decided that it was time to let the matter rest. God would take care of his ministry, thorn or no thorn.

It is a lesson in dialoguing with God. Have we prayed earnestly for an annoyance, a hindrance, to be taken away? Can we really say it's making our mission impossible? If, like Paul, we find we can still operate, then perhaps, also like Paul, we should learn to live with it. If God is allowing it into our lives, somehow, somewhere, it will be for our good. It's natural to pray for an easier life, but it may not be the best in the long run.

Keeping a vision

This is not to say that the 'three times only' rule applies across the board. Paul had been praying for a hindrance to be taken away. But he did not pray just three times for the Damascus road conversion to work for the benefit of others, then let it go. Nor are we, if we have received a vision, an idea, a revelation that delays, to let it go after only three prayers, three days or even three years. 'For there is still a vision for the appointed time; it speaks of the end, and does not lie. If it seems to tarry, wait for it; it will surely come, it will not tarry' (Habakkuk 2:3). And remember Ezekiel: 'The word of the Lord came to me: "Mortal, what is this proverb of yours about the land of Israel, which says, The days are prolonged, and every vision comes to nothing? Tell them, therefore, Thus says the Lord God: I will put an end to this proverb, and they shall use it no more as a proverb in Israel. But say to them, The days are near, and the fulfilment of every vision"' (Ezekiel 12:21–23).

Think of Abraham, holding fast to the vision of more children and descendants than the stars in the sky – for twenty-five years. He knew it was naturally impossible for Sarah to conceive – but God brought it to pass. Remember Elizabeth, giving birth in her old age to John the Baptist; and Mary, cherishing her own vision for nine months until Jesus was born. God is well versed in coping with impossibilities!

Success – despite . . .

At times we need to get both our physical and spiritual adrenalin going, even to get out of the blocks and start on the race. We need a frustration, a hindrance, even a discouragement. 'I'll do it – despite . . .' And, once started, there's often no stopping us. God knew that Paul was so immersed in mission that a bit of a thorn wouldn't stop him; rather, it might spur some more energy out of him and into his preaching.

Let's praise God for knowing us so well!

It's in this 'thorn in the flesh' that we may glimpse at least part of the reason why God is still allowing Satan to roam the earth. If mission for Christ was a walkover, would anyone bother? If hell was not still a possibility for some folk, would there be anyone still trying to avoid it and get to heaven? Satan has his part to play in God's purposes. We don't have to seek his company, he'll foist it on us uninvited; but the way we react to his overtures may make the difference between being simply a good witness for Jesus, and a great one like St Paul.

It must do Satan no good at all to think that his machinations may even thrust greatness upon those who are least interested in it – but who would lose any sleep over the Devil's frustration?

> *Though Satan should buffet, though trials should come,*
> *Let this blessed assurance control,*
> *That Christ has regarded my helpless estate,*
> *And has shed his own blood for my soul!*

> *Horatio G. Spafford, 1828–1888*

Suggested hymns
Father, hear the prayer we offer; God of glory, God of grace; Soldiers of Christ, arise; Thy hand, O God, has guided

Third Sunday after Trinity   *Second Service*
Minding Our Business   Ps. [63]64; Jer. 20:1–11a; Rom. 14:1–17

'If your brother or sister is being injured by what you eat, you are no longer walking in love. Do not let what you eat cause the ruin of one for whom Christ died. So do not let your good be spoken of as evil.'
Romans 14:15, 16

God's contract
God knows we need food, and he's contracted to give us sufficient, providing we trust him with our needs. Some of us feel free to

eat a wider range of his provision than others. Fair enough, says Paul, so long as no one is made to feel uncomfortable or guilty. Physical food, after all, is not the meat and drink of heaven (v. 17). He echoes Jesus' teaching (Matthew 6:33): give the spiritual fruits of 'righteousness, peace and joy' first place, and God will not condemn us for what our bodies consume or set aside.

It's a matter of courtesy

Courtesy in acknowledging others' preferences is a way of honouring their equal status as God's children. Certain food, particularly if taken in excess, can harm or exacerbate already damaged digestive systems; but no physical food can harm the soul (Mark 7:18, 19). This gives us a wonderful freedom in choosing our diet, so long as we eat to live, and not *vice versa*. The miraculous feedings of the thousands, recorded in all four gospels, show Jesus' concern for the physical well-being of his followers; but his gentle rebuke of John 4:32 was designed to teach us that satisfying one's merely physical appetite should always take second place to doing God's business – in this case, discipling a woman who was to lead many Samaritans from that town to him (John 4:39).

Minding our own business means not putting a stumbling block of any kind in the way of another. It means not muscling in on someone else's mission (as Peter tried to do in John 21:21f.). It means not leaving others to learn about Jesus when we could supply their need; nor does it mean shutting off our compassion for their physical needs, if we have the wherewithal to help. There is a line to be drawn, and sometimes this line is so slender it needs a lot of prayer on our part to keep within the will of God. For our example, we can look at how Jesus dealt with his disciples: the patience and forbearance he showed when, time after time, they failed to grasp what he was saying, or gave way to fear, or said or did the wrong thing. When we translate Jesus' concern and courtesy into our congregations and outreach, folk quickly say, as they said of the early disciples, that we have been with Jesus.

Dr Sherwood Wirt once said: 'I have learned there is no point in talking about strong churches and weak churches, big churches and little churches, warm churches and cold churches. Such categories are unrealistic and beside the point. There is only a loving church or an unloving church.'

Wherever love rules, Satan takes an interest, for Christian love is the greatest threat the Devil knows. So if he is presently giving us a torrid time, we can be pretty sure that we are in the will of God. As St Paul tells us, in today's reading: 'If your brother or sister is being injured [e.g.] by what you eat, you are no longer walking in love' (Romans 14:15). If you are out of love, you are in strife; and if you're in strife, you're dancing to Satan's tune, not God's.

To take another example from our Lord: he could easily have got into strife with Judas Iscariot. He knew that Judas was stealing from the mission funds. He knew what Judas was plotting with the chief priests. Our Lord had invested three years of concentrated missionary training on Judas, and he could see all that work heading down to hell. But right to the end, he treated Judas exactly like the others, even to sharing the Last Supper with him (Mark 14:20).

It is surely a lesson to us, that we need to walk together in love until the other party has really passed the point of no return. Many, as well as the penitent thief, have left repentance until the last minute.

Suggested hymns
Bind us together, Lord; Brother, sister, let me serve you; Happy are they, they that love God; We are one in the Spirit

Fourth Sunday after Trinity (Proper 10)
13 July *Principal Service* All for Nothing?
2 Sam. 6:1–5, 12b–19; Ps. 24; Eph. 1:3–14; Mark 6:14–29
'Immediately the king sent a soldier of the guard with orders to bring John's head. He went and beheaded him in the prison.' Mark 6:27

What a waste!
Someone has died so young, and all we can think of is what they could have done, had they been spared! And surely Jesus' own cousin, whose ministry had begun so promisingly, could have been spared for another ten, twenty, or even thirty years! But John had completed his task. Jesus himself was to die fairly soon afterwards – was *that* a waste? If his earthly ministry had lasted thirty years instead of three, couldn't he have done so much more! No, for in the will of God he had completed his task.

With joy

More, he had completed it with joy. We are still on the way to completing our work for God. Are *we* doing the Lord's work with joy? Our aim, surely, should be to give him as much joy as we can, while we can – in some return for all the joy he gives us. John the Baptist lived the frugal, ascetic life – with joy. He preached to those who mainly didn't want to listen – with joy. Jesus, for the joy set before him, endured even the cross. We know we have God's joy, to share with others – and more often than not we do just that. But how often do we reflect on how much joy we are giving to God – not only on others' behalf, but as a special, secret, private 'Thank You' to God from us, in acknowledgement of all that he has given to us? How often do we come into his presence with not only petitions and pleas, but thanksgivings and joyful 'gossip'?

Joyful gossip

Joyful gossip is not forty-second cousin to the ordinary gossip which we should avoid. Joyful gossip is sharing with God the *good* news that has happened to us today – the good experiences we have had, the good things we have thought about. God gave us these experiences and thoughts, so he knows all about them – but our delight in sharing them with him in thanksgiving will bring added joy to us both.

When was the last time you enjoyed a gossip with God?

Starved of joy

The world today is starved of joy. Good news barely gets a mention. It often seems the media folk go out of their way to find the worst, most degrading and sordid news they can. 'Freedom of the press' seems to be freedom at too high a cost.

'John, whom I beheaded, has been raised!' was the startled Herod's reaction to the preaching of Jesus. Did Herod, somewhere deep in his soul, believe that it was possible for John to come back from the dead? Everyone in the banqueting hall at Machaerus that evening had seen John's severed head on the platter. His death could scarcely have been more convincing. Whatever made Herod come out with such a statement?

Fear

The answer is: fear. Nothing less. Fear of what he had done. Herod, in the throes of remorse, was not thinking straight. He had listened to John, when his pagan wife was not hovering near, and he knew he had been trapped into committing a crime he would not have contemplated otherwise. The terrible cruelty of his father had in him been watered down into craftiness.

We need faith, not fear

When we get afraid over something, we can come out with the dumbest things, as well as the wickedest; for fear jettisons not only faith, but reason as well. Yet with faith we can keep both, because our faith gives the Holy Spirit power to work on body, mind and spirit. We have only to look at Jesus' ministry to appreciate its holistic approach. God created us to work for him with soundness of mind and body, as well as faith.

How?

He is still telling us, every day, in whatever circumstances he takes us into: 'If you want the impossible, be prepared to do the impossible – then I'll give you what it takes to do it!' If we want to kick the habit of being afraid, if we want to make our lives beautiful for God, if we want to change the world for God – let's prepare to do it!

And 'Not unto us, Lord, not unto us, but to you be all the glory.'

Suggested hymns

A few more years shall roll; Give me joy in my heart; Now thank we all our God; On Jordan's bank the Baptist's cry

The Fourth Sunday after Trinity
Second Service   **On Fallow Ground**   Ps. 66;
Job 4:1; 5:6–17; or Ecclus. 4:11–31; Rom. 15:14–29

'Thus I make it my ambition to proclaim the good news, not where Christ has already been named, so that I do not build on someone else's foundation.' Romans 15:20

Untrodden land
The Russian Orthodox Christian sees each new day as a field of
pristine snow – untrodden, wonderful in its perfection and
promise. Paul must have known kindred thoughts as he strove to
take the gospel on to fallow ground – preaching to souls who as
yet had not heard it; not to build on another's foundation, not
to follow another man's ploughing, and not to inherit another's
mistakes. How Paul, as so many before and since, longed for the
'open playing field'! How do we bring people to Christ? Not by
preparing a carefully constructed, perfectly manicured speech –
for each person is different – but by praying that the Holy Spirit,
when that time comes, will give us the right words to say: words
that speak not of us (our hopes, fears, good intentions) but of
Christ. We're not in the Marathon, our eternity depending on
whether we've preached more, converted more, helped more, than
our neighbour. Our mission is *our* mission; and if we go to work
for God in all the ways and to all the people he shows us, that is
what he wants us to do, what he has fitted us for doing. It may
be that our mission is to nurture those who already have faith, to
deepen their faith. Or, like Paul, we may be directed towards
those who as yet have no faith. The two are very different, but
complementary ministries.

> *And still there are fields where the labourers are few,*
> *And still there are souls without bread,*
> *And still eyes that weep where the darkness is deep,*
> *And still straying sheep to be led.*

> *Albert W.T. Orsborn*

The world has countless fallow fields, still waiting for the gospel
seed to be sown. We may find good, fertile soil, where the seed
is welcomed, fed, trained and eventually produces a good harvest
– or the ground may be stony, poor and in need of many months,
even years, of hard work before any growth is seen.

> *The good, the fruitful ground*
> *Expect not here nor there;*
> *O'er hill and vale by plots 'tis found,*
> *Go forth, then, everywhere.*

> *James Montgomery*

Round-the-clock availability

As Christians, God requires of us round-the-clock availability for whatever field of mission he calls us into. From one minute to the next, we do not know what new opportunity he may give, or what help or support may be asked of us. There is no such person as an 'off-duty Christian'. We have only to read the gospels, Acts, and the Epistles, to see how not only our Lord but the earliest disciples were always on call – just as the farmer with fallow land waiting to be sown needs to act when God sends the right conditions of weather. If he delays, he may forfeit a harvest. If he gets impatient and sows in haste before God has brought the right amalgam of conditions to pass, the seed may not germinate. Yet – and this is what makes mission exciting – there are times when God seems to work against the odds, but still a harvest is brought to pass. Paul seems to have experienced this on the spiritual front, when he tells Timothy: 'I solemnly urge you; proclaim the message; be persistent whether the time is favourable or unfavourable' (2 Timothy 4:1, 2). We need have no fear on this score. If God has given us the time, it is the right time. May we use it to the full. Then we can say, with Paul: 'I know that when I come to you, I will come in the fulness of the blessing of Christ' (Romans 15:29). The more we experience the fulness of Christ's blessing, the more of it we can give to others.

Suggested hymns

In Christ there is no east or west; Son of God, eternal Saviour; Sow in the morn thy seed; Tell out, my soul, the greatness of the Lord

Fifth Sunday after Trinity (Proper 11)
20 July *Principal Service* **Sheer Faith**
2 Sam. 7:1–14a; Ps. 89:20–37; Eph. 2:11–22; Mark 6:30–34, 53–56

'And wherever [Jesus] went, into villages or cities or towns, they laid the sick in the market places, and begged him that they might touch even the fringe of his cloak; and all who touched it were healed.' Mark 6:56

Even the hem of his garment

> *She only touched the hem of his garment,*
> *As to his side she stole;*
> *Amid the crowds that gathered around him,*
> *And straightway she was whole.*

> *George F. Root*

The faith of these people is awesome. They did not demand a one-to-one interview with Jesus, for diagnosis, consultation or referral. They did not need even to catch his eye, or earn his smile. They may not have touched his hand. Just the hem of his cloak was enough to get perfect healing. How much do we rely on faith in Christ? *That* much?

The acid test
In our times of struggle and trial, sickness and trouble, we can cry for help and lean on Jesus when there is no other visible support. But so often the acid test comes in our times of plenty, when life seems to run on wheels. He wants us to rely on him just as much then, as in the bad times.

Threefold commitment
Remember the threefold commitment that Jesus required of Peter (John 21). Jesus is still asking – three times – for our threefold commitment. Our parents probably made the first for us, at our baptism. We made the second, at our confirmation. And the third is made continually, recurrently, from the day of our First Communion until the hour of our death: every time we affirm the creed, sing the gloria, share Christ's Body and Blood; every time we pray; every time we share the gospel; every time we draw breath, as Christians, we are making that third and crucial, that point-of-no-return commitment: that we belong to God.

Daily contact
Every minute of every day, God is holding us by the power of his love, and by our commitment. There may be times when it seems it's mostly God's love and very little of our commitment that is doing the work; and we can be thankful that God's love never takes a day off, or gets compassion fatigue. Jesus didn't tell Peter

to spend his whole time loving, praying, praising, worshipping. He asked: 'Do you love me?' And having established this, he simply told Peter to translate that love into action.

Difficult work
The work-in-action is difficult, since there are many people out there who think they can get along fine without God. You and I know they can't. But how can they be persuaded that God is essential to their well-being and future existence? St John asks: 'How does God's love abide in anyone who has the world's goods and sees a brother or sister in need and yet refuses help?' (1 John 3:17). Do we accept that, as 'many are called but few chosen', a few non-believers won't be missed? Jesus straightly said that it is not the will of God that *any one* should perish. One day, the non-believers in our village, town or city will be dead, beyond the point of no return. But while they are here, we are surely committed to sharing the gospel with them. That is our part of the deal. God has contracted to do the rest. We cannot save a soul, but he can. We can't always know when, where or how a person may come to him. But he knows.

We are as grass
We are, in a manner of speaking, the grass in his pastures. We may get trodden underfoot, and the lambs and yearlings and sheep may wander elsewhere, or turn out real delinquents, or even not live to eat much of the food we have on offer. But that's not our problem. Our business is to see that what we offer is top quality nourishment: the uncompromised word of God.

Our full potential
Only God knows our full potential. The fact that we are all still here means we haven't yet reached that potential. The best is yet to be. Let's pray that we may keep 'in contact' with our Lord, with the faith that the folk in our reading had. God is no respecter of persons: what he did for them, he'll do for us.

Suggested hymns
Immortal, Invisible, God only wise; Just as I am, without one plea; She only touched the hem of his garment; Thine arm, O Lord, in days of old

Fifth Sunday after Trinity *Second Service*
Divine Help Ps. 73; Job 13:13–14:6 or Ecclus. 18:1–14;
Heb. 2:5–18

'Because he himself was tested by what he suffered, he is able to help those who are being tested.' Hebrews 5:18

Through conflict to victory

Jesus endured what he did, not only to obtain the victory. He already had that. His battle was on our behalf, for our victory. We know this, because daily we live in the hope his victory bought – but it's still something we need constantly to remind ourselves of, lest the enormity is dulled by tacit acceptance. Unless the import of Christ's love and sacrifice is uppermost in our hearts, we shall not have the edge to our work that lifts it above the ordinary – that goes the extra mile, turns the other cheek, forgives when the 'seventy times seven' forgivings have passed their sell-by date.

Magnificently qualified

Thus magnificently qualified, Satan's principalities and powers convincingly overthrown, our Lord's help is freely available to us in every situation. He has been there. He knows to the nth degree what we are facing, how much we can help ourselves, and how much help we need from him. This should give us confidence to face and get the victory in all circumstances.

But in practice it so often doesn't – because we either forget the help he is offering, or think we don't need it. Usually, we don't go so far as to tell him that our problem is beyond him – though at times we act as though we believe it is so. Our hope lies in the fact that God's patience leaves our own far behind.

Can we think the impossible?

We need to make the quality decision to demonstrate our dependence on God, while at the same time doing our utmost for him with the resources he has given us: as St Augustine once said: 'Work as though everything depends on you and pray as though everything depends on God.' If we realize that everything God calls us to do is impossible, we are already well on the way. If we apply to him for help in simple things which we can cope with in the strength he has already given us, he may indeed help, as a

168

means of underlining our gifts – but pretty soon he will make it clear that we have already met and overcome that hurdle. We are meant to *advance* on the racetrack of life, not to take a prolonged respite after the first lap.

But when we are faced with the impossible, that is the time for serious tangling with the powerful help of Christ – showing him that we are prepared to step out in faith beyond our endurance, secure in the knowledge that he will move in and see the job through. It is like waking up on a Sunday morning, with four services to take; you may feel in the deepest throes of 'flu – even convince yourself it is advanced pneumonia – yet if the work to which God has called you is waiting, you set off in faith. And God sees the work through. It doesn't matter how you feel the next day. God will see his work through then as well. *Not* to be in one's allotted place may not only mean a missed blessing, but a lost blessing, for opportunities are not invariably repeated. Impossible? No more impossible than a dead man responding to the call 'Lazarus, come out!' (John 11:43), or the feeding of the thousands with scanty provisions (Luke 9:13). Our Lord's help comes into its own, when we have exhausted our resources.

Only when we're on the wire? Well, perhaps not every time, but too often it seems like that. We may be tempted to think we are being badly used – but self-pity is not of God; it is when we take our eyes off the fulness of God, and focus instead on our own inadequacy.

Lord, deliver us from self-pity and all the harm it can do.

> *When we have exhausted our store of endurance,*
> *When faith seems to fail ere the day is half done,*
> *When we come to the end of our hoarded resources,*
> *Our Father's full giving is only begun.*
>
> *Annie Flint*

Suggested hymns
Guide me, O thou great Redeemer; Lead, kindly Light, amid the encircling gloom; O help us, Lord, each hour of need; Put thou thy trust in God

Sixth Sunday after Trinity (Proper 12)

27 July   *Principal Service*   **Reason to Follow**

2 Sam. 11:1–15; Ps. 14; Eph. 3:14–21; John 6:1–21

'A large crowd kept following him, because they saw the signs that he was doing for the sick.' John 6:2

Come and get well!

'Come and get well!' Dare we put such a sign outside our church? If so, would we shift the emphasis a bit, and qualify our healing ministry as soul-directed rather than physical? But that's not the whole story as Jesus told it. 'Love one another, as I have loved you,' surely covered the preaching, teaching *and* healing he had been doing for three years. Today, we have all but excised the third facet from our ministry. Is it too late to recover it? No, God deals in the difficult.

The people followed Jesus, because they saw he was mega successful. He healed 'all manner of sickness and all manner of disease' (Matthew 4:23; 10:1). That's comprehensive medicine, done for love not money, done to fit folk for life as God intended. And because of his healings, the crowds wanted to stay with him, whether they were well or ill. They were prepared to listen when he preached, and to follow him into towns or villages, up a mountain, or across the Sea of Galilee. Jesus had shown them a love that cared beyond anything they had known, and they were not going to let him out of their sight. With no NHS or insurance, sick people in first-century Palestine had few prospects if they could not cure themselves, begging until death stared them in the eyes. Jesus' coming gave them hope; just how much hope they didn't realize at the time, but they clung on to what they knew.

Where does sickness come from?

We've only to reflect on how comprehensively Jesus dealt with sickness, to realize that ill health and disease does not, cannot, come from God. If we're in any doubt, consider the day when Jesus caught up with a poor woman in the synagogue, bent double with a spinal condition. She had had to wait for eighteen years for Jesus to come and heal her. The ruler of the synagogue, and her fellow worshippers in the court of the women, had not done anything to help. 'Ought not this woman, a daughter of Abraham *whom Satan bound* for eighteen long years, be set free from this bondage?' Jesus asked, indignantly, when folk grumbled at his healing on the sabbath day (Luke 13:16). The infirmity that had stopped her leading a full, normal life, had been from Satan. St Paul was also on the right lines when he identified Satan as the author of his 'thorn in the flesh' (2 Corinthians 12:7) – but in his case God decided that the thorn was not preventing ministry. God is not too concerned with cosmetic surgery for surgery's sake; but if something is really coming between us and his will for us (and our service for him), we can pray for God's power to move in and either to do something about it, or to enable us to knock it out . . . unless we're so attached to it that we want to continue being a martyr to self-pity.

God's surgery
Our work as Christ's disciples is twofold in the field of healing: first, to make his healing power known to others – in teaching and practice – and then to enable others, in turn, to use it. This is not necessarily to boycott the organized medical resources ('Honour a physician with the honour due to him', (Ecclesiasticus 38:1–4), unless felt called to do so; but seriously to seek God's will on each individual case. Many illnesses are not physically induced, and their underlying causes need to be analyzed by faith rather than science.

Love at the heart
It is surely too cynical to entertain the notion that Jesus healed only in order to get folks' attention for his teaching. He healed out of love for them, sharpened into action by indignation that Satan was crippling their bodies and minds. Congenital disease, malformation and malfunctioning, contagious and paralytic – all submitted to his power.

The vast sums expended on medical research today have not yet brought about the comprehensiveness of Jesus' healing. What would he counsel, were he to walk into our sophisticated laboratories and ever expanding surgeries? If the Church today were to practise healing in the Jesus way, there would certainly be an increase in her ranks – unless, of course, people decided that modern science had improved by leaps and bounds . . .

171

For the healing of the nations; Make me a channel of your peace;
Meekness and majesty; Will you come and follow me?

Sixth Sunday after Trinity *Second Service*
Obsolescence Ps. 74; Job 19:1–27a or
Ecclus. 38:24–34; Heb. 8

*'In speaking of "a new covenant", he has made the first one obsolete.
And what is obsolete and growing old will soon disappear.' Hebrews
8:13*

Not destroyed, but fulfilled
Jesus was at pains to assure the disciples that he had not come to
destroy the old covenant (law), but to fulfil it. His coming, and
his forward-pointing gospel that opens out into eternity, had not
written a red line through the old, but completed it with a full
stop. It had served its purpose, its worth was not impugned, but
its day had drawn to a close.

Yet still some were lighting old covenant candles, to try to prolong its day beyond the desired – and designed – limits.

And even now, there are those who cling to what is obsolete –
either from a love of the familiarity that brings comfort without
challenge, or from a longing that somehow history's clock will be
turned back, as though Jesus had never been.

High summer
High summer, with its warmth, holidays and the cessation or at
least reduction of much business pressure, is rarely the time when
we take stock of new beginnings. We put so much on hold until
the autumn which sees a 'new term' for many. But today's reading
surely encourages us to pause in our sun-bathing and to reflect
on how our faith is shedding any encumbrances of obsolescence,
and taking up new help from Christ to meet the new daily challenges. How far have we come, say, in the past month? What new
situations have impacted on our lives? What have they shown us
about our faith, and the faith of others? How 'new' and fresh is
the covenant by which we are living? It is very easy to allow
tradition and convention to intermingle until one is lost in the

other, and combined they serve to blunt our spiritual outlook – in much the same manner that the outlook of the religious hierarchy prevented it from recognizing the Messiah for whom it had looked for so long.

God came to save the world from obsolescence.

Taking notice

If the picture of Christ that we show to the world is clouded by antiquity and complacency, folk cannot be blamed for not recognizing it. If the Christian message we proclaim is obfuscated by traditions irrelevant to today's world, folk cannot be blamed for ignoring it. But show the world a Christ who speaks of new hope, new life, new challenge, new power, new vigour – and folk may take notice (there is no guarantee here; Jesus himself said some wouldn't believe even in the face of a resurrection, but there's a fair chance that others will get the message).

If we cannot get excited about our new covenant, and show to others our Covenant Partner who made it all possible, we shall be waiting a long time for the world even to hear the gospel, still longer for it to be converted.

Holiday reading

When we go on holiday in the coming weeks, can we make our Bible the priority item in our luggage? Can we read (several times, if possible) the Book of Acts, and share again the sheer vitality and enthusiasm that gripped the early apostles firmly enough for them to get the gospel across, not only to folk who had 'open minds' of agnosticism, but also to those who were already heavily committed to other, pagan religions? Can we realize again the conviction with which their message would be preached, to effect such conversions?

Perhaps God is saying, ever so gently: 'I have chosen YOU for my Peter, my Paul, my Tabitha, my Timothy . . . of 2003.'

It would be a crying shame if obsolete tradition or lack of spiritual awareness caused us to miss out on what God may be saying even now to us.

Suggested hymns

For the might of thine arm we bless thee; Hushed was the evening hymn; Jesus calls us, o'er the tumult; O strength and stay

173

Seventh Sunday after Trinity (Proper 13)
3 August   *Principal Service*   **Hunger Appeased?**
2 Sam. 11:26–12:13a; Ps. 51:1–12; Eph. 4:1–16;
John 6:24–35

'Jesus answered them, "Very truly I tell you, you are looking for me, not because you saw signs, but because you ate your fill of the loaves." '
John 6:26

No meal ticket
These people had gone to some trouble to catch up with Jesus, only to be told pretty straightly that they must not look to him merely as a ticket for another free meal. Was this deserved? How would we have reacted? Would we have met his eye and declared we wanted his teaching not his food? Or would we have hung about in case another picnic was lined up? Or would we have bridled, and gone home? God is still challenging us to think ever more seriously about why we are here, what we are doing, and how we are meeting the challenge of mission.

Made for more than picnics
God has made us for so much more than picnics. He has got creation to a fine art. What he makes, he makes beautifully. He's the Master Craftsman, the Master Potter, and he's not in the business of second-hand or second-rate. When he created us, it was for one purpose: to believe in him. Belief in him means keeping his laws and doing his will. His most important law is to love. If we are to love, we are not to be in strife, for the two cannot co-habit in a person. His most important will is to share his gospel, to spread the good news of Jesus. If we're not doing that – if we give people around us the impression that we are not Christians (or even merely nominal Christians) then we are out of God's will.

Upside-down
To be doing God's will as if we meant business means to be turning the world upside-down. This was 'the charge' levelled at the earliest apostles – but had the citizens only known, it was really the best compliment that could have been paid. For the disciples *were* turning the world upside-down – for God; because God's

way and the world's way, were (and still are) diametrically opposed.

'Take care of yourself,' counsels the world.

'Take no thought for food, drink, clothing,' says Jesus.

'Get rich quick!' counsels the world.

'It's easier for a camel to go through a needle's eye, than for a rich person to get to the kingdom of heaven,' says Jesus.

'Make the most of your leisure time!' counsels the world.

'Preach the gospel, heal the sick, raise the dead, and your wages I'll pay,' says Jesus.

No wonder the world makes a poor fist of understanding Christians!

Our caring

But we, as Christians, need to care about the world. If the plight of millions as yet outside the love of Christ doesn't impact on us, we are still outside the love of God.

The world may try to bring goodness down to its level; Christians must seek to bring the world's level of goodness (yes, it does have some goodness!) ever higher until it is on God's level.

The world may say it doesn't matter what a person does, says or thinks. Christians must continue to fight against the set and current of these times.

In telling the crowds to think on a higher level, to see beyond the physical food they had enjoyed, Jesus was not so much reprimanding as encouraging: think high, aim high, live high. God has undertaken to see that his folk do not starve; he wants us to trust him to tell the truth. As Christians, we have accepted the challenge to live, aim and think high – to live as those who will one day die to live for ever; to live as those who are ready at any time to go to meet their Maker; to live as those with a burden for all those who are as yet not ready to die.

Jesus' encouragement

Jesus was seeking to prepare the crowds for the eternity he was preparing for them. A recent illustration of God's encouragement (which shows, also, the Almighty's sense of humour!), was the locust plague affecting parts of China. The worst of its kind for a century, great swathes of the country were in danger of being devastated. To fight the foe, an 'army' of over 700,000 ducks and chickens was mobilized! Foremost in providing these were Christian farmers. Their generosity did not pass unnoticed by the government officials – and the stock of those Christians went up, as many of the local cadres were convinced of their genuineness and unselfishness. Local house churches which had been persecuted were allowed to develop more regular and larger worship services. One missionary remarked, in wonder: 'Only God could have thought to use locusts to turn the tide of Chinese anti-Christian feeling!'

Suggested hymns
Bread of heaven, on thee we feed; Lord, enthroned in heavenly splendour; Lord, teach us how to pray aright; O, Bread of heaven, beneath this veil (*Celebration Hymnal*)

Seventh Sunday after Trinity *Second Service*
That is Wisdom   Ps. 88; Job 28 or Ecclus. 42:15–25; Heb. 11:17–31

'When he gave to the wind its weight, and apportioned out the waters by measure; when he made a decree for the rain, and a way for the thunderbolt, then he saw and declared it; he established it, and searched it out. And he said to humankind, "Truly, the fear of the Lord, that is wisdom; and to depart from evil is understanding."' Job 28:25–28

By faith
In Job, God goes back to the days of creation and the ordering of the elements, in a poetic and poignant definition of wisdom. In Hebrews, the faith of patriarchs and others, including a harlot, continues the theme: look back and consider, is the message. This is how it has been from the beginning. God has initiated all the good. Mankind, in its measure of positive response to the will of God (i.e. faith) leaves a legacy which in turn helps present-day believers. We are not to worship the past, to the extent that we get a jaundiced or cynical view of the world today; but the past is there, with memories to recall it and minds to learn from it. We know what the loss of memory does to a person, how much life is diminished by the inability to relate to the past. Let us acknowl-

edge God's gift of memory, and pray that we may use it aright –
to his glory, not someone else's.

Let us reflect today on the positive aspects of our Christian
life and witness, made possible by our memories (and perhaps
including the memories of others). So long as our memories serve
us to serve God better, they are being used to his glory. This, our
Lord says, is wisdom. Our readings today do not make too much
distinction between wisdom and faith; spiritually speaking, if we
have one, we're pretty certain to have the other.

Our debt to others
Acknowledging not only the fact of God's creativity, but also the
reasons for it, and how they are directed for our good, is wisdom.
Putting our knowledge into practice, is faith. Meditating on the
example of believers who have shaped religious history, is wisdom. Translating the meditative remembrances into Christian
practice, is faith. One goes hand in hand with the other, and
today's is a signal lesson for those Christians who would view
the Old Testament as irrelevant or unnecessary to the Church of
today.

John 21:22 teaches us that we are not to meddle in someone
else's mission business; but let us never be too proud to learn from
what others have done. We all need encouragement from time to
time, and the saints of old have much to teach us. If encouragement, as someone has aptly said, is 'oxygen for the soul', then
Abraham and his ilk have an important part to play in keeping
us spiritually alive.

By the same token . . .
By the same token, our own life and witness may not only be an
encouragement for our friends and families today, but also for
countless souls in time to come. Doesn't this thought encourage
us to make every minute count for God? Let us think of those we
have known, but for whose encouragement we might not be here
today.

The broad-brush acceptance
We are not to judge – to say, for instance, that Abraham's faith
was stronger than Rahab's – but to take the broad-brush approach.
Abraham was a God-fearer; so, too, in her way, was Rahab, though
few would have classed her as such. She took a giant step of

faith, cutting across credal and cultural barriers. Was the step motivated solely by self-preservation? Surely not; she could easily have 'shopped' the spies, alerted her city, and become a local heroine. We are never to despise or belittle the faith of others, for no one knows every detail about another's life, and appearances are notoriously unreliable. Recall that day in the treasury, when Jesus commended the widow who contributed two coins, above the rich who ostentatiously cast almost the Royal Mint into the coffers.

Suggested hymns
Faith of our fathers living still; Give me the faith that can remove; O for a faith that will not shrink; The wise may bring their learning

Eighth Sunday after Trinity (Proper 14)
10 August   *Principal Service*   **Heaven's Bread**
2 Sam. 18:5–9, 15, 31–33; Ps. 130; Eph. 4:25–5:2;
John 6:35, 41–51

'Then the Jews began to complain about him because he said, "I am the bread that came down from heaven." ' (John 6:41)

Is it really so?
There are some parts of Christian belief which are very difficult to accept. We may believe them, but keep the belief to ourselves, finding it too hard to share. What if people were to laugh, or to try to talk us down with logic, reason and commonsense?

Logic and the rest have their place in our ordinary lives; but these ordinary lives don't address the really big questions of life. There comes a day for each of us, when logic, commonsense and reason have to be left behind, and we go forward to the next life with the only thing that matters – the word of God. 'Heaven and earth will pass away,' said Jesus, 'but my words will not pass away.' If we disbelieve a promise like that, everything else is a lie.

'Those who believe in my name, I will never cast out . . . I am with you always . . . Those who believe in me will never die . . .

I am the resurrection and the life . . . I am the way, the truth and the life . . . I am the vine . . . I am the good shepherd . . . I am the light of the world . . . I am the bread of life . . .'

If we believe one of Jesus' statements, we must either believe the others as well or be inconsistent. And an inconsistent Christian is a contradiction in terms. If we take in these promises of Jesus, until the remembrance of them is as natural as breathing, then one day they truly will take over when our oxygen gives out; and the transition from this life to the next really will be as natural as breathing.

Bread of life

'I am the bread of life.' We have one of these great 'I am' sayings of Jesus as part of our gospel reading today. It comes in a passage of the long sixth chapter of St John, that some people will say is 'beyond belief'; they will look us in the eye, apply their logic, reason and commonsense, and say it's impossible to believe.

We can tell them, then, that God deals in the impossible. Jesus came to do the impossible. He calls us to do the impossible. So, when we believe it when he tells us he is the bread of life, make no mistake, we are in good company. We can believe it and keep it to ourselves – but that won't do an awful lot of good for anyone else's soul. Or we can get serious with God, and ask him to show us opportunities for sharing his life-giving bread. There is everything that is best to grasp, in teaching that is destined to outlive earth and heaven.

In his flesh

We meet our Lord so frequently in the elements at the eucharist, that we can lose track of just how mysterious the sacrament can be to non-believers. It was 'in his flesh' that Jesus made the greatest sacrifice of history, 'in his flesh' that he lived the greatest life that's yet been lived. And it's that flesh that he asks us to share, that equips us to live life as he lived on earth. In his living bread we have the capacity to live victoriously, as only he shows us how: to beat the Devil into the middle of next week – and beyond; to intake God's holy word, which will then be with us for all time – and beyond; to relate to God, because every day as the Spirit grows in us, Jesus' living bread multiplies in us, enabling us to take in more and more of God's word . . . And God, looking at us, sees more and more of himself in us, as we grow more and more like Jesus.

More exciting
Then life becomes ever more exciting. The more we take on for God, the more we are given of God; and the more living bread we can spiritually digest, the less we shall be burdened with the confines of logic, reason and commonsense. We shall be able to review each day, and to wonder just what 'impossible' work God is going to do next – in our lives, and in the lives of those we meet.

Without the confines of his incarnation, Jesus has his sights not merely on feeding four or five thousand: he is offering living bread to the whole world.

There's plenty to go round, and absolutely no reason for anyone not to share what they've already been given.

Suggested hymns
Break thou the bread of life, dear Lord, to me; I heard the voice of Jesus say; I hunger and I thirst; Lord, enthroned in heavenly splendour

Eighth Sunday after Trinity   *Second Service*
Take Fresh Hold!   Ps. 91; Job 39:1–40:4 or
Ecclus. 43:13–33; Heb. 12:1–17
'Therefore lift your drooping hands and strengthen your weak knees, and make straight paths for your feet, so that what is lame may not be put out of joint, but rather be healed.' Hebrews 12:12, 13

Bucking up
Bucking up for Jesus means letting the world see that Satan can't get a Christian down. It's not how we enjoy the good times that impacts most on those watching us (and Christians are always being watched), but how we deal when life is tough. God is a loving Father, but not even our earthly fathers like to see their children walking streaks of misery. 'Body language' was important centuries before it was given a name. We may feel terrible, but why give Satan the satisfaction of seeing us present the awful

picture to others? There is enough gloom and apathy in the world without Christians adding to it.

Of our making

If we make our way straight (i.e. keep in the will of God), spiritually speaking, we shall not trip over Satan nor lame our selves into the bargain. We can choose Satan's way, and we can choose God's; but only a moron would deliberately court lameness. How is our mobility for God growing – spiritually, mentally and physically? Are we letting him stretch us in all possible ways? He will not do it unless we pray for the stretching. God wants willing and cheerful operatives in his Royal Service, not recalcitrants.

Taking the power of Christ

One way in which we can build spiritual stamina is to take the power of Christ into places where, as yet, he is not honoured. Praying in his name in such places brings his light into dark corners. A seed is sown; perhaps another will come soon to nurture that seed, or perhaps it will lie dormant for a long time; no matter, we have planted Christ in that place.

Nor do we need to go physically into such places. Christ's power has a mobility that transcends gravity and the laws of time and space. Let us pray him into situations as they come to mind, as we see them on the screen, hear about them on the radio, or read of them in the papers. A lady in Scotland died, well into her nineties. As her nephew sorted through her effects, he found page after page of names and situations for which she had prayed. He estimated her interceding had taken more than two hours each day. She was keeping her way straight in a magnificently simple yet powerful way.

Spiritual athletes

The more we hone our spiritual energy, the more athletic we shall become. Our indwelling Spirit can outpace the Devil by a fair margin, so we need have no qualms about overworking him. He is here, he is waiting, and it is criminally wasteful not to avail ourselves of his great power. We should no doubt bristle with indignation if someone called us 'a couch potato' in physical terms. Let us take as much care on the spiritual front.

No truce while the foe is unconquered,
No laying the armour down;
No peace till the battle is ended,
And victory wins the crown!

Fanny J. Crosby

This ongoing, round-the-clock challenge gives the Christian life its edge. In the modern world we are so programmed into shorter working hours, long weekends, lobbying for more bank holidays, ever more leisure time, pension plans and early retirement. On the spiritual front, these luxuries are unknown. We are never off duty any more than our Captain ever takes a break.

Let us not moan. When we entered the King's Service we knew the conditions. Throughout his earthly ministry, Jesus was at pains to tell his disciples exactly what they were taking on.

And the good news? That's around in plenty, as we do battle in Christ's name. But the *best* news is that we cannot fail, for God is on our side (cf. Psalms 56, 118).

Suggested hymns
Fight the good fight; Lift high the cross; Soldiers of Christ, arise; Soldiers of the cross

Ninth Sunday after Trinity (Proper 15)
17 August   *Principal Service*   **Spirit-filled**
1 Ki. 2:10–12; 3:3–14; Ps. 111; Eph. 5:15–20;
John 6:51–58

'. . . *Be filled with the Spirit, as you sing psalms and hymns and spiritual songs among yourselves, singing and making melody to the Lord in your hearts, giving thanks to God the Father at all times and for everything in the name of our Lord Jesus Christ.' Ephesians 5:18–20*

Enjoying our Lord
How it must give delight to God when we show him we are enjoying our Christianity, by making music for him! We don't need to worry if friends tell us we can't sing in tune; the angels will harmonize our melodies, and see that by the time our music

reaches heaven it's the thought behind it that sings! We have all been born with the gift of music in our hearts, and our Holy Spirit will give voice to it, the more we are willing to sing God's praises. 'To sing is to pray twice,' they say in the Russian Orthodox Church. When we sing, let us put our hearts into the music.

The medicine of music

'A cheerful heart is a good medicine,' said the author of Proverbs (17:22). Let us take at least three doses a day: this medicine comes without prescription, no contraindications, and is free of charge; yet we queue at the doctor's surgery and the pharmacy, and part with our money for unknown quantities coated in bright colours and rattling in little jars or sealed in tin-foil bubbles. These may act as placebos for our mind, but all of them leave the spirit untouched.

Stress-induced ailments take up far too much of the doctors' time. Before they shred our nerves and whiten our hair – and certainly before they stop our heart – can we not make a quality decision before God, that we try *his* medicine before any other? There is little room in a melodious heart for worry; and many have been cured from physical ailments by praise and rejoicing. A lady in Texas was diagnosed with terminal cancer, and immediate surgery was recommended; but she had booked to attend a Christian convention, and her operation was postponed for a week. At a healing service during the convention, she went forward for the laying-on of hands. She believed she had been cured, though her body felt no different. The following week, her doctor ran pre-op tests and was baffled when the scan showed no carcinoma at all. The operation was cancelled, and she returned home in great joy.

'There now!' remarked her sister. 'I told you all you needed was a week's holiday!'

Dear Lord, when you work a miracle, give us eyes to see and hearts to sing all the credit to you!

> Give us hearts to sing your praises,
> Love to help a friend in need,
> Joy to sing in celebration,
> Fellowship in word and deed.

May we all, as the old prayer says so beautifully, cultivate 'courage, gaiety and a quiet mind'.

The song within
In ancient times it was thought that when the logs in the grate burned brightly, hissing and crackling merrily, they were releasing the song of birds who had sung in their branches when the tree was alive. It was only a fable, but the songs we sing to God from our hearts are not dissimilar, for it was the Lord who planted the notes there in the first place. Throughout the Bible – but particularly in Isaiah and Revelation – God shows us that heaven is a place of music: loud music, too, that can make even the doors to the great throne room of the Almighty shake in their sockets (Isaiah 6:4). That is making melody on the grand scale, but somewhere in that orchestral beauty are the notes *we* make – and the more music we make here, the more practised we shall be by the time we get sight of that throne room.

God's love
It tells us so much about God's love and concern for us that he wants us to sing for him, to find joy in his service, to fulfil our duties with a cheerful heart, for the day when we shall know full joy, the complete symphony.

> *There'll never be drapings of sorrow,*
> *No funeral coach in the sky,*
> *No graves on the hillside of glory,*
> *For there we shall never more die;*
> *The old will be young there for ever,*
> *Transformed in a moment of time;*
> *Immortal, we'll stand in Christ's likeness,*
> *The clouds in their brightness outshine.*
> *I'm bound for that beautiful city*
> *My Lord has prepared for his own,*
> *Where all the redeemed of all ages*
> *Sing glory around the bright throne.*

> Fred M. Lehman

Suggested hymns
Angel voices, ever singing; Give me joy in my heart; Songs of praise the angels sang; Ye holy angels bright

Ninth Sunday after Trinity   *Second Service*
In Perpetuity   Ps. [92]100; Ex. 2:23–3:10; Heb. 13:1–15

'Jesus Christ is the same yesterday and today and for ever. Do not be carried away by all kinds of strange teachings.' Hebrews 13:8, 9

Standing firm

A Christian should be known by his ability to stand firm when everyone around him is running hither and thither after a series of distractions. But we need to take to heart the full implication of Christ's stability: what we believe of the first-century Jesus, we must believe of the twenty-first century Jesus. This convincingly answers those who try to tell us that God doesn't act like that nowadays, or that Jesus doesn't work miracles like he did, any more. *The same yesterday and today and for ever* means exactly what it says; and we have to tinker about with semantics (and truth) to make it any different.

Stability

His stability encourages us to stand firm. There is also a hint in our text today, that the stability practised here will be of value Hereafter: an inkling, surely, that in eternity we shall still be working, building on what we have learned in this life. This is God at his most exciting!

Stability in the world today is so often at a premium. Statements are made one day, to be forgotten, altered or simply contradicted the next – or are made in the first place with enough caveats and options as to render them untrustworthy from the start. In an age where proof is elevated above trust, the Christian should stand out as someone whose word is his bond – always. Probably all of us know people who promise things they do not honour: big things, little things, their word cannot be relied upon. But equally there are those who would deny themselves material benefits rather than break their given word. We'd all like to think we fall into this second category – but with the best intentions we sometimes stumble into the first.

Distractions

In a 'get rich quick' society, one invariably finds the philosophy extending from the physical into the spiritual; and today's world has more than its fair share of distractions purporting to give us a quick fix while we live – and sometimes a taste of eternity (or what passes for eternity) before we die. Magic, astrology and occult practices have never been so numerous; and, as in ancient days, have sufficient mystery to attract the sophisticated, and sufficient drama to seduce the gullible.

There is a warning here for all Christians. If people say they find the Christian faith boring, is this because of the way in which we are portraying it? For, as our Lord introduced it, his gospel has surely all the mystery and drama anyone could wish for!

How much do we care that Jesus is presented to the world yesterday, today and for ever? How much does it impact on us, that souls may be lost because we do not present Christ to them in the right way? We are not raw recruits, learning the ropes while the top brass make the decisions. We are the front-line fighters; the 'other side' sees us first, before they meet Jesus. That is a sobering thought, and one we'd do well to ponder.

Always the same
But because Jesus is always the same, we can have the blissful confidence of reading the gospels and putting ourselves in the position of eyewitnesses: he is saying this to us; he is inviting us to accompany him up to the Transfiguration mount, to Bethany, Gethsemane, Calvary . . . He is preaching to us his Sermon on the Mount; we are the light of the world . . . Whatever he says to the earliest disciples, he is as surely saying to us, because he is the same yesterday, today and for ever. This is why he can say: 'Heaven and earth will pass away, but my words will not pass away.'

Nothing of Jesus can ever change.

Not even his wounds.

Suggested hymns
And can it be that I should gain; For ever with the Lord; O Jesus, I have promised; Yesterday, today, for ever, Jesus is the same

Tenth Sunday after Trinity (Proper 16)

24 August *Principal Service* **Standing Armour**

1 Ki. 8:[1, 6, 10–11]22–30, 41–43; Ps. 84; Eph. 6:10–20;
John 6:56–69

'Put on the whole armour of God, so that you may be able to stand against the wiles of the devil.' Ephesians 6:11

Six vital pieces

Truth, righteousness, peace, faith, salvation and the word of God. But these six pieces of armour don't just wing their way through the ether and stick to us like honey on a bear's paw. Neither can we trot down the High Street and obtain them with cash or credit card. This armour has to be prayed on, to be prayed into position, and then to be prayed constantly into action. Prayer is a business. God wants us to take it seriously, to prepare for it as thoroughly as we do our daily work. God wants us to operate, if you like, on 'special pleading'; he is prepared to listen, to reason and to respond. And, on occasion, as Abraham found when he interceded for Sodom, God may even change his mind in answer to special pleading.

Power and authority

The power and authority of God's armour can turn an impossible situation upside-down and right side out. It can turn the negativity of evil into the positivity of good. It can cut Satan down to size and thwart the old Devil's machinations, as nothing else can do. We need never imagine that time spent in meditating, reading, learning and sharing the word of God is wasted. No one yet has memorized the whole Bible from Genesis to Revelation – though some through the centuries have learned vast portions of it.

The better will be our armour

We can know for certain that by the time we die, we shall still have much to learn about God's word – but the more we do learn of it, the better will be our armour in the war against evil. 'Search the scriptures,' said Jesus. And again he said, 'Learn of me.' We can do both simultaneously.

Truth
Jesus is the truth (John 14:6). If we wear the truth of Jesus, we have a protection against the falsehood of the Devil – we can identify lying for what it is, even though Satan is well versed in the art of wrapping up lies in an innocuous covering to look more like the truth.

Righteousness
This breastplate covers the heart, from which right thoughts, intentions and actions have their birth. If the Spirit rules, OK. If Satan rules, our breastplate needs polishing to reflect out the light of Christ. On the instant we find evil coming at us, let us firmly put the breastplate of righteousness between us and the foe.

> *Jesus, victor in the strife,*
> *Jesus, who has loved me so,*
> *Dowered me with eternal life,*
> *Stand between me and the foe!*
>
> W.J. Govan

Peace
With the gospel of peace round our feet, our way to God is protected. If Satan has put any snares in the way, our gospel footwear will protect us. There is a gospel word of Jesus to meet and overcome any snare that the Devil can concoct. We can take immense and peaceful comfort from the knowledge that our Commander has already sussed out the armoury of the enemy.

Faith
Faith's shield is small enough to be grasped and moved into any position against Satan's flak – yet powerful and deadly enough to give complete protection, even though it may be the only thing between us and the demolition squad. The more we build our faith in the quiet times, digging into the word of God, praying in private and joining in corporate worship, the stronger will be its protection when the battle hots up.

Salvation
This helmet protects us from the top. While we are this side of eternity, we need our vision, voice and all the brains God has

given us – and Satan is powerful in launching airborne missiles like devious religions, wicked thoughts and lying suggestions.

The word of God
This is the *crème de la crème* of the armour. Without it, we are sunk. Let us pray it into our hearts, so that – as with Jesus in the wilderness – we have the right answer every time.

Suggested hymns
A charge to keep I have; A Sovereign Protector I have; Soldiers of Christ, arise; Stand up, stand up for Jesus

Tenth Sunday after Trinity   *Second Service*
Combined Operation   Ps. 116; Ex. 4:27–5:1;
Heb. 13:16–21

'Pray for us; we are sure that we have a clear conscience, desiring to act honourably in all things. I urge you all the more to do this, so that I may be restored to you very soon.' Hebrews 13:18, 19

On the home front
Ask any missionary, preacher or evangelist what is the Number One way in which you can help, and the answer will invariably be: 'Pray for me.' 'Pray for me, that I may be able to stand firm.' 'Pray that I may become what God wants me to become.' 'Pray that I may handle God's word in the right way.' 'Pray for me.'

And this is the plea of Paul (or whoever wrote Hebrews) – 'Pray for us . . . I urge you . . . to do this.' Yet often prayer can be the most difficult of ministries. In our fast-paced world, those who are rushing around looking busy are deemed to be the busiest folk. It can be hard to sit at home praying for those whom one may not know, or may never even meet.

A missionary the other side of the world gets a sudden uplift, a fresh burst of courage, a lightening of the load, or deliverance from a dangerous situation. He may never know who it was – but someone, somewhere, had lifted him in prayer to God.

Self-sufficiency? No!

There are those who pride themselves on being self-sufficient, but these don't include true Christians, who know not only their need of God but also their need of others' support. It can be humiliating to accept charity: far easier to go it alone. But we all stand in need of prayer support, and the early apostles quickly appreciated this. Not that we should take refuge in prayer when action is called for; there is no substitute for practical help in many cases – but the value of prayer should never be under-estimated. (It cannot be over-estimated, because it is incalculable.) James urges us to get the balance right: 'If a brother or sister is naked and lacks daily bread, and one of you says to them, "Go in peace, keep warm, and eat your fill," and yet you do not supply their bodily needs, what is the good of that?' (James 2:15, 16); yet 'the prayer of the righteous is powerful and effective' (15:16).

The necessity of prayer

Most of us can detect a mega need for prayer, such as peace negotiations between nations, an outbreak of serious disease, an accident or natural disaster of flood, earthquake or avalanche. But it is easy to assume that 'the great and the good' don't need prayer. Today's text knocks that theory on the head. We are to pray seriously for those in authority, for those whose lives are affecting many others, as well as for the child next door who sits an examination tomorrow. Prayer enhances the value of life – of both the pray-er and the person being prayed for. It's no wonder that, as Christianity advances across the world, its diamond-studded filaments of prayer becoming stronger by the day, Satan lashes out in ever greater fury. Well, let us lose no sleep over Satan's fury.

> *Give us joy to do your will,*
> *Promises we can fulfil;*
> *Grace to go beyond our strength,*
> *Knowing it is yours at length;*
> *Praying hearts for every day,*
> *Give us, Lord, the will to pray.*
>
> *Keep us loyal, keep us true,*
> *Ever watchful, Lord, for you;*
> *Ever wary of the foe,*

As we on your business go;
Praying hearts for every day;
Give us, Lord, the will to pray.

Give us hearts alive with love,
Likenesses of those above;
Hearts of pity, not of stone,
Ever, only, yours alone.
Praying hearts for every day,
Give us, Lord, the will to pray.

When the Devil tries his best,
Make us equal to the test;
For we know that on our side
Greater forces are our guide;
Loving, gentle Lord, each day,
Give your children power to pray.

Suggested hymns
Brother, sister, let me serve you; Help us to help each other, Lord;
Lord, teach us how to pray aright; Prayer is the soul's sincere desire

Eleventh Sunday after Trinity (Proper 17)
31 August *Principal Service* **God v. Tradition**
Song of Sol. 2:8–13; Ps. 45:1–2, 6–9; James 1:17–27;
Mark 7:1–8, 14–15, 21–23

'[Jesus said] "You abandon the commandment of God, and hold to human tradition."' Mark 7:8

Back to basics
'Oh, it's traditional!' we say, and the implication is, we're going 'back to basics' – to some observance, some rule, that was given before whatever it's being contrasted with. The old is better, and therefore should be followed.

In first-century Palestine, the Jews had buttoned themselves into such a straitjacket of tradition that it was hard to find the original law: their modifications and interpretations had largely become the law for them. Many portions of the old law (as is often the case today) were never read; and succeeding generations of rabbis felt obliged to add to the man-made traditions, merely increasing the confusion.

Jesus cut through the red tape of obfuscation. Human tradition, even at its best or with the best of intentions, post-dates the commandment of God.

God is the greatest

Whether the problem is social or sexual, sacred or secular, somewhere in the Bible God has something to say about it. We can choose to abandon what he says – but our abandoning doesn't wipe God's commandment off the record. We can come up with our own modifications and interpretations – but let's not forget that GOD MADE MAN BEFORE MAN MADE PROBLEMS. There's no problem going that's bigger than God. And there's no problem going that man can solve on his own without God. If we want to solve our problems, then a combined operation is needed. Just as it takes three persons to make a marriage – a man, a woman, and God – so it takes two persons to effect a commandment: the one who gives it, and the one who accepts and keeps it. Any rule of our own making is, in some way or another, an accommodation, second-best (in some cases, far worse than second-best).

Authoritative implementation

We may deck out our problem with different names and modern camouflage; but, strip the impedimenta away, and you're left with the Angst that has been troubling man since Eden.

Well, God had the answer to Eden.

At Calvary.

And Calvary is the answer to everything since. 'Once, only once, and once for all,' had the precious blood to be shed. Jesus came, not with a reversal of the old laws, but with an authoritative implementation of them – an understanding of God which transcended the Gemara and the Mishnah and their ilk. His was a thoroughgoing attitude too stringent for most to take on board. And Jesus didn't even go halfway to meet them. He challenged them for all they had. 'Be perfect . . .' (Matthew 5:48). And they couldn't take it.

What you can

Even those nearest and dearest to him had problems. At the end of the first century, a little manual, *The Teaching of the Twelve*

Apostles (*Didache*) was written. It contains the very honest, very modern-sounding teaching: 'Do all the words of the Lord – or, if you cannot manage them all, do what you can.'

And we're still trying to do what we can. It may fall short of 'as much as we can' – but with God's grace, the average creeps up all the time.

Our mission
Looking ever more closely into their religion, many of the Jews of Jesus' day had forgotten how to look outwards. They had let go of mission, as some have today. Being involved in mission is not an optional extra for any church. It is what the Church is all about, what undergirds Jesus' teaching, and what characterizes a Christian.

Suggested hymns
A new commandment I give unto you; Inspired by love and anger; Lord, thy word abideth; There is a book who runs may read

Eleventh Sunday after Trinity
Second Service **Shine Out!** Ps. 119:1–16;
Ex. 12:21–27; Matthew 4:23–5:20
'[Jesus said], "You are the light of the world."' *Matthew 5:14*

So familiar
Seven little words, and they're so familiar. They waft over us, like a warm summer breeze, and we let them lull us into contentment. But Jesus wasn't singing them as a lullaby. He meant these seven little words to impact. He was not saying the disciples were the light of Galilee, but the light of the world. An old gospel hymn says:

> *Do not wait until some deed of greatness you may do;*
> *Do not wait to send your light afar;*
> *In the simple daily duties to your Lord be true,*
> *Brighten the corner where you are.*

> *Ina Duley Ogden*

And that's fine. Our little corner will always benefit from a bit more of the light of the gospel. But we have been commissioned as light for the world. By the power of prayer our mission knows no bounds; by the wonders of technology, prayer can be translated and transmitted in more ways than the early Christians could have thought possible.

Getting the light to go

While we are bogged down by the parish share, the church roof, the power bills, how to fill the pews and a hundred other items that take their monotonous turn on the meeting agendas, we're not getting our light to go out very far beyond our parish boundaries. The first-century disciples found it hard, too, with their country in the stranglehold of Roman occupation. They had the equivalent of curfews and black-outs, embargoes and restrictions, that any modern country has when it is occupied by an alien power. They also had opposition from the established church, whose members were mostly hell-bent on killing Christians. Jerusalem and the surrounding area was no health resort for anyone who claimed allegiance to Christ. Who could have blamed the earliest disciples, if they had gone into diplomatic hiding, and let the rest of the world go hang?

Praying for guidance

We need to pray for guidance in shining God's light on our world. Praying has the divine sanction and guarantee of approval and excellence. We are very busy with all our advanced technology, while God has a single purpose in mind: to get the world evangelized. And the world, we are sometimes told, is getting smaller as telecommunications advance. We can call up a place the other side of the world on the Internet at the touch of a button. We can reverently wonder how St Paul would have made this technology work for him! Each year, 50,000 new Christians in China alone are being baptized; many more in Africa and parts of Asia are being converted from long-held pagan traditions. Alpha, Emmaus and Cursillo groups are spreading ever further.

There's a Sunday School hymn that never loses its impact:

> *Jesus bids us shine,*
> *With a pure, clear light,*
> *Like a little candle*
> *Burning in the night.*

> *In this world of darkness*
> *We must shine –*
> *You in your small corner,*
> *And I in mine.*

> *Anon.*

Professorial simplicity
Its simplicity reminds one of Karl Barth, perhaps the most eminent theologian of the last century. The professor of theology was once asked by Dr Billy Graham: 'What do you consider the most profound truth of Christianity?' Barth thought for some moments, and Billy waited in anticipation of a great, high-falutin' reply. Then the professor smiled and said, simply: 'I think the greatest truth of Christianity is this:

> *Jesus loves me, this I know,*
> *For the Bible tells me so!'*

It may also seem a very simple matter, to share the gospel message, the gospel light, with someone. But it could be a matter of life and death – for us, as well as for the other chap.

Suggested hymns
Give me oil in my lamp; Light's abode, celestial Salem; Shine, Jesus, shine!; The light of the morning is breaking

Twelfth Sunday after Trinity (Proper 18)
7 September *Principal Service*
Taken by Surprise   Prov. 22:1–2, 8–9, 22–23; Ps. 125; James 2:1–10[11–13], 14–17; Mark 7:24–37
'From there [Jesus] set out and went away to the region of Tyre. He entered a house and did not want anyone to know he was there.' Mark 7:24

The unusual
In each case of these healings something unusual happened – over and above the actual miracle of healing. The Greek woman is

remembered particularly because she was drawn into a real argument of pleading. Jesus at first told her, in so many words, that she was not a candidate for a miracle, because she was a Gentile. Then in the Decapolis, noted for its mixed population, Jesus heals again but tells the man and his friends to keep the miracle a secret. But they ignore him, and make a better job of spreading the good news than do the more conservative Jews.

God is a professional in the art of taking people by surprise. And it's from verses such as today's Markan reading that we get an inkling of how the mission of Jesus developed by surprise. Primarily, Jesus was sent to the Jews, for the salvation of the Jews. Yet in the time of Isaiah, and even of Abraham, it had been acknowledged that one day all nations would come to God, and that the Saviour-to-come would be 'the Desire of all nations' (Haggai 2:7; AV). Jesus was not averse to travelling through the Decapolis where there was a mishmash of nationalities and where crime was rife. Yet in the case of the Greek woman, he seems to have shown reluctance to accede to her request. Was he really trying to draw out her faith? We don't know. It's impossible not to be reminded of the wedding feast at Cana, when the wine ran out. Remember that when Mary put the problem to him, Jesus replied quite sharply that his time had not come. But Mary ignored his reluctance, and went ahead with her order to the servants – just as the Greek woman refused to take no for an answer.

Faith-filled perseverance
Why should we imagine God would be unwilling to respond to faith-filled perseverance today? He is still saying: 'Come now, let us argue it out' (Isaiah 1:18). He wants us to order our case with care, zeal and perseverance, in the longest-term investment ever.

These healings in today's reading show us that Jesus' mission was not set in stone. He had the freedom to go where he pleased, and to act as he was moved – in the will of God, by the faith of others. As God deals individually with us, so Jesus felt free, within God's will, to deal with those whom he met as individuals.

Divine variation
He could heal by touch, as with the man of the Decapolis. He could heal at a distance, 'by remote control', as with the Greek woman's daughter. He could effect an instantaneous change from death to life, as with Lazarus and Jairus' daughter. He could heal

in two stages, as with the blind man who began to see men as trees walking, and who later saw everything clearly. He kept within God's will – but God's will nevertheless provided ample freedom. The freedom not to sin has always, in the divine wisdom of God, been greater than the freedom to sin.

Utter freedom
You shall know the truth, Jesus told his disciples, and the truth shall make you free.

Free from leprosy, free from mental weakness, free from blindness and the diseases that afflict mankind. As Christians, we stand in the freedom and the truth of God. We stand together, recognizing that we are servants of a great mandate to take Christ to our world, through words of truth and deeds of kindness. We do it, because the gospel of Christ has no fear of the twenty-first century, and is still God's way of changing the world.

A fine verdict
The Decapolitans passed a fine verdict on Jesus. There could have been irony in a verdict being passed on him who was to go on to become the Judge; but this verdict was one that Jesus would wish could have come also from his own people, the Jews: 'He has done everything well' (Mark 7:37).

If such a verdict could be passed on our lives, when we get to the Pearly Gates wouldn't it make our present trials and troubles worth while!

Suggested hymns
Happy are they, they that love God; In heavenly love abiding; Sometimes a light surprises; When all thy mercies, O my God

Twelfth Sunday after Trinity   *Second Service*
Our Debt – Others' Debt   Ps. 119:41–56; Ex. 14:5–31; Matthew 6:1–18

'[Jesus said], "And forgive us our debts, as we also have forgiven our debtors."' Matthew 6:12

The broader view

Houses and money – though we are not to rely on them, and certainly not to worship them – are nevertheless two of the most important things in this life. The possession of them brings some problems, but generally the lack of one or both brings more. But we are only addressing a part of the problem of debt on the world view, unless we also take on board the issue of faith: lack of faith, compromised faith, persecuted faith, the building of faith. If houses are provided for the homeless, that is good; but it only solves part of the problem. If a country's National Debt is paid, or at least alleviated, it's good, but it's only part of the problem. If individual debts are paid, it's good, but it's still only part of the problem. In order to initiate real, long-term growth, we need to go to the root of these troubles. We need to attack the evils that have been working in governments, in local areas and in individuals.

Planting faith

We need to plant faith where there has been fear, faith where there has been rapacity, faith where freedom is threatened, faith from the Bible into people's hearts. Because where you have people operating in the Christian faith – whether on the home front, or at local or national government level – you have progress: progress towards democracy, respect for human life and values, and growth; food, clothing, money, prayers, Bibles, teaching materials, agricultural equipment – whatever is given in faith in the love of God, gives God the opportunity to work ever more mightily in any situation.

Aid for countries in debt and distress is nothing new; for thousands of years godly men and women have been doing what they could, under God's guidance, to alleviate the problem in many and varied ways; and their success has been given many interpretations and understandings.

If you move faith to operate in a situation, that situation can be changed from the unbelievable to the believable; and if you can believe it, it can be redeemed. This divine equation can be seen many times in the Bible.

Begin at home

But before we can help the world out of debt, we need to begin at home. As Christians we start with an advantage, for the debt of sin with which Adam lumbered us has been paid – at Calvary. Yet our account may not be clear, for we have almost certainly managed to run up smaller debts by sinning: whether little sins or big sins, black or white, public or private, doesn't matter. It is all sin, and needs to be brought to God every day so that we do not sleep on it for even one night. At some point in that night we could be ushered into the presence of God, too late to get rid of unconfessed sin.

Others' debts

The NRSV rendering of this text implies that we dare not come to God asking for forgiveness unless and until we have forgiven anyone who is indebted to us. It is not a question of demanding, but of forfeiting our 'pound of flesh'; not of standing up for our own rights, but of looking to the rights of others; not of saving our face, but the other person's. To lend, looking for eventual return, is human; to look for no return, divine.

It is not God's will that any should be in debt, so if we have landed into it, we need to get serious with the Lord to discover where and how we have gone wrong: our own plight should also make us more tolerant and understanding of others who may be in a far worse situation.

The world has been promoting the 'buy now, pay later' philosophy for many years. Perhaps today's text, so familiar as to be often taken for granted, may enourage us to see any areas of our lives where so-called 'acceptable debt' can be jettisoned.

Suggested hymns

A debtor to mercy alone; A new commandment I give unto you; Be thou my vision; I feel the winds of God today

Thirteenth Sunday after Trinity (Proper 19)

14 September   *Principal Service*   **In Return for Life**

Prov. 1:20–33; Ps. 19 or Canticle: Wis. of Sol. 7:26–8:1; James 3: 1–12; Mark 8:27–38

'[Jesus said] "For what will it profit them to gain the whole world and forfeit their life? Indeed, what can they give in return for their life?"' Mark 8:36, 37

Our precious birthright

God took clay – dust of the earth – the nucleus of a seed – and gave it flesh and bones, and the senses of hearing, seeing, smelling, tasting, feeling. And he called it a dog, a lion, a tiger, and a thousand and one other names. And then he took some more dust, and gave it all these things, and a soul besides. He gave it the capacity to relate to him, to love him, serve and worship him – and through him to relate to, and love, serve and honour others.

It's a precious birthright, wholly undeserved; but with it comes the capability to part with it, even as Esau sold his birthright to Jacob. We can exchange our God-given soul for 'something else' *in the short term*. But, as Esau found, there will come a time when God reminds us that our responsibility for it is ongoing.

Selling the soul

Of men like Adolf Hitler – and, perhaps, more recently, Harold Shipman – it could be said: 'They have sold their soul to the Devil.' And the world is for ever holding out short-term alternatives to God. We can sell our souls not only to outright vice, but also to apathy, luxury or worry. Yes, we can. And the price can seem, at the time, so reasonable as to be a bargain. And, by contrast, God's way can seem too expensive in terms of Angst and effort. But as Jesus tells his friends in today's gospel reading, whoever lays down his life for God will really be taking it up. Whoever puts God first is thereby insuring his life for eternity. And taking up one's cross for Christ is surely an insurance premium with the longest-term benefits on offer!

Grace to press on

A missionary in Singapore said recently, as part of his understanding of the gospel message: 'God's grace is available to press on!' To stand still with one's cross is to increase its weight; but as soon as we begin to move forward with it, the weight is distributed through a greater number of stress-bearing muscles. In spiritual terms, through new opportunities, situations and circumstances.

If ever the Church needed people to take up the cross and make their lives count for God, it is in these early years of the twenty-first century. We have so many opportunities. God is opening so many doors, that we may even get the impression he is overworking us. Let's not work ourselves into a nervous breakdown over that; God will not ask of us more than he knows we can give.

Nor will he ask less.

And if we give him less than our all, one day he'll want to know the reason why.

No exchange
There is no viable exchange for life. There are those, like Judas, who get themselves to a point where the thread of life and the will to hang on to what God has given, becomes too much to bear. It is not for us to know what happens after that: '*C'est* son *métier*', observed Henri Heine. Our work is to make the best of our life here count for Jesus. If we keep in mind this aim and no other, we shall not fail.

All for Jesus
When the cross seems heavy, remind yourself that the work is all for Jesus. When you are misunderstood, misrepresented and everything goes wrong, take heart: all the suffering is for Jesus. When God appears not to answer prayer, or gives an answer you were not wanting, recollect that the struggle is all for Jesus. And when things go well, and the gospel light extends and brightens, thank God, take no credit for yourself; it's all for Jesus.

> *What though all my earthly journey*
> *Bringeth nought but weary hours;*
> *And, in grasping for life's roses,*
> *Thorns I find instead of flowers!*
> *If I've Jesus, 'Jesus only',*
> *I possess a cluster rare.*
> *He's the 'Lily of the Valley',*
> *And the 'Rose of Sharon' fair.*

> *Hattie M. Conrey*

Suggested hymns
Jesus, I my cross have taken; O Jesus, I have promised; Take up thy cross, the Saviour said; They who tread the path of labour

Thirteenth Sunday after Trinity

Second Service   **As You Would Have**   Ps: 119:73–88;
Ex. 18:13–26; Matthew 7:1–14

'[*Jesus said*] *"In everything do to others as you would have them do to you; for this is the law and the prophets."* ' *Matthew 7:12*

Sharing the bread

If we were starving, and our neighbours baked an ovenful of bread, the wonderful aroma would be of little use to us unless some of the food came our way as well. So it is with Christians who attend worship regularly, and probably do much good work besides, but allow their near neighbours none of the spiritual food that keeps them sustained. 'Oh, they're not interested!' is an excuse commonly heard, even before disinterestedness has been proved to be the case. The initial contact with unbelievers is the most difficult, and we postpone it until ... someone else makes the move.

The counsel of Hillel

Round about the time of Jesus, there were two rival rabbinical schools in Jerusalem, one headed by the hardliner Rabbi Shammai, the other by the moderate and much loved Rabbi Hillel. One day, a cocky young man presented himself before Hillel with the challenge: 'You'll make a proselyte out of me, if you can tell me the whole law while I stand on one leg.' With the modifications, interpretations and accretions of generations of rabbis, by this time the 'law' had become an unwieldy instrument. But Hillel calmly returned the young man's gaze, and replied: 'What you would not do to yourself, do not do to another. That is the whole law. The rest is commentary. Go and learn' (TB *Shabbat*, 31a).

A right way, and a wrong way

The law in itself is good, but there is a right and a wrong way of interpreting it. The Jews had concentrated on the letter of the law, and had become preoccupied with the technicalities of its operation. Equally, at the end of the first century, Jesus was to castigate the church in Ephesus for being cold and intolerant in its observance of religion (Revelation 2:4). Zeal had overtaken the tender loving care that Christians should have for each other: the sort of care that heals someone on the sabbath day; that gives hospitality to any, even those with whom we may feel we have little in common; the sort of love that can break with convention when convention gets in the way of the will of God. God gives us the freedom to impose restrictions. Why can't we be more ready to use his freedom to let them alone?

'No one can be considered useless in this world who has lightened the burden of it for someone else,' said Charles Dickens. Let us make burden-lightening in the name of Jesus our Number One priority. Jesus spent three years in concentrated seed-sowing. We have a wider mission field, but, after all, he promised that his followers would do greater works than he had done.

Our own experience
Our Lord does not ask us to get into the mindset of others. There is always at least one factor in someone else's life of which we know nothing. He tells us, rather, to measure their need by our own experience – to use our preferences as a yardstick. It's a fair assumption that what would come amiss to us, would not be to another's benefit either.

It may take us a lifetime to get it right every time. But a lifetime is precisely what God is giving us.

Suggested hymns
Brother, sister, let me serve you; Can I see another's woe; Help us to help each other, Lord; Make me a channel of your peace

Fourteenth Sunday after Trinity (Proper 20)
21 September   *Principal Service*   **Love of Self**
Prov. 31:10–31; Ps. 1; James 3:13–4:3, 7–8a;
Mark 9:30–37

'[Jesus said], "The Son of Man is to be betrayed into human hands, and they shall kill him, and three days after being killed, he will rise again . . ."
. . . But they were silent, for on the way they had argued with one another about who was the greatest.' Mark 9:31, 34

Negative response

Jesus had been telling his friends of the approaching Passion, but they had not responded positively. They may have listened, but didn't like what they heard; or perhaps they didn't listen properly; or perhaps they listened, but didn't understand what they heard. It was probably a bit of all three. They were out of their depth – so, to cover their confusion, they started discussing a subject that was less taxing: themselves.

We still do it. If in doubt, fall back on yourself! In general we love the subject, we'll even get round to it without thinking; this could be why psychiatrists have such long waiting lists. Jesus knew the human propensity so well. He didn't interfere. He let their tongues run riot – but then, at journey's end, he gave them a salutary lesson about forgetting the ego trip, and becoming as uncomplicated and outgoing as little children.

It's all about focusing on God.

Religious of centuries past called it 'recollection' – being alert to what God is saying to us, how he is moving in our lives, which way he is directing us. If we take recollection seriously, it's a full-time job attending to God.

And why should it be otherwise? God works on attending to us twenty-four hours a day. Whenever we feel like praying, talking to God, fellowshipping with God, isn't it the greatest blessing to know that we're never outside his surgery hours? It's such a great blessing, and sometimes we take it for granted.

Minds set on God

But these fine, articulate, muscular minds that God has given us, can flit from one thought to another with the speed of light. Perhaps a physicist would say we can race ahead of light. The story is told of a knight riding down a country lane. He drew level with a monk walking on the verge. 'I'll give you my horse, if you can recite the Lord's Prayer through without any deviation,' offered the knight with a smile. The monk's eyes lit up with anticipation, as he took in the rippling sinews of the satiny-black thoroughbred. 'Our Father . . . ,' he began, confidently. He had reached the petition, 'Forgive us our trespasses . . .' when his gaze took in the gaily decorated saddle. 'Oh!' he exclaimed, shyly, 'Do I get that lovely saddle as well?'

God is telling us to work at what he is saying; really to think about how he is daily moving in our lives. We may not fully understand, but we are not to give up on that score. It will come out right in the end, for all things work together for good to those who love him.

Only human
Yet we are still human; not one hundred per cent human, for we have the Holy Spirit implanted in us; but we often have what has been rather bluntly termed the 'thirty-second sound byte' mentality. Is it because we cram, or try to cram, so much into our days? Not really. Those first-century disciples of Jesus were pretty much the same; at least, until Jesus had been resurrected and ascended, and the Spirit had been given.

God normally manages to get people's attention at times of birth, marriage and death – but where do these 'three timers' go, when there isn't such an occasion to get them to church? We who come regularly to meet God in worship, know the value of the exercise. But we have a responsibility to reach out in Jesus' name to those who are not yet recollected to God. The disciples were at a loss to know what Jesus meant – but after the Holy Spirit had come, life was very different.

We who have the Spirit already should need help to misunderstand him – help that, for once, we can do without.

Suggested hymns
I heard the voice of Jesus say; I hunger and I thirst; Jesus, stand among us; Son of God, eternal Saviour

Fourteenth Sunday after Trinity
Second Service   **Spiritual Awareness**
Ps. 119:137–152; Ex. 19:10–25; Matthew 8:23–34
'Suddenly they shouted, "What have you to do with us, Son of God? Have you come to torment us before the time?"' Matthew 8:29

The time appointed
The demons know they have an appointed time when Jesus will torment them to oblivion. Both sides in the spiritual world have an awareness that makes our own look tiny by comparison. They have tangled since the dawn of time (and perhaps even before

then), have witnessed the rise and fall of Lucifer, the victory of Calvary, and the ongoing frustration knowing that their time is measured. The Bible is rich in snippets of information about this spiritual dimension, where so much is happening that it makes the earth and our machinations look pedestrian in contrast.

The two madmen whom Jesus met recognized him with the speed and accuracy of spirit meeting with spirit. Our Lord must have wished that his own people could have shown similar awareness; but this startled recognition has some encouragement for Christians, for it tells us that Satan and his like are not only aware of what is in store, but are dreading the 'torment'.

There are some, particularly in the Eastern Church, who see in the Book of Job evidence for a final pardon for Satan. Certainly, God and Satan are on speaking terms, as far as Job is concerned, Satan urging for a free hand in tormenting poor Job, and God allowing him a fairly long rein but stopping short of killing Job. This is still a pretty tenuous peg on which to hang a theory of eventual pardon. Were Satan to be forgiven, one would surmise his 'angels' would be, too – and there is no hint of this in today's reading.

Sad irony

It is a sad irony that the demons were in no doubt as to Jesus' mission and identity, while many of those he had come to save were too blind, preoccupied, ignorant or antipathetic to recognize him.

> *Amused in someone's kitchen, asleep in someone's boat,*
> *Attuned to what the ancients exposed, proclaimed and wrote;*
> *A Saviour without safety, a Tradesman without tools,*
> *Has come to tip the balance with fishermen and fools.*

> *John L. Bell and Graham Maule*

Proclaimed by the deranged, scorned by the sane; fêted by the poor, derided by the rich. Such was the reception for the Saviour of the world. Can we make sense of a God who operates like this, when he could have employed *force majeure* at any time, in any way, to get his message across?

No, we cannot – because God does not work according to sense, but out of sheer love. And sheer love makes a nonsense of anything less. Only when we are over the last hurdle, and face to face with Love, shall we understand why it had to be this way – if by that time it will really matter, for God may already have filled our minds with other missions.

A very narrow divide
At times such as this meeting of the demoniacs with Jesus, we see that the divide between the human and the spiritual is not so wide as it may seem for much of the time. *It can be crossed*, as Saul found when the Witch of Endor called Samuel from the dead. But God says, Don't do it; don't make the crossing outside my will. It may be intriguing to contemplate the tremendously *busy* world of the spirits, but let us leave it there. One day, God willing, we shall be a part of that spiritual activity. Then will be time enough to experience it in the freshness of introduction.

Perhaps that is why Jesus on several occasions told the spirits to be quiet, when they cried out to him in recognition.

Suggested hymns
Angel voices, ever singing; Around the throne of God a band; There is a land of pure delight; Ye holy angels bright

Fifteenth Sunday after Trinity (Proper 21)
28 September   *Principal Service*   **Word of Truth**
Esth. 7:1–6, 9–10; 9:20–22; Ps. 124; James 5:13–20; Mark 9:38–50

'My brothers and sisters, if any among you wanders from the truth and is brought back by another, you should know that whoever brings back a sinner from wandering will save the sinner's soul from death and will cover a multitude of sins.' James 5:19, 20

Working out
These verses are the climax of a letter that seems to show us how to realize the word that has been grafted into us (implanted), James 1:21, in working it out in practical ways for the benefit of others. James sees the divine implantation much as a physical operation which opens one up, inserts an implant, and closes up the incision

so that the implant cannot be removed but is there for as long as we function.

God's word, which empowers and enables us to reach out to others with his love, is locked on to our spiritual DNA, for our Holy Spirit to work on – as Jesus said, to remind us of things we might otherwise forget (John 14:26).

Divine implementation
If we follow the AV 'grafted', surely, yes, we can see the word, using what we *are*, growing and expanding on its own account – subject to pruning, nurturing, maturing and blossoming. But how does this square with the word also being *sown* in us? Can it be implanted, grafted *and* sown? Yes, if we recall the four ways in which the seed grew (or failed to grow) in Jesus' parable of the sower. When we welcome the word into our lives, it comes to stay. When once we have the word, we have life. When we have it, we have power. We are no longer totally human – but, dare we say it, partly divinely spiritual. If this does not inculcate an awesome awareness of God's love in bestowing his word, it's hard to know what will.

The word's good
Keeping our eyes on God's word increases the value of good in us, in a world where evil in a thousand manifestations is competing for our attention. It takes a real effort to lift one's mind off a problem on to something so true, honourable, just, pure, pleasing, commendable and excellent (Philippians 4:8) as the word of God – but if we don't do it, we shall die. It's as simple as that. The more we accept even the thoughts of grief, worry, gloom and whatever else Satan rolls along into our lives, the faster we are heading down the high road to hell. The only thing that can drag us off that road, on to the straight and narrow way of Jesus, is the word.

Health warning
Many a time it's a lot easier to go on worrying about evil of one sort or another – but it carries a health warning. Worry kills. The word gives life (James 1:21).

The true word
The word is truth, says Jesus. Because of this guarantee of integrity, we can share it in abundance, knowing that whether we use it verbatim in one-to-one contact, or in prayer, perhaps over long distances, its veracity impacts positively. It may lie dormant for many years in a person; but it has been implanted, and God will safeguard his word, come what may.

We're used to fuel, and even some food, having a star rating. But God's word comes with all the stars of the universe backing it! 'Can you count the stars?' God once asked Abraham. 'Your seed will be as these stars for multitude.' So Abraham kept looking, every night, at those stars – and he kept on keeping faith, holding on to God's word.

Can we count the worth of God's word?
Can we figure out its power?
Well, let's just keep treasuring it, reading it, taking it in, and sharing it for all we're worth.
For without it, we're worth nothing.

Suggested hymns
Father of mercies, in thy word; Lord, thy word abideth; There were ninety and nine; Thou art the way, by thee alone

Fifteenth Sunday after Trinity
Second Service   **True Authority**   Pss 120, 121;
Ex. 24; Matthew 9:1–8

'[Jesus said], "But that you may know that the Son of Man has authority on earth to forgive sins" – he then said to the paralytic – "Stand up, take your bed, and go to your home."' Matthew 9:6

Speaking with authority
'He speaks with authority, not as the scribes,' was the verdict on Jesus, part-way through his ministry. And, right at the end, he underlined his universal authority: 'All authority in heaven and on earth has been given to me' (Matthew 28:18) – while we, as his disciples, have his authority to go out in his name. Let us not

arrogate to ourselves what is Christ's, but neither let us be remiss in taking the authority he has given us.

It is the authority to do and dare all in his name: the authority that carries infinite weight because it has infinite power behind it, even to the problem of sin. 'Whatever you bind on earth will be bound in heaven, and whatever you loose on earth will be loosed in heaven,' Jesus later told Peter (Matthew 16:19).

The needful breadth

Jesus need not have brought sin into the healing of the paralytic; he could have kept the miracle on the physical plane. But he intended the breadth of his authority to be seen. The man was being healed, not simply because it would be better for his body, but also for the health of his soul. There is the inference that sin had somehow been instrumental in the man's physical condition – or even that he had sinned as a result of it, perhaps stealing food he could not earn or beg. We don't know. On another occasion, Jesus plainly affirmed that neither the man born blind nor his parents had sinned to produce his condition. But this case, for some reason, is different.

Our Lord knew, also, that to link forgiveness of sin with physical healing was asking for criticism from those who had been unable to do either. In fact, it may have suited some to see in the paralytic a man suffering as the result of sin. The world is very quick to point the finger at the vulnerable, whether they are rich or poor, healthy or sick.

Immediate cure

The man was apparently not asked to confess, before being cured, but his future life was expected to portray his repentance and renunciation of whatever sin had been forgiven. This is not to say the paralysis might return if he slipped back into the old ways. Jesus gave him the best of healing, and implicitly asked for the best of responses. It is the divine magnificent unfairness that we meet every day. God doesn't work with the caution of commercial money men: he invests lavishly in each person he has made – because, unlike a suspicious banker, he knows to the nth degree what we are capable of achieving with his grace. Unquestionably, it's far more than we estimate, or he would not be so generous. Can we possibly take time to reflect on all he has given to us – and evaluate how much *more* we can be returning to him, in time, talents, and (what he's looking for above everything) grateful love!

The value of friends
One of the best gifts from God is a friend – and here, too, God is munificent. Even the paralytic had four good friends who carried him to Jesus; four who obviously had faith that the new Rabbi could do something for their friend. There is no finer ministry than bringing our friends to Jesus. Why, after all, do we think God has given them to us? Those men could easily have considered their friend's case too hopeless to bother Jesus, yet they went to some trouble to struggle through the crowds with him. Who knows what other ministry they would go on to do, with the remembrance of this miracle spurring them on?

Is someone waiting for us to bring them to Jesus? To help them get to Sunday worship? To share the word of God with them? Let's do it – NOW, before we think up a string of reasons why we shouldn't – and before it's too late.

Suggested hymns
At even, ere the sun was set; In heavenly love abiding; Jesus calls us, o'er the tumult; Put your hand in the hand of the Man of Galilee

Sixteenth Sunday after Trinity (Proper 22)
5 October   *Principal Service*   **Is It Lawful?**
Job. 1:1; 2:1–10; Ps. 26; Heb. 1:1–4; 2:5–12; Mark 10:2–16

'Some Pharisees came, and to test him they asked, "Is it lawful for a man to divorce his wife?"' Mark 10:2

Legal eagles
The Pharisees, out to trap Jesus, had pitched on the question of divorce. They knew full well that the Mosaic interpretation had been an accommodation – but they wanted to hear it categorically from Jesus' lips. So, 'Is it lawful?' And Jesus told them straitly: 'Divorce is possible – but it's wrong, so don't do it.'

It isn't God's method to take all the options but the right one out of our way. What would be the point of making it impossible for us to sin? Into whatever situation he calls us, he expects us to ask: 'Is it lawful?', and then to choose the right. But when a Christian asks, 'Is it lawful?', the question is not only on the temporal plane, but 'Is it lawful in the eyes of Jesus? Would Jesus do this, say that, go there . . . ?'

From the start
This has been God's *modus operandi* from the start of creation. God gave – and still gives – the challenge: 'Keep my rules and live life to the full. Break my rules, and you will then struggle.' God could easily have left the forbidden tree out of Eden. Instead, he presented Adam with the challenge: 'Here is the fruit, but I'm telling you not to eat it. You have the choice – but don't do it!' He gave Adam a companion, a woman, because in his great goodness he believed it wasn't right for Adam to be the only form of humankind. He didn't remove the capacity of Adam to separate from Eve, but he said: 'I'm giving you to each other, as man and wife. You have the choice to alter that union – but don't do it!'

The other side
Someone said, the other day: 'If God is a good God, won't he see that any contact with the saints – the good people who have died – is impossible? Won't he let them rest in peace? The folk who dabble in the occult, and call up spirits – won't they be *evil* spirits?'

This is not a strange question. It's one that surfaces pretty regularly, as more and more people seem to be thinking about 'the other side'. There's no reason why we shouldn't think about it – but there are ways of getting there that we should not take. God works in certain ways – ways of challenge, tempered by love. He put the fruit in Eden, but said, 'Don't do it.' He gave the holy sacrament of matrimony, and said, 'Don't break it.' And he shows us another world – a world of spirit life rather than physical life, but he says, 'Don't meddle with it, outside my will.'

The Witch of Endor
When Saul of Israel was finding life hard he disguised himself (because he knew he was breaking God's law), and asked the Witch of Endor to call the prophet Samuel back from the dead. She did as requested, but Samuel reprimanded Saul in no uncer-

tain terms, and after that Saul didn't have too long to live to regret his action (1 Samuel 28).

Now the thrust of this story is not only the sin of Saul in consulting a medium – but the fact that Samuel could be recalled. God is saying: 'Yes, it can be done – but don't do it! Don't seek to know more of the spirit world, unless and until I tell you.'

The other world is there. The forbidden fruit was there. The possibility of divorce is there. BUT DON'T DO IT! says God. It is not lawful!

No compromise

Jesus could have concentrated on his preaching, and ignored the immorality and evil around him. But he couldn't do that and be true to himself and to God. He had to get involved at all points. He had to pitch in against evil, whenever and wherever he saw it. He didn't care about 'rocking the boat' of what passed for the established religion of his day.

In the trick question of today's text, Jesus was given the opportunity to choose the easy option: there would be some among his listeners who had taken advantage of the Mosaic accommodation. But Jesus didn't opt for second best. Ever.

Suggested hymns

Living Lord; Love Divine, all loves excelling; O love that wilt not let me go; O perfect love, all human thought transcending

Sixteenth Sunday after Trinity   *Second Service*
Comprehensive Policy   Pss 125, 126; Josh. 3:7–17; Matthew 10:1–22

'Then Jesus summoned his twelve disciples and gave them authority over unclean spirits, to cast them out, and to cure every disease and every sickness.' Matthew 10:1

Four gifts

When we were baptized, and a cross was traced on our forehead, we were given our 'name-in-Christ', our 'Christian' name. And when we were confirmed, in the laying-on of hands we were given the Holy Spirit. Two great gifts from God, marking us out as his

213

disciples. By the resurrection of Jesus, we've also been given the hope of eternal life. A name. A Spirit. And life.

But there's another gift which is not only linked to these three, but is also a gift which shows we have them: the gift of the authority of Jesus, in all whom he calls to be his disciples. It's the authority that takes us through and beyond the world's gossip and slander and vindictiveness; the authority that can meet evil and overcome it, that can turn disease into health, and sickness into strength.

We may not use it – certainly we don't use it to the full – but we have been given it.

Power cut off
A Christian who is not using the authority he has been given is like a woodsman attacking a tree with the power supply to his chain saw cut off. Just imagine the difference it could make to our day – any day – if on rising we made a conscious decision to put our all-powerful, indwelling spiritual dynamo to work, in every meeting God leads us into, every piece of mail the postman delivers, every telephone call we make or receive . . . everything we look at, hear or read. Our dynamo pack inside is permanently charged up and ticking over, ready to go into action. And what do we do? Too often we act like the woodsman pushing the chain saw through the timber without activating it – acting as though the power wasn't there.

Turning up the heat
Get a little British heatwave, and life changes. On the roads, drivers become as eager as their French counterparts to sound their horns; coughs, sneezes, stomach upsets afflict all ages; heart attacks either fill the hospital wards or the mortuaries and crematoria. 'It's the heat!' is the reason given for whatever crisis. But our indwelling Spirit never complains when we turn up the heat and give him more work. When we tap into the power and authority of Jesus, it increases in energy. In our reading, Jesus gave his disciples sufficient authority for everything, without any danger of their power source overheating.

Blanket healing
God is not in the business of falling short, or of admitting defeat. The disciples were given the means for blanket healing, and they

put their authority to good use. They kept their spiritual engines running. *Every* sickness, *every* disease – that is, no germ or bacterium excepted – gave way before their healing.

Remember when Elijah was assumed into heaven. Before he left, he asked Elisha: 'What do you want when I've gone?' 'A double portion of your spirit,' said Elisha, boldly. That's like asking a racing driver who's been winning prizes in his four-litre Maserati, for an eight-litre Ferrari. And Elisha got it. If we ask God boldly for big things, he will never say: 'Sorry, I've not got that in stock.' But if we ask, we need to be prepared, like Elisha, to use what he gives. We need to have the courage and faith of the disciples, to put the authority we've been given to the best possible use.

God is munificent in his providing – but he's economical, too. When he's given us the authority to heal, he won't exile us to solitary confinement. We shall find candidates for healing coming into our lives – as God says, as plainly as if he stood behind a BBC microphone: 'Here's a God-given opportunity to use what I've provided.'

Suggested hymns
For the healing of the nations; I sing the almighty power of God; Meekness and Majesty; Thine arm, O Lord, in days of old

Seventeenth Sunday after Trinity (Proper 23)
12 October   *Principal Service*   **Only Follow**
Job 23: 1–9, 16–17; Ps. 22:1–15; Heb. 4:12–16;
Mark 10:17–31

'As [Jesus] was setting out on a journey, a man ran up and knelt before him, and asked him, "Good Teacher, what must I do to inherit eternal life?"' Mark 10:17

At his word
And Jesus took him at his word. 'You must keep Numbers One through Ten of the Commandments, and, in your case, go the extra mile: get rid of all your possessions, and follow me.' Only by following Jesus, unencumbered by his wealth, could the man

really discover the answer to his question: 'What must I do to inherit eternal life?'

To inherit usually means waiting until someone has died. In essence, Jesus was saying, 'Cut all your ties, and follow me – and learn what it means to inherit eternal life after I have died at Calvary.' But the conditions proved too stern for the earnest enquirer. He went off sad at heart, back to his millions (or what passed for millions, in first-century Palestine).

Correct identification

The man had not identified the situation correctly. He had probably not identified Jesus correctly, though he had courteously called him 'Teacher'. Jesus was to spell it out on another occasion: 'Believe, *in my name*, and be saved.' In other words, *Know who you're dealing with*, and work from there. There is only one name under heaven whereby we can be saved. If we put our trust in any other, we're on a hiding to hell.

Around the time of her hundredth birthday, Queen Elizabeth the Queen Mother visited a nursing home in London. Going up to an old lady sitting in a chair, with her lovely smile the Queen Mother asked: 'Do you know who I am?' 'Oh, dear, if you have a problem with you who are, ask the nice man at the desk in the hall, and he'll help you,' came the quick reply.

A question of identity.

One Man needed to die so that we could inherit eternal life. He went to Calvary, and he died. And we, as his beneficiaries, inherited. Then he rose from the dead, having plumbed the depths of hell and fulfilled all the conditions that God had written into *our* eternal contract.

Earning is impossible

The man who went to Jesus that day wanted to earn his eternal life by good works. He may have been used to helping the poor and contributing to good causes. But he could not cotton on to simply believing in the name of Jesus. He identified his own good deeds, but he fell short on identifying Jesus as the source and finale of all that was good in him.

The equation works like this: a person can keep all the commandments, and even top up his goodness by giving away every penny of his fortune; but if he doesn't believe in Christ – if Jesus is not his reason for living, and giving – he is *only* 'a good man'. He's not a saved man. He's not an inheritor of eternal life. But if he believes in Jesus, that belief not only qualifies him for eternal life, it also motivates him to do good anyway. A believer in Jesus who doesn't do good works is a contradiction in terms.

We are close to St Teresa d'Avila's festival (15 October), so let's share one of her prayers:

> May your will, O Lord, be fulfilled in me,
> by all the ways and means
> that you, Lord, are pleased to use.
> If you want it to be through hard work,
> then give me the strength I need
> and let it be so;
> if it is to be through persecution,
> sickness, dishonour or poverty,
> then I am ready;
> I will not turn away from it,
> nor is it fitting
> that I should turn my back on you.
> Since your Son gave you even this will of mine
> in the name of all
> it is not right that I, for my part,
> should fail to keep my promise;
> but for me to do it,
> grant me the grace of your kingdom,
> that he has asked for me,
> and use me as your own,
> according to your will.

The Way of Perfection

Suggested hymns
All for Jesus, all for Jesus; Jesus, I my cross have taken; Oft in danger, oft in woe; Will you come and follow me

Seventeenth Sunday after Trinity

Second Service **A Busy Life** Ps. 127[128];
Josh. 5:13–6:20; Matthew 11:20–30

'Then he began to reproach the cities in which most of his deeds of power had been done, because they did not repent. "Woe to you, Chorazin! Woe to you, Bethsaida!"' Matthew 11:20, 21

Tantalizing glimpse

This is a tantalizing glimpse of an extended ministry of which we know very little. The four canonical gospels are precious, but they are all too short. They tell us enough of Jesus – but from verses like Matthew 11:20f. we see that there was much more in those three years or so of ministry. God tells us some, but much more is hidden. One day, perhaps, we shall meet some of those who met our Lord yet whose particular healings or questions have not been included in our gospels.

Least expected

But the thrust of these verses is that it is often from the least likely source that due recognition comes; the down-and-out area produces the better harvest; the persecuted community shows more compassion; the poor exceed the rich in loving service; the unsophisticated people accept their God-given authority to heal and raise the dead, while 'traditional religion' relegates such authority to the first century. Sodom had been such a vice-ridden place, that not even a handful of good-living citizens could be found there, though Abraham had daringly negotiated an exceedingly generous deal for them with God. Yet Sodom, Jesus roundly says, would have repented if it had seen him and had experienced his miracles as Chorazin and Bethsaida had enjoyed.

From those to whom much has been given, much (more) will be expected; but God's goodness is so often taken for granted. Was this why Jesus extended his ministry into the mishmash of nationalities that made up the Decapolis? Or made a point of conversing with Samaritans, whom no self-respecting Jew could tolerate? Or elevated women to positions from which the society of the day largely excluded them?

Our ministry

It behoves us to examine our own ministry, our church, our community. Have we shown real gratitude to God for his goodness? Does our love reach out to the areas where Jesus would go if he were here today? Are we too good at examining ourselves, to the detriment of places and people where there is a great need for the gospel? It's not only those people who can fellowship with us in God's word, whom we should be meeting (though this ministry is important), but the un-churched who, unless we tell them, are not likely to pick up a Bible for themselves.

God will safeguard his word

God will safeguard his word. His honour is not at risk, and neither is ours if we are faithful to him. Better far to have the world's ridicule or animosity, than the world's indifference or even praise because we are hiding the fact that we are Christians. At least by scorn and enmity the world is paying us the compliment of sticking our heads above the parapet. And let us not be slow to speak out for the truth, even though we startle. Jesus' words here must have startled the respectable citizens of Chorazin and Bethsaida – hopefully to some purpose. If we are not startling people for God, we are not doing much to get the Devil riled either.

The day of judgement

On the day of judgement we have Jesus' warning assurance, that those who have received benefits from God and have misused them, or failed to appreciate them, will be judged more harshly than those to whom less has been given. It is not our mission to evaluate who has been given more or less than we have – but to make the best possible use of what we have; to ask God for all he is willing yet to give; and to share all he gives with others.

It is a full-time work – but the stakes are the highest ever.

Suggested hymns

A Man there lived in Galilee; Forth in thy name, O Lord, I go; Onward, Christian soldiers; Strengthen for service, Lord

Eighteenth Sunday after Trinity (Proper 24)
19 October   *Principal Service*   **The Daring Truth**
Job 38:1–7[34–41]; Ps. 104: 1–9, 24, 35a; Heb. 5:1–10;
Mark 10:35–45

*'And they said to him, "Grant us to sit, one at your right hand and one
at your left, in your glory."'* Mark 10:37

Confidence-building
A verse like this gives us great confidence – confidence in the
veracity of the gospels. It's so brutally frank, honest and open.
We'd need help to disbelieve it. Here's Jesus, knowing full well
what lies ahead of him in Jerusalem. But, nothing daunted, he sets
out to walk right into the Passion and all it means. For company
he's got a collection of disciples, on whom all his hopes for his
Church are pinned. But they're not listening eagerly to what he
has to say; they're not rehearsing what they'll be preaching when
he has gone. They're not jumping for joy at the prospect of doing
and saying great things for God. At least two of them are angling
for preferment.

And all of us at times still do it.

Jesus' patience
Thank God that Jesus' patience outlasts ours, by a very fair margin.
The other disciples' reaction was so predictable; yet Jesus, who
had the most cause of all to be indignant, reacted so mildly, with
compassion and understanding. We may even reverently believe
that he would rather have such enthusiasm than a lukewarm disinterestedness. That's not to say we have a green light to go ahead
with getting ahead. But at least let's give God a notion of our
enthusiasm for what is in store. He is doing all the preparation,
and for us to live as though eternity has nothing to do with us,
must surely sadden him.

The contrast of Job
By contrast, Job had received quite a chiding from God. You
weren't around when I was putting everything together! is the
message in our Old Testament lesson. The difference is marked:
God is dealing with the earliest days, and a man who is sincerely
questioning his fate. Jesus, with eternity and two disciples who

are frankly curious and eager. Was God being fair with Job? Yes, because he reserves the right to deal with each of us as individuals. Remember the labourers in the vineyard, and the seemingly unfair 'penny for the day'.

Following in his footsteps
As we follow in the footsteps of Jesus, we shall also meet up with seemingly unfair situations. Some of them, we shall be able to deal with. Others, we shall need to leave with God. When Jesus had first met James and John on the shore of Galilee busy mending their nets with their father at the boats, he had invited them simply to follow him. They had obeyed immediately. The nets would get repaired. They had new work to do.

Similarly, the disciples would get over the tension caused by the brothers' request. Until we reach our last breath, everything comes – to pass; and we have to go on, living with whatever decisions we have made at a particular time. Looking back, we can no doubt identify really mega decisions which have instigated major turns in our lives; but for every one of these there have been countless others, mostly forgotten. During his sufferings, Job looked back along his life, to decisions he had made, paths he had followed. Did James and John believe that their humble origins would preclude high status in glory? Don't we, also, value lineage, position and power, translating our earthly structures into the future which may be nothing like them at all?

It does no harm to ponder such questions. God's love for Job, and Jesus' love for James and John, was unabated. But we need to learn from them, and to draw the line between pondering and pride. The former, God willing, leads on to the heavenly mansions; the latter, to quite another place.

Suggested hymns
At the Lamb's high feast we sing; Glorious things of thee are spoken; Lord, when thy Kingdom comes, remember me; Thou art gone up on high

Eighteenth Sunday after Trinity   *Second Service*
Knowing Mercy   Ps. 141; Josh. 14:6–14;
Matthew 12:1–21

'[Jesus said], "I tell you, something greater than the temple is here. But
if you had known what this means, I desire mercy and not sacrifice, you
would not have condemned the guiltless. For the Son of Man is Lord of
the sabbath."' Matthew 12:6–8

Greater than the temple
Forty-six years had seen the magnificent temple slowly rising out
of ruins. To the Jews, it was the flagship of their religion, standing
sentinel over Jerusalem and the Kidron Valley. When one crested
the Mount of Olives, the temple was the first building in the
city to catch the eye. That foreign influence was to be seen in its
colonnades and porches didn't worry the Jews unduly. Solomon's
temple, after all, had been redolent of Phoenician design. That the
whole edifice (apart from a few huge courses, now known as 'the
Wailing Wall') would be fired and tumbled into ruins in the Roman
sack of Jerusalem in AD 70, was mercifully hidden from the Jews
of Jesus' day.

Who was this carpenter's Son, to cast doubts on the pre-
eminence of their temple? To tell them that God preferred mercy
to all the sacrifices which took up so much of the temple's day?
To proclaim that he took precedence over the sabbath itself? Since
the sabbath had been constituted by God, Jesus did not need to
spell out his credentials; the point was clear. At a stroke, the
carpenter's Son overrode three of the staples of Jewish religion:
temple, sacrifice and sabbath.

Our Christian staples
What are our staples today? Do they promote or inhibit our
religion? Our 'temple' may be our church buildings, some of which
have an insatiable appetite for resources which could otherwise
be channelled into mission outreach, Bible translation or many
other projects which so often miss the agenda in favour of the
parish share or the quinquennial recommendations.

Our 'sacrifices' may be our various liturgical observances, which
often appear to become more intricate and time absorbing than some
years ago. Well, they help to identify our particular persuasion.
Much of their ritual is 'cast in stone'. Could we indeed live without

them? What about the non-liturgical (often 'family') services? What about the times when we join with other denominations? Those wonderful united services during the Week of Prayer for Christian Unity – could we have them at other times too?

A difficult question: Do we worship (or rely on) the liturgy – or what it stands for?

Our 'sabbath' (Sunday, for Christians) is, of the three, the one which probably causes us the least heartache. Some churches have a Saturday evening service, and few of those attenders will be seen again at the Sunday services. Many Christians find no problem with shopping on a Sunday after the morning service. The secularization of Sunday is pretty far advanced. Most of us stand in no danger of making a god out of Sunday observance. Just the reverse. Far less time is spent at worship than in running after a variety of secular pursuits.

With the secularization of Sunday, our world has lost a vital respite in the 'making money, having fun' culture of modern times. Many Christians are giving God less time than, say, even a generation ago did. Jesus' words in today's lesson are a challenge to us to review our religious priorities before it's too late. It may take longer than we think – but we need to make a start.

A vicar noted for his long sermons was eventually challenged by his churchwardens, and in the end replied: 'I'll see what I can do, but it might take me a long time to make them shorter!'

There will come a time when, if we haven't done anything, there won't be time to start.

Suggested hymns
And can it be, that I should gain; Father of heaven, whose love profound; This is the day the Lord hath made; Today thy mercy calls us

Last Sunday after Trinity (Bible Sunday)
26 October   *Principal Service*   Reading Aright
Isa. 55:1–11; Ps. 19:7–14; 2 Tim. 3:14–4:5; John 5:36b–47

'[Jesus said], "You search the scriptures because you think that in them you have eternal life, and it is they that testify on my behalf. Yet you refuse to come to me to have life."' John 5:39, 40

Taken for granted?
With so many English versions of the Bible to hand, do we take it for granted? Or do we search its pages with avidity and the absorbing concentration that characterized our early reading? Do we compare the versions, even learn Hebrew, Greek or Latin, so that we can get behind the English text?

Jesus was castigating the religious grandees of his day – the dons whose life's work was to study the scriptures. They had analyzed the texts for years, and had committed whole scrolls to memory. Yet when the very object of the prophecies came, they failed to recognize him. We, too, can become so familiar with a Bible truth in a certain context that we fail to take it out of that well-known setting and apply it to our lives today.

The precious word
In some parts of China today, no material on which words have been written is thrown away or treated without respect. We in the West are not so scrupulous, and we sometimes take language for granted – until we visit another country and don't understand what the natives are saying, or a stranger who can't speak English drifts across our path, and we suddenly find communication has broken right down.

A closed book
Pick up a Bible in Japanese, Gaelic or even shorthand. In an instant, from being the most recognizable book in the world, the Bible has changed into 'a closed book' for us. No amount of searching these scriptures will advance our spiritual knowledge.

Disciples – apostles?
When Jesus ascended back to heaven, he left eleven men who were no longer just disciples, but apostles: men literally 'sent' out. Jesus had told them to stay in Jerusalem until they had received the Holy Spirit, which they did. But then, even after Pentecost, they continued to hang about – until it took an extra stiff dose of persecution to winkle them out of the city, to Pella, and from Pella the *real apostleship* began.

But someone had gone before them, and was already doing the work out there. Paul was preaching as though his life depended on it. He had answered the call of duty (he had been taught by the eminent scholar, Rabban Gamaliel), and he was going where no one as yet had taken the Christian gospel.

His twenty-first century counterparts are still being called to preach the uncompromised word of God, to search the scriptures; and, as ever, there is a shortage of both preachers and Bibles. A pastor in China was asked recently: 'What do you and your people need?' 'A million Bibles,' came the quick reply. 'Oh!' exclaimed the questioner. 'Er – and anything else?' '*Two* million Bibles,' came back, even more quickly.

Increase in demand
We may have a surplus of Bibles on our bookshelves. We may see Bibles being offered for sale at coffee mornings or church bazaars. But the world's bestseller is still so much in demand, in so many countries, that the Bible printing presses can't cope with the demand. And it's not just the new believers, nor the unbelievers, who are requesting Bibles. Across the world, in every Roman Catholic parish, with the encyclicals since Vatican II, all catholic lay people, as well as the priests, are now permitted to own and study the Bible for themselves. It has meant a welcome increase in demand, and is such a great step forward.

May we never let the mis-use of the scriptures, hinted at by Jesus in today's reading, dissuade us from studying the Bible for dear life, which will be life eternal.

Suggested hymns
Father of mercies, in thy word; Lord, speak to me that I may speak; Tell me the old, old story; There is a book who runs may read

Last Sunday after Trinity *Second Service*
Show Gratitude Ps. 119:1–16; 2 Ki. 22; Col. 3:12–17
'Let the word of God dwell in you richly; teach and admonish one another in all wisdom; and with gratitude in your hearts sing psalms, hymns and spiritual songs to God. And whatever you do, in word or deed, do everything in the name of the Lord Jesus, giving thanks to God the Father through him.' Colossians 3:15–17

Saying 'Thank you'

When we're growing up it often seems we're forever being told to say 'Thank you'. It's recognized that showing and saying thanks, is good manners. 'Be thankful,' 'give thanks,' also feature in various forms in the gospels. When Jesus sent the ten lepers on their way, when he discovered he was healed, only one turned back to give thanks. In the upper room, on the night of the arrest, Jesus took bread and wine, and gave thanks. Just as he had done when he fed the multitudes. Just as he was to do on Easter evening at Emmaus.

Being thankful for what God gives should be part and parcel of our daily life; and Paul repeats the advice in these verses. He goes further: *Whatever* we do, let's do it in Jesus' name. That in itself is a 'Thank you' to God for the sacrifice of Calvary.

All the time? How can we do this all the time? Shouldn't we have to take vows and retreat to a convent or monastery? No, all we need, for starters, is to go to Nehemiah 8:10, 'The joy of the Lord is your strength.' Through his joy – the joy of knowing and serving the Lord, walking and talking with him, God will give us strength to do *all* in the name of Jesus.

'I can do all things,' says the power of positive thinking – which isn't bad; at least it's not negative thinking. 'I can do all things.'

But, 'I can do all things, *through Christ who strengthens me*,' says the Christian. And that's a lot better.

Depression weakens

There's no Christian living will make his or her mark for Christ in a mood of despair, of depression, of doom and gloom. These merely sap what strength we have. Our physical strength drains away as we allow feelings of negativity to take us over. Watch it! If you get out of bed the wrong side one morning, and allow yourself to be at odds with the folk you meet, chances are you'll attract the first cold or 'flu germ that drifts your way.

But by the same token, if you feed on the word of God – if you attend to the Holy Spirit living somewhere between your breastbone and your spine – God will give you joy, and that joy will be your physical, mental and spiritual strength. And there's no germ living which can tangle with the Holy Spirit's joy when it's coursing through a person at a rate of knots.

226

Joy abounding

We can't get too much of the joy God is offering us. Today's Christians need this joy in abundance – because out there the world is ready to offload a megatonne of doom and Angst on to us. We need to ask God for his joy all the time.

Lord, you've led me into such-and-such a circumstance. You've brought me to this point, Lord. I need your strength to cope with it. I need your joy to see me through. Abounding joy, Lord. I ask for nothing less. Lord, I'm looking to praise you for that joy, in Jesus' name.

Praying such a prayer means that it won't be long before the joy of the Lord *is* our strength. We shall be able to look back and think: 'My! Such-and-such a problem wasn't really a problem, after all!'

Because God doesn't deal in problems. He calls them all solutions.

Nothing fazes God. And if we're walking in the joy of his strength, there's no problem on earth with the power to faze us either.

St Athanasius was hounded into exile more than once, for preaching the uncompromised word of God. He was vilified, tortured, ridiculed – but each time he would smile, and say calmly, ''Tis but a little cloud, and will soon pass!' The worst that Satan can threaten us with will pass, if we meet his onslaught fairly and squarely in gratitude for the strength of the Lord's joy.

Suggested hymns

Come, sing with holy gladness; Happy are they, they that love God; I sing the almighty power of God; O strength and stay

Fourth Sunday before Advent 2 November

Principal Service **Seeing the Light** Deut. 6:1–9; Ps. 119:1–8; Heb. 9:11–14; Mark 12:28–34

'Then the scribe said to him, "You are right, Teacher, you have truly said ... this is much more important than all whole burnt-offerings and sacrifices."' Mark 12:32, 33

The coming order

It is encouraging to see one of the scribes far-sighted enough to envision the superceding of sacrifices by love for God and one's neighbour. That he was probably not quite so intuitive is likely, however; but such has obviously been read into his considered response to Jesus. It had been recognized (in theory, at least) from the time of Hosea, but the sacrificial system had been made such an integral part of Judaistic religion for so long that the temple hierarchs were determined to cling to it while they could. Particularly in view of the Roman presence, they would resist any changes to their traditions on principle.

Jesus' overriding

Jesus had no hesitation in overriding traditions and principles that conflicted with his message. The sacrifices had almost had their day; their official time would run out at 3 p.m. on Good Friday. But only he who was to take the place of those innocent animals had the authority to announce their cessation. Other religions demanded sacrifices, some human; but only Jesus would die as the innocent victim for the sins of others. Only the Almighty Lord had enough love in his heart to effect the salvation of the world so magnanimously, so convincingly, so vicariously.

Encouragement

Our Lord must have been encouraged with the open-mindedness of this scribe. It was evidence that some theologians in the temple were thinking for themselves, rather than going along with the hardline philosophy of Annas and Caiaphas. Already, too, the Sanhedrin member, Nicodemus, had been won over. Any majority vote among the religious grandees would still go against Jesus; but his message had begun to get through to some. Perhaps our individual ministries are like this, with one or two listening and asking for more, while most don't evince an interest at all. We must not be discouraged. Jesus was content to proclaim his message and leave its implementation with his Father. If we are tempted to think our work has counted for little, let us reflect that Jesus could easily have asked God for a longer time to consolidate his mission. But God had decreed that three years was long enough.

Letting go

It's difficult to let go when we are part-way in helping someone to a knowledge of the Lord: to approach ministry in the dedicated yet detached way of Jesus. Always on the move, yet never hurrying, he loved as much as he could at every step, but could always move on – to the next town, the next opportunity. We, with our less nomadic lifestyle, may try to slow down the purposes of God (or may do so unwittingly). Let us live as those who are ready to die at any time, with peace of mind that each day we have done our best. Others will build on our work. Let's make sure we leave them solid foundations. Relatively few of God's work-force see a matter through from beginning to end; it's all part of the challenge of ministry. Those times when people to whom we have ministered make a full commitment and take up their cross with zeal and integrity, are gifts of God to encourage us along the way; we cannot book them as we would order a season ticket: they are completely in the timing of the Lord.

A breakthrough

Our lesson shows that even in unlikely quarters, God's word can take root and grow until it manifests itself in revelation. Some come to God in sheer, naked faith. Others may weigh the matter long and hard – but their decision, once made, will often be deep and lasting.

Can we consider today how we came to Jesus, thanking God for those who helped us on the way. Can we also lift to him any whom we are helping just now, and who may be asking searching questions, such as that posed by the scribe who came to Jesus. With him in mind, we can reverently suppose that considerable heart searching lies behind the asking of such questions. May God give us grace to come out with the right answers.

Suggested hymns

Jesu, lover of my soul; Love is his word; Thine be the glory; When I needed a neighbour

Fourth Sunday before Advent   *Second Service*
Water of Life   Ps. 145; Dan. 2:1–48 (or 1–11, 25–48);
Rev. 7:9–17

'For the Lamb at the centre of the throne will be their shepherd, and he will guide them to springs of the water of life, and God will wipe away every tear from their eyes.' Revelation 7:17

Vision of contrast
As St John, obedient to God's command (Revelation 1:11, 19) writes all he sees in the vision, the waters of the Aegean would stretch from his Patmos island thirty-five miles or so to Miletus, the nearest port in Asia Minor. He would contrast these salty waters with the pure 'springs of the water of life' – and would probably long for his exile to be over and to be translated to glory where the life-giving waters were springing. Meanwhile, he had work to do – for who would know of the excitement of the spirit world, and the wonderful and impeccably arranged eternity planned by God, if John did not faithfully record these visions and arrange somehow for their despatch to the mainland?

The Shepherd Lamb
A lamb is usually looked after by a shepherd, but the Lamb of Calvary is seen by John in the centre of the throne, and the visionary is told that this Lamb will be the shepherd. It is he, Jesus, who has made eternity possible for us, who has paid the price of our admission there. As the Lamb, he will bear the scars that Calvary cost him, for ever. Again, as the Lamb, he is emphasizing the sacrifice that bought salvation. And, as shepherd, he will still be our guide, mentor and upholder in eternity, as he has been here, the only difference being that here he is our guard against the Devil; in eternity there will be no evil from which to guard us.

Living water
As living water flows from Jesus, so he will guide us to the springs of this pure nourishment and cleansing. If we have drunk from his inexhaustible supply here, we shall continue in eternity.

> *The well is deep, and I require*
> *A draught of the water of life.*
> *But none can quench my soul's desire*

For a draught of the water of life.
Till one draws near who the cry will heed,
Helper of men in their time of need,
And I, believing, find indeed
That Christ is the water of life.

Albert W.T. Orsborn

Jesus, Son of God, Shepherd, Lamb, Mediator . . . Jesus of the many names and yet the one great name, Saviour, is the real author of Revelation: it is his own (1:1). He dictates the Seven Letters to the Churches (chapters 2 and 3), and features in the visions, nowhere more prominently than in today's reading. His place in eternity is special and assured, because it is he who has made eternity possible.

Joy replacing sorrow

There's no disappointment in heaven,
No weariness, sorrow or pain,
No hearts that are bleeding and broken,
No song with a minor refrain.
The old will be young there for ever,
Transformed in a moment of time.
Immortal, we'll stand in Christ's likeness,
The clouds in their brightness outshine.

Fred M. Lehman

God himself – what condescension and love! – will wipe away the last vestiges of the tears we have shed on earth. Let us remember this, when torn by grief or pain. Nothing we endure here will endure in heaven; not even our tears (so precious to God that he counts them) will outlive the grave. The only memory of sorrow and pain in eternity will be the five wounds of Christ.

Suggested hymns
Jerusalem the golden; Light's abode, celestial Salem; O sacred head, sore wounded; There is a land of pure delight

Third Sunday before Advent (Remembrance Sunday, q.v.)   9 November   *Principal Service*

God's Work   Jonah 3:1–5, 10; Ps. 62:5–12;
Heb. 9:24–28; Mark 1:14–20

'And the Spirit immediately drove him out into the wilderness.' Mark 1:12

Giving credit where it is due

Throughout his life on earth, Jesus gave the credit for everything he said and did, to God. 'Of my own self, I can do nothing,' he told the disciples on one occasion. Right from the start, Gabriel had said that the holy thing to be born in Mary would be of the Holy Spirit (Luke 1:35). And at the other end of his earthly life, on the cross, Matthew tells us that he gave up his spirit (Matthew 27:50; AV); while St Peter collects it together: 'Jesus was put to death in the flesh, but quickened by the Spirit' (1 Peter 3:18; AV). At some point between 3 p.m. on Friday, and sunrise on Easter morning, God's Holy Spirit came again into Jesus, with resurrection power.

Divine availability

In the thirty-three years or so of his time on earth, Jesus made himself available to be directed by the Spirit. He could have 'done his own thing' – he had the freedom to do it, as we have. But he chose the even greater freedom not to sin, to be obedient to the Spirit. 'Not my will, but yours be done,' he prayed to his Father, that night in Gethsemane. One can reckon that wasn't the first time, by a long chalk, that he had prayed such a prayer. And the reward for such dedicated and faithful obedience? 'All authority in heaven and on earth has been given to me,' he told his disciples. 'Now [YOU] go therefore and make disciples of all nations...' (Matthew 28:18, 19).

Divine allowing

As we meditate on the life and faithfulness of Jesus, doesn't our awe and wonder increase? We can tremble at the thought of him *allowing* the Spirit to drive him into the wilderness to be at the mercy of Satan's temptations for forty days. Isn't that dreadful! But, he's *Jesus*! He can come out of it the Victor!

'All authority . . . has been given to me . . .' Mighty words, for a mighty God, from a mighty God. But how often do we complete these mighty words? How often do we dare? – for Jesus, from describing his own situation, suddenly turns to us: 'All authority . . . has been given to me . . . [Now you] go and teach all nations'!

Early interpretation

For a while, the early Church took these words to heart, recognizing them for what they were: not merely a nice suggestion for some of our leisure time, but a full-blown, full-time, Spirit-filled command. There are not too many interpretations of such a clear command. It's encouraging to trace the history of the early Church, how the gospel was taken out from Galilee and Jerusalem to many countries of the old Roman Empire. But today, in many parts of the Church, the energy and driving force of the Spirit is not being used anywhere near to the full. We have become so locked on to our man-made structures, that ecclesiology has in some areas stifled mission. We have become so busy on the home front, while 'some corner of a foreign field' is still waiting to hear the gospel.

Why Spirit-driven?

Why was Jesus driven by the Spirit into the wilderness, if not to prepare him for ministry and mission? Do we today need to listen more to our Spirit? Do we need to stand back from parochial busyness, to hear what God is saying? When the face-to-face meeting comes between a Christian and God, and we are asked how we have put the commands of Jesus into practice, one guesses he won't spend too long on the parish share or the church roof. But he is bound to ask: 'Have you shared my gospel? How far and how fast have you gone with it?'

Still time

We still have time: time to tell the world of God. These seven little words encapsulate the Christian's Spirit-driven mission. It's a mission so big, the temptation is either to sit down and think about it, or to decide it's meant for 'someone else'. Jesus had been preparing for ministry for thirty years. People, drawn to hear John, were crowding round, ready to accept the carpenter's Son as a new prophet at the very least. Yet, with potential power and preaching in sight, God said, in effect: 'Go into retreat for six weeks, and run the gauntlet of Satan at his worst.'

Thank God, Jesus didn't stop to think about it, or decide it was really meant for 'someone else'.

Suggested hymns
Forty days and forty nights; Filled with the Spirit's power; Jesus, still lead on; What a Friend we have in Jesus

Third Sunday before Advent   *Second Service*
Believe Me!   Ps. 46[82]; Isa. 10:33–11:9; John 14:1–29 (or 23–29)

'Jesus said to [Thomas], "I am the way and the truth and the life. No one comes to the Father except through me."' John 14:6

Integrity
Dr Billy Graham was once asked. 'Billy, when you die, what would you like the first line of your obituary to be?' And Billy replied: 'I guess I'd like for them to say, "He had integrity."' Who could ask for a better remembrance?

In our reading, Thomas and Philip have been asking Jesus questions. He tells them they should have known the answers, yet he is patient with them, nevertheless, because in him lies all power and all authority to reveal. He is the Way to God; he is the Life that has come into the world and which will continue into the next; and he alone is the Truth that gives all this from God, and that enables us to receive it all from God.

Jesus had time, and he took it to explain matters of life, death and eternity to Thomas and Philip; but on the cross, when the penitent thief cried, 'Jesus, remember me when you come into your kingdom' (Luke 23:42), there was no time to launch into a considered explanation. Yet with integrity he could not ignore the desperate cry.

God's integrity
God's integrity is so magnificently complete and dependable, we can always be certain of him. We're never certain of what he is going to do next, because he's a God of the unusual, the inventive, the surprising – even the shocking – but we can always be certain of *him*; certain that he is here, listening, constant.

He is Truth. He is Integrity. He cannot be untrue to himself. He has promised to help us, to show us his way, his truth, his life. And he will not go back on his word. There are over seven thousand promises of God in the Bible, and it's never too late to start digging these out and applying them to our lives, claiming them for our own spiritual journey, praying them also into the lives of others. Nowhere in the Bible does God ever limit any of his promises to a select one or two. They are for all who believe in him.

What is truth?

'What is truth?' Pilate asked, and the Living Truth stood right before him. Perhaps Pilate wondered this same question three days later, when Jerusalem was on fire with rumours of an empty tomb, a missing body, and angels in white.

Truth is standing firm for what we believe to be right. Truth always riles Satan, because the two are incompatible. But the old Devil still fights; he still has not realized that with God's truth on our side we cannot fail. 'The Lord is on my side. I will not fear' (Psalm 118:6; AV). It is a wonderful promise and comfort, and we can't remind ourselves of it too often. It means we can stand firm and press forward. It means we need never be disgusted, discouraged or disheartened. It means we can remember that opposition is very often the sign of coming success: 'The Lord is on my side. I will not fear.' Just consider the armament there, to fight Satan and his miserable lies, criticisms, beastly insinuations and distortions.

We have the Lord on our side. That means we have love, joy, peace, long-suffering, gentleness, goodness, meekness, faith and temperance on our side; and we have integrity on our side, for we fight under the banner of truth.

Yet all the spiritual ammunition at God's command (and God's War Budget knows no limits) – all this vast weaponry is not an atom of use if we don't realize we have it.

St John tells us that the law was given by Moses, but 'grace and truth came through Jesus Christ' (John 1:17). Jesus was made Man, and was yet God ... 'and we have seen his glory ... full of grace and truth' (John 1:14).

The law of Moses kept some people on the road to God for centuries. But then with Jesus came a new law, a new testament, a new covenant, full of grace and truth. Please God, with Jesus the Truth on our side, let us live so that one day folk can say of us: 'They had integrity.'

Suggested hymns
A charge to keep I have; Thou art the way; Thou whose Almighty Word; When God of old came down from heaven

Second Sunday before Advent
16 November   *Principal Service*   **Beware!**
Dan. 12:1–3; Ps. 16; Heb. 10:11–14[15–18], 19–25; Mark 13:1–8

'Then Jesus began to say to them, "Beware that no one leads you astray ... When you hear of wars and rumours of wars, do not be alarmed; this must take place, but the end is still to come."' Mark 13:5, 7

Keeping on guard
Somehow, it's easier to anticipate the great thrill of eternity than to keep watchful among the little hindrances and frustrations of daily life. Yet, the more we become aware that these impedimenta have been brought into contact with us for a purpose, the more clearly we begin to see that God is constantly doing little things divinely well in us and through us every hour.

The Catholic hymnwriter Sir Frederick Faber, used to stress the importance of saintly awareness in everyday life. His hymns, such as 'There's a wideness in God's mercy' and 'My God, how wonderful thou art', are well-known; but here is something he once wrote in prose:

Remember that the opportunity for great deeds may never come; but the opportunity for good deeds is renewed day by day. The thing for us to long for, is the goodness, not the glory.

'Beware that no one leads you astray.' If we keep our sights on what is good – absolute good – this is the yardstick with which to test whatever comes our way. Most of us can't walk around in constant prayer; we have many practical things to do. But let's offer up to God those times, for his praying, his watchfulness, to suffice.

Lord, I shall be very busy this day.
If I forget thee,
Do not thou forget me.

Sir Jacob Astley

Looking ahead

In our reading, Jesus is looking ahead to a time with which we can empathize – when the disciples, like us, would be without his visible presence. God's will must be done before the End, but Jesus knows all that will come against his followers before the End arrives.

Our highest ambition, as Christians, is to become what God has planned for us. All our plans are to be laid before him. His will is to be our will – and then he will lead us to that life which will be for us the most beautiful, most honourable and most blessed. If we would have God's thoughts to live out in our lives, we must go to God for them. We need to sit down often with him in the silence. We need to open our Bible and ponder its holy sentences. We need to pray. We shall not have heavenly visions if we never look up for them. God knows better than we do, that if we haven't anything up front to hope for, to look forward to, we might as well be dead.

Uppermost in Jesus' mind was the thought that the disciples whom he loved so much would need all the divine help on offer, if they were to navigate the spiritual minefield between his ascension and the end of their mission. We perhaps only begin to realize the complexity of our own minefield when with hindsight we can see how God has already preserved us.

Each new morning

Each new morning needs to be handed back to God, for him to take full control of our waking as well as our sleeping hours. He has plans for us this morning that have never been operated before. He has brought us to a place where those plans can be worked out. Morning by morning, he brings us – not to the same place, but to a new starting point, an untrodden length of the race course, a lap twenty-four hours closer to the finishing line.

Every day. Every single day.

When we wake, we step into his plan. How far we progress is our choice, his invitation. And it would take more than a day of doom and gloom, worry, hassle, fear, grief, sickness or trouble, to make God forget his plans for us. We'd better believe it – on the good days, and the bad.

Suggested hymns
Come and see (We worship at your feet); Morning has broken; My God, I love thee not because; There's a wideness in God's mercy

Second Sunday before Advent   *Second Service*
Clearing out the Evil   Ps. 95; Dan. 3 (or 3:13–30);
Matthew 13:24–30, 36–43

'[Jesus said] *"The Son of Man will send his angels, and they will collect out of his kingdom all causes of sin and all evil doers. And they will throw them into the furnace of fire, where there will be weeping and gnashing of teeth. Then the righteous will shine like the sun in the kingdom of their Father."* ' Matthew 13:41–43

In the dark
It can be well nigh impossible to contemplate an end to evil when one is in the throes of trouble and no respite is in sight. But Jesus says plainly that evil will come to an end – a pretty violent and convincing end; and God is not directing his judgement merely against the evil itself, but against the root causes (Satan and his angels), and those who have chosen to make compromise with Satan. Whatever wickedness will be manifested in the earth, will not carry over into God's eternity.

We may cry, as Christians have been crying for two millennia: 'Lord, how long?' But this is God at his most encouraging. The length of time involved is the period it will take to get the gospel published in all nations (Matthew 24:14; Mark 13:10) – so, instead of asking 'How long?', we need to be up and doing in that work. We don't have to wait for glory, to shine with the light of Christ. We are that light now (Matthew 5:14), whether we share it so that others can benefit, or hide it away from them. The world is far more starved of light than is heaven; and we cannot exhaust our power supply, no matter how much we use it.

The End in focus

Jesus could have restricted his training lectures to the disciples' earthly ministry; but in these preparatory talks, as well as in the Transfiguration experience, he intended the extra anticipation, the extra *joy*, of what was to come Hereafter, to infuse their witness. God does not keep us in unadulterated unknowing suspense. If we want to examine not only the gospels and Revelation, but the whole Bible, we shall find hundreds of pieces of information about the new order, the new life, that will be ushered in when we Christians have fulfilled our commission to evangelize the world.

Like a father who has spent much time and effort, as well as love, in constructing a beautiful present for his child, God is in effect saying: 'Look at the glorious eternity I have prepared for you! Can't you thrill with excitement about it?'

How much do we care?

But how much do we care that no one whom we may be able to help will end up being thrown into the furnace of fire? Such a one doesn't have to be a murderer: the 'fearful' (Revelation 21:6; AV) head the list of those who will perish.

Can we pause for reflection on this one?

And what about the millions who die before they have heard of Jesus? Those who have not heard the word of God, much less owned a Bible of their own? Those who, as yet, don't even have any part of the Bible translated into their minority language or dialect? Can we imagine how difficult our walk with God would be, if we had no Bible?

White heat

Can we take the heat out of the furnace for some, by getting white-hot ourselves in the spreading of God's word? It can be daunting to think that we, Christians of today, are standing between someone and salvation – so don't let's spend too long thinking about it and getting fearful. Let's be up and doing, sharing this precious word of God every which way we can: getting on fire, to keep out of the fire.

Suggested hymns

Go, tell it on the mountain; O Jesus, I have promised; Stand up, stand up for Jesus; Tell out, my soul, the greatness of the Lord

Christ the King (Sunday next before Advent)
23 November   *Principal Service*   **Past, Present
and Future**   Dan. 7:9–10, 13–14; Ps. 93; Rev. 1:4b–8;
John 18:33–37

*'Grace to you and peace from him who is and who was and who is to
come ... from Jesus Christ, the faithful witness, the first-born of the
dead, and the ruler of the kings of the earth' Revelation 1:4, 5*

The Master
Each of the synoptic gospel accounts tells us that when Jesus died
at Calvary he 'cried with a loud voice' (AV). He died with power,
power that no death could hold; power that was going to resurrect
the crucified body; power that was going to knock the living daylights out of Satan. Jesus was Master of his life, his death, and his
resurrection. Satan wouldn't need an amplifier at Calvary, to tell
him what was coming.

Later, in Revelation, John says: 'The devil is come down to you,
having great wrath, for he knows that he hath but a short time'
(Revelation 12:12; AV). Satan lost face when Jesus powered
through the kingdom of the underworld – and he's still smarting,
dangerous as a wounded lion, with shame and injured pride. But
he's vulnerable, and every Christian needs to be aware of the
Devil's Achilles' heel. It is the weapon Jesus used to such good
effect in the wilderness (and at other times): the true, uncompromised word of God. Satan may use it himself (he did, in the
wilderness) – but, in the mouth of a Christian, the Devil has no
defence against it.

Just as Jesus was, and is, and is to come, so is the indestructible
word of God. It's always available, and the more we make ourselves familiar with it, the better are we equipped for emergencies
(for Satan rarely gives advance notice of his arrival).

Jesus is King of Alpha-time – before time was.
He is King of the present, Christian-time (Anno Domini).
And He is King of Omega-time – after time.

Christ's revelation
John, writing on Patmos, exiled to work in the quarries there
because of his Christian faith, writes the revelations he is given –

not as the old prophets, who wrote in their own name – but in the name of Jesus, the *ipsissima verba Christi*, linking and intermingling past, present and future, in an outline of God's plan for mankind. There are letters to Church communities, visions of war and glory – but the overriding message of today's reading is that these heavenly communications come from the One – the only One – who was dead and who is now very much alive. Only Jesus can speak with such authority. He is the faithfullest of witnesses. We can have supreme confidence that what he says is the truth.

Who is this Jesus?
The drama of Revelation is breathtaking in its colour, speed and scale. Is this the Jesus of our prayers who is telling us such news? Can it really be the Child of Bethlehem, the Man on the Cross? Do we, having studied Revelation, need to revise our ideas of Christ? Does the Revelation Jesus whisk us off our spiritual feet – this mighty Lord who can keep up such a pace in heaven, yet care for each of us so tenderly?

No, we cannot stretch our minds round that one. But we could do far worse than focus on the Jesus we know: in Bethlehem, at Calvary, and greeting us outside the empty tomb. Yet to focus is not to confine him; we need to read Revelation regularly, to inculcate an ever increasing awareness of the glorious 'otherness' of Jesus, of which one day we shall be a part. We can become so circumscribed by the mundane that our senses become atrophied. As we need the aesthetic beauty of the spring flowers after the winter, so our souls need the benefit of the glory to which they belong. They – we – are only sojourners on earth.

God's starting point
Although Revelation is the last book of the Bible, in a special way it is God's starting point; for as he reveals more and more of the Life to come, we get more insight into the meaning of what has gone before. If there was no other scripture available, Revelation would be enough.

Suggested hymns
Around the throne of God a band; Lord, her watch thy Church is keeping; Of the Father's love begotten; Ye watchers and ye holy ones

Christic the King   *Second Service*   **King-makers**
Ps. 72; Dan. 5; John 6:1–15

'When Jesus realized that they were about to come and take him by force to make him king, he withdrew again to the mountain by himself.' John 6:16

Yet it happened
In a way, these prospective king-makers would make Jesus a king: on Good Friday, when a non-believing Roman would sentence him to crucifixion under a regal *titulus*. He would reign from the tree, to the puzzlement and frustration of the Romans, and the thwarted antipathy of the Jews. King of the universes beyond the universe, no one would be able to confine him once his voluntary confinement to human limitations had ended. But even now, as these well-intentioned folk try to hold him, he will not let himself be manipulated.

The art of confinement
We have confinement to a fine art, building our churches to contain rather than pour out; hedging our worship round with traditions that have the comfortable aura of familiarity . . . Wouldn't we have joined those people in seeking to make Jesus a king, and thus keep him as our own tame monarch? Well, this may be too severe a criticism of their intentions, but in any case Jesus was having none of it.

Temple history
The Jews had moved away from the impermanent, transportable tabernacle of Mosaic times. David – once money, manpower and a fairly settled existence had come his way – had collected vast sums for his own house, and had laid the foundation funds for a temple. Solomon had outspent his father in building an 'exceeding magnifical' temple. Zerubbabel had built its successor. Third in the line came Herod's building, outshining, outclassing, and by a very fair margin outpricing the others. The Jews felt secure in their religion, while the temple stood as a physical proof of God's glory.

But they wanted a king for even greater stability. A king who would restore the Davidic monarchy, oust the Romans, and elevate their religion to the glorious heights of the Solomonic 'golden age'.

And today?

And today, what do we rely on for our faith? Our King crucified and risen? Our prayers? Our Christian heritage of manpower and masonry? Our Bibles, filling ever more shelves as new versions are published?

Or do we value most the words of God we have treasured in our hearts? The words that our King's Spirit brings to mind when a need arises? Do we value most this Spirit's prompting, in the multitude of opportunities with which God presents us?

The workings of God defy rationalization, logic, or any other tidy pigeonholing we may try to devise. One sows, another reaps. We can labour, struggle, fret, fume, toil and sweat – but the strength for living Christ's way comes from a King; the means of doing it comes from a King, and the outcome and reward of doing it, come from a King.

> *We give thee but thine own,*
> *Whate'er the gift may be;*
> *All that we have is thine alone,*
> *A trust, O Lord, from thee.*

William Walsham How, 1823–1897

In the King's Service we are paid from his munificent wealth – but his coinage is not that of the world. When Mother Teresa died, a few years ago, her worldly wealth consisted merely of two little blue-and-white saris, and a bucket for washing. It is strange to reflect that, had she lived two, three or even four thousand years before, she could have left pretty much the same. All the developments in technology, all our modern sophistication, all the advances of one sort or another, of which our age in general is so proud – all that 'ology' and this 'ology' which has cluttered up so much of the world with material possessions – had left Mother Teresa (and those of her ilk) unmoved and untouched. She couldn't offer her King any possessions, but she offered him a far richer and more permanent gift: a little life dedicated in a big way to his service.

As another Church year draws to its close, what do we have to offer to our King?

Suggested hymns

King of glory, King of peace; Lord, enthroned in heavenly splendour; Our God reigns; The King of love my Shepherd is

243

SERMONS FOR SAINTS' DAYS AND SPECIAL OCCASIONS

St Andrew, Apostle 30 November
What Is Heard Isa. 52:7–10; Ps. 19:1–6;
Rom. 10:12–18; Matthew 4:18–22

'So faith comes from what is heard, and what is heard comes through the word of Christ.' Romans 10:17

The first missionary
Because Andrew, on hearing the call of Jesus, went straight away and brought his brother Simon Peter to the Lord, he has been called the first missionary. We get a hint of the Galilean ministry already carried out by John the Baptist, in that the gospel of John states that Andrew had been one of John's disciples. Then he 'heard' the call of Jesus, and answered it. He is thought, after the ascension, to have gone as a missionary to Scythia, and eventually to have suffered martyrdom on an 'X'-shaped cross. Scotland took him as her patron saint, and this cross is to be seen on the country's flag.

Andrew was one of the inner circle of disciples, present at the miraculous feeding of the multitude, and there when Philip introduced some Greeks who were wanting to see Jesus.

Ears to hear
We do not know how many prospective disciples Jesus called, who did not respond positively. The Andrews of this world are in the minority; but history has shown that when a need is there, God motivates someone to answer it. His Church was destined to continue against all the odds, because it had been founded by the Lord who does not admit defeat.

Taken from the fisherfolk of Galilee, Andrew could have looked at the immensity of the task before him and decided to quit. He was one of the fearful, huddled behind locked doors, on the evening of the resurrection day; but this is the last time that any of the disciples are on record as being afraid. The seed that Jesus had sown on the day he called him suddenly blossomed with the joy of his Lord's resurrection – and from there it was forward all the way.

The blossoming
Have we experienced this blossoming joy? Have we reached the point where, whatever comes in the way of trouble, we can outride it in the resurrection joy of Jesus? Is there that steel inside us that is nothing of us but everything of the Spirit, that says: 'Greater is he that is in [me], than he that is in the world' (1 John 4:4)?

Many of us have experienced the feeling of vulnerability, when the Driving Test is successfully behind us, the L-plates have been taken off, and the new licence carefully signed. There's the elation – but also the qualms, as the road suddenly seems narrower than before, full of potential hazards, and we are on our own with no experienced driver in the front seat beside us.

The disciples quite possibly felt equally vulnerable, when Jesus had ascended; but the joy he had infused seems to have out-weighed everything else (Luke 24:52). It was strong enough to take Andrew and the others out from their homeland, to a life of itinerant preaching, teaching and healing. Just three years before, Andrew had heard the call of a Man he scarcely knew – but in his call to others he was now able to add three years of personal testimony to his faith.

How far do we make our personal testimony count for Christ?

Suggested hymns
A Man there lived in Galilee; I heard the voice of Jesus say; Jesus calls us, o'er the tumult; Will you come and follow me

St Nicholas of Myra   6 December
The Children's Bishop   Isa. 61:1–3; Ps. 68;
1 Tim. 6:6–11; Mark 10:13–16

'[Jesus said], "Let the little children come to me; do not stop them; for it is to such as these that the kingdom of God belongs."' Mark 10:14

Lover of children
Bishop of Myra in the fourth century, Nicholas is remembered as one who used his God-given talents and miraculous powers to help children and young people. He rescued three girls from prostitution, healed many youngsters from sickness and disease, and was known as 'the children's bishop'. For long, his festival has

been kept as a day for giving presents, though in many parts now this custom has been taken over by Christmas. Nicholas is one of the patron saints of Russia.

Looking ahead

As the little children crowded to Jesus, attracted as children always are by goodness, he saw in them the next generation of Christians. Unlike their parents, who would fête him, try to make him a king, throw palms before him and then cry for his crucifixion, these children would grow up as his Church was growing up. He may have seen, in their high-pitched voices and innocent smiles, men and women who would go out from Jerusalem with the apostles, to spread the gospel; theirs would be the kingdom of heaven.

Precious seed

We need to be conscious of our children of today, that some of them will do greater work for Christ than we have done. Was our faith taken seriously when we were their age? Were we made to feel that we were special to God? The things we are now doing for Christ, were we encouraged to start when we were young? The gospels leave us guessing – but who can doubt that the young people whom Jesus met and helped would make good as adults? – Jairus' daughter, the boy raised at Nain, the young boy with the loaves and fishes, the Syro-Phoenician's daughter . . . and the little ones in our text. Jesus gave each one the opportunity to listen, learn and act on what he had told them and had done for them.

Four centuries later, Nicholas of Myra used his compassion and prestige to help the young ones of his day. He was not too worldly wise or heavenly minded to see and appreciate the value of children. Today's children challenge us no less: their innocence and directness, their openness to listen and to learn, need to be directed to Christian precepts before the caveats and caution of age strangle all the mystery and wonder of the faith.

Perhaps on this day, when we commemorate the faith of Nicholas in the preciousness of children, we may reflect on how we could involve children more in our church and parish – yes, perhaps also in telling us the news from the pulpit!

Suggested hymns

Jesus, Friend of little children; Loving shepherd of thy sheep; One more step along the world I go; When a knight won his spurs

St Ambrose, Bishop   7 December
Bishop by Request   Isa. 41:9b–13; Ps. 20; 2 Cor. 5:16–21; Luke 22:24–30

'[Jesus said] "For who is greater, the one who is at the table or the one who serves? Is it not the one at the table? But I am among you as one who serves."' Luke 22:27

Rising to the challenge

Ambrose (339–397) was of an aristocratic family, taking an early interest not only in secular government, but also in the furore caused in the Church by the Arian controversy. His diplomacy and scholarship encouraged the ecclesiastical hierarchy to offer him the bishopric of Milan, even though he was not yet baptized. With some reluctance, he allowed his nomination to go forward, and within eight days had been baptized and had gone through the various stages up to his consecration as a bishop.

He was an episcopal success. Milan was far enough from the Court for the Church to enjoy relative calm, though Ambrose needed staunchly to defend the Church against State interference. He argued energetically against Arianism, became noted for the power of his preaching, and baptized the newly converted Augustine (who later became Bishop of Hippo).

While in Constantinople, Ambrose's contemporary and an even more eloquent preacher, John Chrysostom, was too close to the Imperial Court for comfort, Ambrose in Milan had the freedom to compose hymns, and is credited with introducing hymnody to the church services. Some of his verses are still sung today.

Servant bishop

Ambrose was a worker bishop, using his power and position to help the struggling and underprivileged. He saw the episcopacy as an open door of opportunity to reach people he would otherwise have missed, to reach a wide audience with his preaching, and to give the Church the distance from the State which he saw was necessary and beneficial to both. He likened his secular beginnings in government to Jesus' years in the carpenter's shop at Nazareth, learning what life was all about outside the rarified atmosphere of synagogue and temple.

It is sometimes easier to serve God than to serve our fellow men, until we realize that the two are really one. Ambrose was not too heavenly minded to be of no earthly use. Nor did he neglect to use all the privileges and perks of his episcopal office when these could help others. A comparatively recent example of similar expediency was seen in the Second World War, when the sailor-turned-priest, Vice-Admiral the Revd Alexander Woods was not averse to using his title to obtain much-needed food and bedding for bomb victims in his East End parish!

May we, too, use every opportunity and open door that God provides, to help those in need.

Suggested hymns
Captains of the saintly band; Forth in thy name, O Lord, I go; O strength and stay (St Ambrose); Pray when the morn is breaking

St John of the Cross 14 December
Kindled in Love Song of Sol. 2:8–17; Ps. 121;
1 Cor. 2:1–10; John 14:18–23

'Jesus answered [Judas, not Iscariot], "Those who love me will keep my word, and my Father will love them, and we will come to them and make our home with them." ' John 14:23

Meeting of saints
John of the Cross (1542–1591) was born into a poor family in Avila, Spain, where, having lost his father early in childhood, he went to a charity school. He became a nurse, and having entered the Carmelite Order, before long met Teresa d'Avila, who was much impressed by his piety and devotion to duty. John became the superior of several Carmelite houses, but was eventually exiled to Andalusia by those who objected to his energy for work as well as his mysticism. After a painful illness, he died at the age of forty-nine.

A prolific writer, John's *Ascent of Mount Carmel* and *The Dark Night of the Soul* are the best-known of his mystical works; but his *Spiritual Canticle* and *Poems* are also redolent of the spiritual energy and longing for closer union with God, which characterized his life.

Fervent love

The fervent love for God which saw John through much trouble and soul-searching, is the love that Jesus is outlining to Judas in our text today. It's a love that is inspired by pure, passionate devotion; a love that puts God first every time; a love stronger than any evil, any wickedness – stronger than death itself.

It's a love that sees another living without Jesus, and which reaches out to bring the two together. It's a love that is active, dynamic, willing us to do what Christ wants – not because we think we should, but because we love him too much to want to do anything else.

In this poem, John tries to explain this love of God that energizes him:

> O living flame of love
> That, burning, dost assail
> My inmost soul with tenderness untold,
> Since thou dost freely move,
> Deign to consume the veil
> Which sunders this sweet converse that we hold.
>
> O burn that searest never!
> O wound of deep delight!
> O gentle hand! O touch of love supernal
> That quickenest life for ever,
> Puttest all my woes to flight,
> And, slaying, changest death to life eternal!
>
> And O, ye lamps of fire,
> In whose resplendent light
> The deepest caverns where the senses meet,
> Once steeped in darkness dire,
> Blaze with new glories bright
> And to the loved one give both light and heat!
>
> How tender is the love
> Thou wakenest in my breast
> When thou, alone and secretly, art there!
> Whispering of things above,
> Most glorious and most blest,
> How delicate the love thou makest me bear!

St Stephen, Deacon and Martyr
26 December   **Looking into Glory**   2 Chr. 24:20–22;
Ps. 119:161–8; Acts 7:51–60; Matthew 23:34–39

*'[Jesus said] "Jerusalem, Jerusalem, the city that kills the prophets and
stones those who are sent to it! How often I have desired to gather your
children together as a hen gathers her brood under her wings, and you
were not willing!"' Matthew 23:37*

The first of many
Stephen was the first of many, many Christian martyrs – how
many, only Jesus knew, as he waited on his feet in glory for
Stephen to join him. Imagine the Lord of Heaven getting up from
his throne to welcome a table waiter! But Stephen had been so
much more than a waiter; he had been eager to witness to everyone. He had made a spirited and courageous defence before the
Sanhedrin, ranging over the whole of Jewish history. And now,
at his martyrdom, he showed only forgiveness for those who were
taking his life. Of no one could it be more truly said that he was
following his Master's example.

The cruel city
The city that had crucified the Saviour was now martyring one of
his most ardent followers. Yet Jerusalem had had a chance to
change her spots, but she had refused. Basking in the sun, her
honey-coloured buildings giving the city the appearance of a
tawny lion, she would continue to extend the list of prophets
stoned and executed, to evangelists and disciples of the emerging
Church. This proud city, even though presently suffering the
Roman army of occupation, would not humble herself to be gathered into the arms of Mother Church, as a hen takes her chickens
under her wings.

Slings and stones
We can probably identify some of the stones that are presently being slung our way: the disappointment of a missed opportunity; the job that went to someone else; the friend we lost to cancer; the deal that backfired; the holiday that was a disaster . . . Do they seem small in comparison to the stones that knocked out Stephen? Only with hindsight: at the time, it seems that we're attracting more flak than anyone else. It's perhaps the major difference between the first and the twenty-first centuries, that today most people think that trouble shouldn't happen. From the beginning, since Adam sent chaos back into the order that God had created, trouble has been an inevitable part of life. Stephen had already tested the water, in the Sanhedrin; he knew that to press on with his defence of the gospel would get him in to ever deeper water.

But he pressed on, with the blessed disregard that sees trouble only as a stepping-stone to glory. And God rewarded him by giving him an advanced vision of glory, while he had breath enough to tell everyone within earshot.

It's fitting that even in the midst of our Christmas celebrations, we take time to thank God for the table waiter turned preacher.

Suggested hymns
Forgive them, O my Father; Good King Wenceslas; Of the Father's love begotten; Thou didst leave thy throne

St John, Apostle and Evangelist   27 December
The One Jesus Loved   Ex. 33:7–11a; Ps. 117; 1 John 1; John 21:19b–25

'This is the message we have had from him and proclaim to you, that God is light and in him is no darkness at all.' 1 John 1:5

Protector of Mary
To John, Jesus from the cross had entrusted his mother Mary; and, according to tradition, John died in good old age at Ephesus, so we may suppose he cherished Mary for as long as she needed him. John the apostle and John the evangelist may not have been one and the same; but traditionally the Church has kept this day as the celebration of both functions under the one name. As

apostle, John was the son of Zebedee and brother of James – 'the disciple whom Jesus loved', one of the inner circle of his friends, who reclined next to his Lord at the Last Supper and asked who was the betrayer. John the writer of the fourth gospel has given an account of Jesus' life and ministry which differs from the other three (synoptic) gospels, in that it is more theological, delving more deeply into the Old Testament prophecies fulfilled in the coming of Jesus, and the meaning behind when he came, where he went, what he said and why he did what he did.

All light

This Jesus was the *true* light that came into the world as a light for everyone, John tells us. Looking back, the evangelist has appreciated how dark the world had become – in faith and morals. Jesus had come to light up the hearts and minds of people, to take light into corners that sin, ignorance, obfuscation and indifference had clouded.

It's from John that we learn of the light that dawned, even in the darkness of night, on Nicodemus; light that shone out in a benighted Samaritan village, after an immoral woman had met a Stranger at the well; light that was let into a tomb at Bethany, when Jesus raised his friend Lazarus from the dead; light that shone from the cross when Pilate's regal *titulus* was read, and when a Son gave his mother to his best friend.

The list could be continued. John's gospel is so different, so precious, so unique as one man's theological interpretation of his Best Friend's ministry. Even in the rush of Christmas, can we today find a space to read at least a chapter of the Fourth Gospel – to read it as 'a best friend's tribute'? And while we read, may we also reflect that, if John the evangelist and 'the disciple whom Jesus loved' really are one and the same, then the Blessed Virgin Mary (even if she only lived a short time after the crucifixion) would probably have contributed not a little to it.

Suggested hymns

Abide with me; God is working his purpose out; Jesu, lover of my soul; Thine be the glory

Feast of the Holy Innocents   28 December
The Price of Survival   Jer. 31:15–17; Ps. 124;
1 Cor. 1:26–29; Matthew 2:8–18

'God chose what is foolish in the world to shame the wise . . . God chose what is weak in the world to shame the strong.' 1 Corinthians 1:27

Too high a cost?
Moses was born under a pharaonic edict whereby all male Hebrew children were to be killed. The megalomanic ruler had seen the rise in Jewish numbers as a threat to his position and to the balance of power in Egypt.

But Moses was preserved and protected. God knew exactly what he would have him do, when the time was right for the exodus.

And so Jesus was born in the days of another megalomanic ruler. For thirty-three years Herod the Great's paranoia made life dangerous for his family and subjects. As soon as he realized that the Magi were not going to reveal the whereabouts of Jesus, Herod lashed out in blind fury at all the eligible children in the area.

But Jesus was preserved and protected. God knew exactly what he would have him do, when the time was right for Calvary.

Still today
The Pharaohs and Herods are still around today, still believing they can thwart God's purposes, still inflicting grief and torment in an effort to preserve their position – for all the world as if they thought they would go on ruling and gaining power instead of dying like everyone else. One would think, with the benefit of history, that by now we should have found a way of curtailing such megalomania. Well, in 1945, a prime example was stopped – but the awful effects of his wickedness live on.

Why?
Why does God allow it? Why had so many innocent children – in Egypt and Bethlehem – to suffer? Why do God's plans sometimes cost such a lot? The truth is, God's plans are *always* expensive, but we are only aware of the cost in such cases as Moses and Jesus. Satan, the wounded lion who knows that his time is running out, is constantly trying to frustrate God's plans and to impose his own. While the Devil is still around, there will be a price to pay for all the good that can happen.

But since God apparently believes that the cost is not too high, the price will need to be paid.

Out of danger
The little children who had been exposed for such a short time to the powers of evil, were quickly transferred and transformed back to glory. We can only reverently wonder at the work that they may have been doing there. Please God, one day we shall know. It's a strange fact, that although we know this life is only temporary – and certainly far less glorious – even Christians cling to it with great ingenuity and determination. Death when it comes is seen as being 'too soon'. Perhaps God wonders at times if his followers could not summon up a little more enthusiasm for glory.

Suggested hymns
How vain the cruel Herod's fear; In dulci jubilo; There is a land of pure delight; Unto us a Boy is born

Naming and Circumcision of Jesus 1 January
The Right Time Num. 6:22–27; Ps. 8; Gal. 4:4–7;
Luke 2:15–21
'But when the fulness of time had come, God sent his Son, born of a woman, born under the law.' Galatians 4:4

Strange preparations?
Insurrections, plottings, mystery cults, financial shenanigans, an army of occupation – these seem strange preparations for the coming of the Saviour of the world. Yet in the midst of such unrest, God decided that it was *the right time* for Jesus to be born. His birth was unique, but then the well established customs and formalities slipped easily into place; on the eighth day, circumcision and formal naming. The Saviour of the world had chosen to take on human form; human laws and practices would therefore be observed.

Names are important
Christians are not required to undergo physical circumcision, but our names today are as important as they ever were. And in a

very special way, at our naming we take on also the name of Christ, as 'Christians'. We don't have to save the world from inherited sin – Jesus did that, once for all time. But we are obliged by our Lord's commission, to bring as many people as we can to a knowledge of him by preaching, teaching and sharing the gospel.

Jesus' Name

This is 'the Name high over all' (Charles Wesley). It had been decreed by God at the announcement of his conception, that he would be so called. Mary and Joseph would recall how John the Baptist's name had been fore-ordained (Luke 1:13), and how, when he had been born, certain people objected (Luke 1:61); but when Elizabeth stood firm, and Zechariah had supported her, God showed his approval by healing Zechariah's dumbness. There was to be no hesitation in the case of Jesus. Mary and Joseph, even if their family had objected, were standing firm.

But it is a measure of the importance that God attaches to names. One's thoughts inevitably go to Revelation, where God shares with us the knowledge of his precious Book of Life. Entries in this book cannot be bought – but they can be blotted out.

> *Lord, I care not for riches,*
> *Neither silver nor gold;*
> *I would make sure of heaven,*
> *I would enter the fold.*
> *In the Book of thy Kingdom,*
> *With its pages so fair,*
> *Tell me, Jesus, Lord Jesus,*
> *Is my name written there?*
>
> *M.A. Kidder*

The hand of the Almighty has written our names in that wonderful Book. There they shine, in brilliant red, on the pure white pages. Written in the Blood of the Lamb – for it was the Child whose naming we celebrate today, whose sacrifice made our inclusion in that Book possible.

Suggested hymns

At the Name of Jesus; How sweet the Name of Jesus sounds; Jesus, the Name high over all; There is a Name I love to hear

Week of Prayer for Christian Unity
18–25 January   **Divine Unity**   Acts 16:16–34;
John 17:1–19[20–24]

'[Jesus said], "As you have sent me into the world, so have I sent them into the world."' John 17:18

The ideal

The divine unity of the Trinity is the ideal set before every Christian. The Father, Son and Holy Spirit are co[n]substantial, co-eternal – Three Persons in one Substance. We sometimes like to simplify matters by seeing God the Father as Creator, God the Son as Saviour, and God the Holy Spirit as Indweller – but from Jesus' beautiful prayer to his Father in John 17, there is no distinction between the Persons of the Godhead; and this is picked up in the Proper Preface for Trinity Sunday:

> *Who art one God, one Lord;*
> *not one only Person,*
> *but three Persons in one Substance.*
> *For that which we believe*
> *of the glory of the Father,*
> *the same we believe of the Son,*
> *and of the Holy Ghost,*
> *without any difference*
> *or inequality.*

> Holy Communion Service, BCP

Full agreement – on the divine scale!

In practice

But in practice how do Christians cope with unity? Not too well. We should not need a Week of Prayer for it. We should practise it already. But at least this week focuses our minds on the problem, and most parishes have a few interdenominational services; but next week we'll all be back on our own patch, doing our own thing – probably doing it pretty well, with love and devotion – but how far, really, does this week of special observance take us forward on the unity road? How often, in the rest of the year, does unity surface on our agendas? To be fair, probably more often than it did forty, thirty, or even twenty years ago.

For the right reasons
When the Church in China began to revive after the Maoist years, it looked to the West and saw our mishmash of denominations, and their deleterious effect on the Body of Christ. And it decided, in so far as was possible, not to go down our road. China is a very big country, and there are varying denominations within her Christian ranks, but their scale has been kept to a far lower level than in the Western Church. Can we learn from this? Can we share the gospel with people, not necessarily with a view to getting them to join 'our' church, but the Church of Christ? The more we subsume our denominationalism under the gospel, the greater will be the gospel light we are sharing.

If we can sink our differences for one week of the year, then perhaps we should have these annual weeks more often!

Suggested hymns
Bind us together, Lord; In Christ there is no east or west; Thy hand, O God, has guided; We are one in the Spirit

Conversion of Paul   25 January   **Holy Boldness**
Jer. 1:4–10 or Acts 9:1–22; Ps. 67; Acts 9:1–22 or
Gal. 1:1–16a; Matthew 19:27–30

'For several days [Paul] was with the disciples in Damascus, and immediately he began to proclaim Jesus in the synagogues, saying: "He is the Son of God!"' Acts 19:19, 20

A brave man!
Such a volte-face was bound to cause suspicion and raised eyebrows, as people heard the arch-persecutor of the Christians preaching Christ! Paul was nothing if not fervent; all the energies he had channelled into hatred against the Church, were now directed into zeal for it! Truly, God has ingenious methods of attracting folks' attention! But Paul had been through a nerve-racking experience on the Damascus road, followed by days of frightening blindness. He had quickly become aware that Jesus

had not been to all that trouble for nothing. This was a Jesus he could follow, a Saviour he could preach with conviction. And he didn't care what people said, or how many fingers of derision they wagged.

Cautious consideration
Not for Paul cautious consideration. He had been a man with a mission – and so he still was, but now his mission had changed. If people didn't accept the change, so be it. Perhaps, if there was an increase in this holy boldness today, the Church would give more people more to talk about – which is far preferable to a lukewarm disinterestedness. 'I wish that you were either cold or hot,' Jesus told the pathetically lukewarm Christians at Laodicea (Revelation 3:15).

And then – Jerusalem
Paul (as Saul) stayed in the local synagogues, preaching Christ to all who would listen, for three years after his conversion, and then he went to the heart of the matter, taking his message to Jerusalem itself. With Jerusalem's history, he could hardly expect an unqualified reception, and he was not disappointed. Perhaps the Holy Spirit brought to his mind an encouragement Jesus had once given to his disciples: 'Beware when all men speak well of you!' Paul, for all his problems, did not have that one!

Sense of urgency
Paul had recognized the urgency of God's action on the Damascus road. The fervent persecutor had not been stopped in his tracks to admire the scenery, nor even to bask in the realization that God had noticed him – but to get up, get out and get working on his mission.

And God has noticed each one of us. Isn't that wonderful, that the Lord of the Universe has so condescended! But he hasn't noticed us merely to give us a nice warm feeling; so what are we going to do about it? Are we certain about what he is telling us to do? Then let's do it. Are we not so sure? Then let's pray him for a bit more guidance. God really *works* at noticing his people, and Paul, to give him credit, noticed what God was doing. When did we last notice God?

Suggested hymns
Go, tell it on the mountain; Lord, her watch thy Church is keeping;
O the deep, deep love of Jesus; Oft in danger, oft in woe

St Polycarp, Bishop of Smyrna   23 February
Will He Desert Me Now?   Wis. 5:15–20; Ps. 34;
Rev. 2:8–11; John 15:1–8

'Do not fear what you are about to suffer. Beware, the Devil is about to throw some of you into prison so that you may be tested, and for ten days you will have affliction. Be faithful until death, and I will give you the crown of life.' Revelation 2:10

'Dear Smyrna . . .'
This text comes from the Letter to the Church at Smyrna, dictated by Jesus to St John on Patmos in which the Smyrnian Christians are warned about impending trouble. It duly came . . .

Polycarp (*c.* AD 69–155) had been Bishop of Smyrna for forty years when persecution hit the city. He was arrested, but was offered a pardon if he would deny Christ. Drawing himself up proudly, Polycarp looked his interrogators in the eye, and said, 'Eighty-and-six years have I served my King, and he has done me no harm. Should I desert him now?' Wood was gathered for a fire, and the saintly old bishop was martyred. His disciples collected the remains and reverently interred them outside the city, where began the practice of celebrating the eucharist on this anniversary day.

Loyalty to Christ
Our Christian loyalty may not be tested in such a dramatic way – but our tests do come, in many smaller ways, every day: the half-truth that we recognize but don't admit; the speed limit we exceeded because no police car or camera was in sight; the undercharging at the supermarket or garage, that we didn't rectify; the programme we switched on, only to find it compromised our faith – yet we let it run a while; the argument we got into (that was started, of course, by the other chap) . . . 'You will be tested,' warned Jesus. And he was so right.

Be faithful

Polycarp had been faithful for many years. Now, with glory only just ahead anyway, he wasn't going to blow it by compromise. It's not what we have that counts – but whether we can leave what we have at any time, without a twinge of regret. And even on the spiritual front, it's not what we have that counts, but what the Holy Spirit has of us. Is our worldly wealth dear to us? Is our spiritual wealth deposited with the Spirit?

We never know when the next test is coming, as Satan does not generally give advance warning of his approach. And Polycarp's testing is an example of the wisdom of Jesus' caution to be faithful until death. Even after eighty-six years of loyalty, Polycarp's dedication would have counted for nothing, had he fallen at the last hurdle.

The prize

But the prize for our faithfulness is munificent. Who can put a price on 'the crown of life'?

Jesus did, at Calvary.

So it costs us nothing beyond faithfulness.

Suggested hymns

Be thou my vision; In the cross of Christ I glory; O for a faith that will not shrink; O Jesus, I have promised

St David, Patron of Wales   1 March

Bishop Dewi   Ecclus. 15:1–6; Ps. 16; 1 Thess. 2:2–12; Matthew 16:24–27

'As you know, we dealt with each one of you like a father with his children, urging and encouraging you and pleading that you should lead a life worthy of God, who calls you into his own kingdom and glory.'
1 Thessalonians 2:11, 12

The ascetic monk

Born in the fifth century, David (Dewi) became a monk and embraced the rigorously ascetic Rule of the Egyptian desert monks. Elevated to the bishopric, he is believed to have founded the monastery at Menevia (St Davids), and a number of other houses. He has been commemorated on this day as the patron saint of Wales since at least the twelfth century. Always mindful of his duty and love for the poor and the sick, the celibate David indeed 'dealt . . . like a father with his children', using the prestige of his office to ease the burden of many of his flock.

Help and discipline
St Paul is advocating not only material help but also spiritual discipline. The two were always together in the life of David. It is no use holding out 'pie in the sky' to non-believers. Jesus never gave his followers cause to believe that the Christian way was anything but challenging. Perhaps today we tend to talk up the benefits and to play down its challenge. So many people say they love a challenge, yet stay out of the Church. Are we presenting the gospel with too much suffocating cottonwool, tarted up with tinsel and pretty ribbons? Or are we sticking faithfully with the principles as set out by Jesus in the gospels?

The Order of Friars Minor
When St Francis of Assisi founded his Order of Friars Minor, his principles were severely ascetic, but as time went on accommodations were introduced. Perhaps it was thought that more would be encouraged to join if the rigours were relaxed. Francis had advocated no settled home, no possessions, no books, no money, a life of begging for food, much prayer and not a little work. It was a standard that frightened off many prospective recruits.

But the accommodations grieved him deeply, and he relinquished his place as head of the Order – not leaving the brethren, but allowing another to lead while he maintained his original principles.

What is essential?
With the media trying to persuade us that whatever they are promoting is essential to life and well-being, prioritizing is a difficult business these days. But today, as we reflect on the asceticism and simple lifestyle of David, can we perhaps run a dispassionate eye over how our possessions and daily schedule are impacting – for better or worse – on our walk with God?

Suggested hymns
Jesu, gentlest Saviour; O the love of my Lord is the essence; Pray
when the morn is breaking; Prayer is the soul's sincere desire

St Patrick, Patron of Ireland   17 March
Another Country   Isa. 51:1–11; Ps. 96; Rev. 22:1–5;
Matthew 10:16–23

*'And there will be no more night; they need no light of lamp or sun, for
the Lord God will be their light, and they will reign for ever and ever.'*
Revelation 22:5

Captured – and consecrated
Patrick (*c*. AD 390–460) was born in England, but taken as a slave
to Ireland by raiders, at the age of sixteen. He escaped after about
six years, and went to the Continent, where he trained as a priest
and was attracted to the monasticism of Martin of Tours. Returning
to Ireland as a bishop, he set out on an itinerant mission to evangelize the island. He aimed to replicate the diocesan system he
had seen in Gaul, but it proved impossible. After severe opposition
and some success, he died on 17 March 460.

Another homeland
Just as Patrick spent the greater part of his life in a country other
than the place of his birth, so in Revelation we hear of the other
country that is awaiting us. The Englishman took the gospel to
Ireland; the mortals of earth will put on immortality in heaven.
As the light of the gospel is gradually lighting up this world, so
the world to come will be *all* gospel – light, brighter far than
human eye can bear. The energy responsible for this super-light
is the energy that took Patrick back to Ireland, and that takes us
to others with the gospel.

It may be that we are witnessing for Christ in a country other
than our homeland. The place is immaterial: wherever we are
shining Christ's light, we are in his will. Consider how St Paul
gave no heed to country, culture or creed, so long as he was
preaching Christ, and Christ crucified.

By any means
By all and any means, God will get his gospel published. The monk behind cloistered walls spent hours copying and illustrating the scriptures. Patrick, trekking from town to town, had the vision of a Christian Ireland.

What is our particular vision? Do we know what we'd like to do for Christ? Has he made it clear to us? Have we asked him recently? If we do ask, we need to be prepared for an exciting life, for God will pack our days with surprises all the time. And if we don't allow ourselves to be surprised by God, he'll one day likely ask the reason why.

Out of thought
It teases the imagination out of thought, to envisage a light that comes from nothing natural. But the light of God is a positive brightness; there will be no dingy corners in heaven to spotlight: God's light will be crystal clear, in a dimension that knows no adulteration. Can we let these words from Revelation sink into our hearts today, as we reflect on the bishop who wanted such a light to shine in Ireland?

Suggested hymns
Be thou my vision; Hail, glorious Saint Patrick, dear saint of our isle (*Westminster Hymnal*); I bind unto myself today; Inspired by love and anger

St Joseph of Nazareth   19 March   Seed of David
2 Sam. 7:4–16; Ps. 89; Rom. 4:13–18; Matthew 1:18–25

'It depends on faith, in order that the promise may rest on grace and be guaranteed to all his descendants, not only to the adherents of the law but also to those who share the faith of Abraham (for he is the father of us all.)' Romans 4:16

Of David's line
In fulfilment of the prophecy that the Saviour would be born of David's line, Joseph was God's chosen husband for Mary – and to all intents and purposes the father of Jesus. He could also have been the strong, silent type, for not a word from him is recorded

in the gospels, and yet there he was at the centre of the Christmas story! He was a good man: we can infer this from the fact that God chose him; but he was also obedient to the angelic dreams he received, not breaking with Mary as (with some justification) he had considered doing; taking note of the warning to move Jesus out of Bethlehem into Egypt, and back to Nazareth after Herod's death. He was there supporting Mary at her Purification; there, searching for the missing Child when Jesus, aged twelve, had gone missing to talk with the doctors.

And then – no more. Did he die when Jesus was in his teens? We don't know. In Luke 4:16 we have a hint that Joseph and Mary had inculcated a pattern of regular sabbath worship in their Son; but Joseph could have died many years before the start of Jesus' ministry (although, when folk in his home town Nazareth called Jesus 'the carpenter's Son', the inference may be that Joseph had been working his trade until fairly recently).

The right line

Lineage was very important to the Jews, no less than in many areas today. It mattered from whom one was descended. Because of Joseph's lineage, the birth of Jesus took place, as prophesied, in Bethlehem. Because of Paul's Roman birthright, he could appeal to Caesar, so that God could get his man where he wanted him – to the heart of the Empire. God's forward planning is breathtaking in its awesomeness.

If there was something special about Mary (on whom, we are told, God's favour rested), then we must surely believe that Joseph was – at the very least – a good man. He must also have been a physically strong man; to set out on a 250-mile journey to Egypt, with a wife and baby, is no tea-time stroll. And he was in good standing with his neighbours: his Son was welcomed back to Nazareth at the start of his ministry (even though the mood changed when he began to tell them who he really was).

To be the nominal father of the Saviour of the world, without letting it go to one's head, is surely a sign that Joseph was a very special person. And surely Jesus had him in mind, when he told his listeners about the father who delights to give good gifts to his children.

A Man there lived in Galilee; Come, sing with holy gladness; Father, I place into your hands; For the beauty of the earth

Annunciation of our Lord to the Blessed Virgin Mary   25 March   The Favoured One

Isa. 7:10–14; Ps. 40; Heb. 10:4–10; Luke 1:26–38

'And [Gabriel] came to her and said, "Greetings, favoured one! The Lord is with you." But she was much perplexed by his words and pondered what sort of greeting this might be.' Luke 1:28, 29

The angel Gabriel

What did he look like, this archangel? Did he come in his glory, or in the form of a man? And how had Mary merited the favour of God? By special piety and devotion? By clean living and strict observance? Or just by being a natural young woman of no outstanding beauty, learning or charm? We don't know. But we do know that from this day of annunciation onwards, Mary was anything but ordinary.

'The Lord is with you'

Of course, he is with each one of us, but he was with Mary in a very special, unique, intimate way. Through no natural means, he gained access to her womb, and implanted there what St Luke, according to the AV, calls 'that holy thing'. It is striking that a doctor of medicine can come up with no more precise explanation than this.

The next time, Jesus will come in glory. There will never be a need for another *Theotokos*. For eternal ages, Mary alone will bear this title.

Much perplexed

Mary's perplexity was understandable – particularly if Gabriel came to her when she was at home, perhaps busy with housework. But the angel seems to have taken her diffidence for granted. Similarly, when God approaches us, in prayer or a dream or a certain set of circumstances, and what he seems to be saying is hard to understand, he is not fazed when we don't cotton on straight away. He knows it sometimes takes a long time for us to home in to his wavelength.

There is a tendency to think that if we don't understand what God is saying, we're somehow off course. This may be so in some cases, but let's not forget that Mary was perplexed. She didn't pretend to know what the angel was saying, but simply gave her *Fiat*, and trusted that God knew what he was about.

Celebration
The feast of the Annunciation has been observed in the Church since at least the fourth century. It marks the time of the initiation of Mary's joy, that sent her over the hills to share it with Elizabeth, herself six months into the pregnancy which was to give John the Baptist to the world.

Since it had been a woman who had made compromise with evil in Eden, God was now using two very special women to produce the Messiah and his Forerunner, thereby showing the world that if one woman could choose sin, it did not put the rest of womankind beyond the pale.

At the End of time, when the accounts are made up, it's pretty certain that more people will remember Mary, than Eve.

Suggested hymns
For Mary, Mother of the Lord; and from *Celebration Hymnal*: Maiden, yet a Mother; Mary Immaculate, Star of the morning; Protect us while telling thy praises we sing

St George, Patron of England   28 April
(transferred from 23rd)   My Gospel
1 Macc. 2:59–64 or Rev. 12:7–12; Ps. 126; 2 Tim. 2:3–13; John 15:18–21

'Remember Jesus Christ, raised from the dead, a descendant of David – that is my gospel, for which I suffer hardship, even to the point of being chained like a criminal.' 1 Timothy 2:8, 9

Personally mine
In his letter to the Romans, Paul twice mentions 'my gospel'; here he says it again. It was not the gospel with which he had grown

up; he had sat at the feet of the learned Rabban Gamaliel, but Gamaliel had not pointed him to Jesus. Yet Paul had taken it up after his conversion, and could now with justification call it his; he had suffered for it, more than anyone else.

St George may not have been an Englishman, but England took him to her heart and made him her patron saint. He had proved himself strong and courageous, and had fought in a good cause.

Soldier and martyr

George the soldier is believed to have lived in Palestine in the early fourth century, suffering martyrdom at Lydda in or around AD 304, when the Diocletian persecution was getting under way. The dragon-slaying may have arisen from illustrations depicting Michael Archangel and the war in heaven described in Revelation. At any rate, even before the Norman conquest churches in England were being dedicated to St George, though it was not until after the Crusades that George replaced Edward the Confessor as England's patron saint.

For the truth

Standing up and fighting for the truth of the gospel is important; but when the defence is made of the gospel we can call our own, it is a hundredfold more important. The difference hangs on Jesus' words to his disciples: 'I call you servants no longer, but I call you friends.' Because of this, his word is ours, his light is ours, his truth is ours, his gospel is ours. It's the way by which we live, the life by which we die, and the truth by which we enter eternity.

The Great Martyr

People called George 'The Great Martyr', but surely everyone who suffers martyrdom deserves this title. Jesus reprimanded a man for calling him 'good' ('There is none good but one, that is God'). Perhaps he would have given George another title. That said, it is somewhat satisfying to have such a man as one's patron saint!

Christus resurrexit

'Remember Jesus Christ, raised from the dead,' Paul counsels Timothy. Whatever our preoccupations, however many distractions we have, we are to remember this, the cornerstone of the gospel. If we base our preaching and teaching on anything else, we are off track. But today, let us give thanks for our country, for the Christian faith it has accepted and preached for many centuries, for its saints and martyrs – and for a man probably born 'in some corner of a foreign field', not far from where our Lord himself was born, who is remembered as 'The Great Martyr'.

Suggested hymns
And did those feet; I vow to thee, my country; O faith of England, taught of old; O God, our help in ages past

St Mark the Evangelist 29 April (transferred from 25th) Inspired to Write Prov. 15:28–35 or Acts 15:35–41; Ps. 119:9–16; Eph. 4:7–16; Mark 13:5–13

'When they bring you to trial and hand you over, do not worry beforehand about what you are to say; but say whatever is given you at that time, for it is not you who speak, but the Holy Spirit.' Mark 13:11

The boy in Gethsemane
Was Mark the boy who wriggled out of the soldier's grasp in Gethsemane on the night of Jesus' arrest, leaving his clothing in the man's hand, and running away naked into the night? Perhaps. What we do know is that he was a Jew, the cousin of Barnabas, and that he accompanied Paul and Barnabas on their first missionary journey. He was scheduled to go on the second, but a dispute with Paul meant that Mark joined Barnabas on a mission to Cyprus. Later, with the rift between them healed, Mark caught up with Paul, and then Peter, in Rome. He became Peter's secretary, and it was from Peter that Mark would receive much material for his gospel.

Tell it straight
Mark's gospel moves quickly, almost impulsively. It also is brutally frank in parts, letting in the daylight on to the disciples' failings and fears, and giving the impression of St Peter walking to and fro, dictating with the freshness and vivacity of an eyewitness. If Mark at any time protested that Peter, in particular, was getting a bad press, can we not hear the old apostle replying: 'No, no, it happened this way. Tell it straight!'

Imperative publication
The Parousia was delaying. Peter, the key witness, was in Rome.
But, hundreds of miles away, he thought of his compatriots. 'Get
this written down, Mark! They must know about it before I die!'
he would say. And so Mark was faithful to his task. It is a nice
compliment to our saint of today, that his gospel is generally the
one memorized in English and studied in Greek, by theological
students the world over.

It had to be written. Mark 13:10 is a key verse: 'Jesus said,
"The good news must first be proclaimed to all nations."' Can
we reverently imagine Peter pausing as he reached these words
in his dictation, and exchanging a glance and a smile with Mark,
as if to say: 'Well, we are helping the good work along!'

Let us thank God for all the thousands of Peters and Marks since,
who have helped the good work along, by copying, translating,
printing, publishing and distributing the precious scriptures. And
St Mark's day is also a good time to reflect on how we, too, are
helping the work along. Because it still has a fair way to go, the
fields are still white for the harvest, and the labourers are still so
few.

Suggested hymns
Father of mercies, in thy word; Hills of the North, rejoice; Thou
whose Almighty Word; We've a story to tell to the nations

SS Philip and James, Apostles   1 May
Gift of Grace   Isa. 30:15–21; Ps. 119:1–8; Eph. 3:1–10;
John 14:1–14
*'Although I am the very least of all the saints, this grace was given to
me to bring to the Gentiles the news of the boundless riches of Christ.'
Ephesians 3:8*

Little known
Philip was of an outgoing spirit, though we hear little enough of
him in the gospels, and this mostly in St John. Having met Jesus,
he immediately found his friend Nathanael, and introduced him
to Jesus. It was Philip who was the spokesman at the feeding of

the five thousand; Philip, too, who asked the questions that called forth Jesus' 'Final words' to the disciples.

James the son of Alphaeus is usually known as 'the Less', to distinguish him from James the son of Zebedee. We know little of this James. The church in Rome, where the relics of Philip and James are believed to be, was dedicated on 1 May 560, since when this day has been observed as their joint festival.

Bringing the news

God gives us all the grace we need to share all the good news we can with as many as we can. To each of us he gives unique opportunities, and no one should look at another and feel either triumphant because we seem to be doing better, or despondent because the other party seems to be having an easier ride or greater success.

It is tempting to focus on high profile apostles like Peter and Paul, and to imagine that others like Philip and James did not have such opportunities, or didn't make the most of the opportunities that came their way. It is none of our business. One day, perhaps, we shall learn just how busy Philip and James were, in the years after Christ's ascension.

If our thoughts do wander into someone else's life, God has a habit of halting us in our tracks, and getting personal: 'How is *your* witness coming along?' Well, how is it? We probably don't make the headlines that Peter and Paul would have made, had they been here today – but if we should die tomorrow, would anyone have cause to remember us as the witness who brought them to Christ? Philip left precious little information about himself – but at least Nathanael would always think: he's the chap who brought me to Jesus.

My Saviour

A preacher gave a series of Lenten sermons, to which a man came whom he knew was thinking about becoming a Christian. At the end of the final service, he came to the preacher and announced he wanted to be baptized. 'Fine!' smiled the preacher. 'Er – which of my sermons clinched your decision?' 'Oh, it wasn't anything you said,' replied the man candidly. 'As I left the church last week, a lady stumbled on the path, and I caught her before she fell. "Do you love my Saviour?" she asked. And it was then that it hit me, that Jesus has died *for me*. He *is* my Saviour!'

270

Who knows how many people in heaven now have cause to thank Philip and James for their witness – whether it was high or low profile?

Suggested hymns
Be still, for the presence of the Lord; Be still, my soul, the Lord is on thy side; For all the saints, who from their labours rest; O, the love of my Lord is the essence

St Matthias the Apostle   14 May
Plugging the Gap   Isa. 22:15–25 or Acts 1:15–26;
Ps. 15; Acts 1:15–26 or 1 Cor. 4:1–7; John 15:9–17
'And they cast lots . . . and the lot fell on Matthias, and he was added to the eleven apostles.' Acts 1:26

Judas' defection
While ever the twelfth place among the disciples was vacant, Judas' defection would impact. There would also be the consideration that other disciples had shown loyalty throughout the three-year ministry, and had witnessed the post-resurrection Jesus, thus qualifying for apostolic status. And, as St Luke points out, Jesus had talked of the twelve in glory sitting on thrones judging the twelve tribes of Israel. Probably each of these reasons had a bearing on the apostles' decision to plug the gap left by Judas.

And the lot fell on Matthias. It had left God the opportunity to decide for them, and we hear of no questioning of the decision. And this is practically all we know for certain about Matthias; yet another disciple who had been so close to Jesus for so long, and had managed to rate not a single mention in the gospels.

There are churches where some members of the congregation have a high profile ministry, while others come and go so quietly that they may hardly be noticed. Yet the ministry of one is no less significant in God's eyes than that of the other. Man looks on the outward appearance, but God on the heart. It would probably never have crossed the minds of Jesus' disciples that one day they would be known worldwide, would be featured in the world's bestseller, and would have festivals observed in their honour.

Fame by default?

If we set out to carve our name with pride in the annals of the Church, we might as well forget our mission. No one in the pages of the New Testament was conscious of being God's prime preacher, key witness or greatest gospeller. Others may have given them such accolades, but they didn't claim the glory for themselves. We shouldn't worry if the world does not remember us when we have gone (though if the world does remember, please God let it be for the right reasons).

Today's gaps

If we have any vacant places today – on our committees, councils or synods – can we try to fill them? A vacancy is a most unsatisfactory witness; it doesn't cut much ice in preaching, teaching or healing either. We need all the manpower we can get, for the maximum opportunities for encouragement, service and support. Let's take a leaf out of the disciples' book; had they not elected a twelfth member, we might have had no reason to celebrate Matthias' festival today.

Suggested hymns

Help us to help each other, Lord; Jesus, I my cross have taken; Put thou thy trust in God; Teach me, my God and King

The Visit of the Blessed Virgin Mary to Elizabeth 31 May Rejoicing in Hope

Zeph. 3:14–18; Ps. 113; Rom. 12:9–16; Luke 1:39–56

'Rejoice in hope, be patient in suffering, persevere in prayer. Contribute to the needs of the saints; extend hospitality to strangers.' Romans 12:12, 13

Franciscan beginnings

This festival was inaugurated in 1263 by a Franciscan Order General Chapter, but it was fairly rapidly adopted throughout Europe. With the rise of the Protestant Church its spread increased; for, though it was a Marian feast, it carried biblical authority, and it also included Mary's beautiful *Magnificat*, with which Protestants had no quarrel.

Mary, in visiting Elizabeth to share her good news, and in staying to help her elderly cousin for the last three months of Elizabeth's pregnancy, was putting into practice the teaching of Paul in today's lesson from Romans. We are often quicker to seek the sharing of sorrow, than to share our joy with another. Mary could quite easily have stayed at home and hugged her joy to herself – but she intuitively divined Gabriel's intention in telling her of Elizabeth's miraculous condition.

Hopeful joy

There are two kinds of joy: the celebration of a past or present gladness, and the anticipation of a future one. In the Christian life, the two coalesce, because we cannot recall Calvary without remembering what it purchased; and we cannot thrill with anticipation for eternity, without recalling Calvary that made it possible. Mary's joy would be an amalgam of wonder that she of all people had been chosen by God; that the old prophecies which had hung in abeyance for so long were at last to be fulfilled; that God alone must be responsible – for who else could effect a virgin birth? The Lord who had worked the impossible in the life of Elizabeth would take care of Mary.

Believing against the odds

We probably believe that God can still work the impossible in the world of today – but do we believe he can operate so divinely in our own lives? If he has given us an impossible vision, idea, inspiration, aspiration – do we believe he can bring it to pass? It's so impossible, only God can do it?

Do we believe? If not, why not?

Well, there may be a verse in the Bible that conveniently tells us it can't be done; but while we're looking for it, we could be doing something much more worthwhile – like sharing a joy with someone, or comforting someone in trouble, or having some quality prayer time with God, or sharing our home and a cup of coffee with someone who just may be wanting to share something of their own with us.

Suggested hymns

Hail, Queen of heaven; I'll sing a hymn to Mary; Maiden, yet a Mother; This is the image of the Queen (from *Celebration/Westminster Hymnals*)

St Barnabas the Apostle 11 June

Antioch Crusade Job 29:11–16 or Acts 11:19–30;
Ps. 112; Acts 11:19–30 or Gal. 2:1–10; John 15:12–17

*'News of this came to the ears of the church in Jerusalem, and they sent
Barnabas to Antioch. When he came and saw the grace of God, he rejoiced,
and he exhorted them all to remain faithful to the Lord with steadfast
devotion; for he was a good man, full of the Holy Spirit and of faith.
And a great many people were brought to the Lord.' Acts 11:22–24*

A stout fellow

Barnabas must have been a good man to have on one's team:
generous of spirit, he had accepted the young Mark when Paul
would have nothing more to do with him (though later the two
buried their differences). After Paul's conversion, it had been
Barnabas who had smoothed his path and convinced the other
apostles of his genuineness. Now it's Barnabas who goes virtually
as Jerusalem Nuncio to Antioch, to see for himself how successful
has been the 'crusade', to encourage the faithful, and to bolster
the number of conversions even further. As stout a fellow as ever
was! St Luke is generous in his assessment, and doesn't forget
that the credit is due to the Holy Spirit.

Full to the brim?

Are we full to the brim, *Spirit-filled* crusaders for Christ? If we ask
the Spirit to fill us, we have to want it. We have to be prepared
for him to take us at our word.

Getting rid of a fortune

Barnabas (like Joseph and Matthias prior to the casting of lots,
Acts 1:21ff.) may have been with Jesus for at least part of his
three-year ministry. He is not listed as one of the twelve apostles
in the gospels, but he was certainly one of the key workers in the
early Church. Having got rid of his house and acreage, he gave
the money to the Church and became a whole-hearted missionary
and preacher. A Levite from Cyprus, it was to this island that he
took Mark, after the quarrel with Paul. According to tradition, he
suffered martyrdom on Cyprus, in AD 61, and today pilgrims
visit the little church there that bears his name.

Christian diplomats

There are those, like Peter, who are noted for saying the wrong thing at the wrong time, of stepping in where the angels would fear to tread. There are those, like Paul, whose zeal sometimes makes them short-tempered. And there are just a few, like Barnabas, who have the gift of pouring diplomatic oil on troubled waters, bringing opposing sides together, encouraging with exactly the right words at the right time.

They are the salt of the earth.

But let's remember, Jesus included *us* in this designation . . .

Suggested hymns
Great is thy faithfulness; Help us to help each other, Lord; Lord of the dance; When I needed a neighbour

Birth of John the Baptist   24 June
What Will He Become?   Isa. 40:1–11; Ps. 85;
Acts 13:14b–26 or Gal. 3:23–29; Luke 1:57–66, 80

'All who heard [these things] pondered them and said, "What then will this child become?" For, indeed, the hand of the Lord was with him.'
Luke 1:66

Pre-natal blessing

The unborn John had leapt in Elizabeth's womb, at the time when Mary visited to share her own good news, three months previously. In a way, John had been the youngest and earliest to register delight at the news of the Saviour. This encouraged the early Church to see 'the hand of the Lord' on him from before his birth, and has been largely responsible for this festival of his birth being given more prominence than that of his death.

Luke tells us that until the start of his public ministry, John was in the wilderness, becoming 'strong in spirit'. He would need all the strength the Spirit could give, because his preaching was to break new ground. It also needed to pierce the protective layers of security that the Jewish hierarchy had built up around their traditions.

Retreat
It is surely significant that before either of their public ministries, both Jesus and John were moved to go for a time into the wilderness. St Paul, too, spent three years in virtual retreat, before he took on Jerusalem. (Even so, he needed the support and mediation skills of Barnabas, to get a hearing among the apostles.) We can only reverently imagine what John would have made of our fast-paced world. He would have risen to the challenge, because the Holy Spirit can outpace the twenty-first century; but he might have found it a little more difficult to find a prolonged, quiet retreat.

The place of solitude
Yet places of solitude are there for the finding; and we all need to draw aside from the bustle and noise, to catch up with ourselves and with God. It may take quite a time to get our Filofaxes and schedules out of our minds – Jesus and John had long retreats – and if God is there in the solitude with us, so also will be Satan. Two's company, but three's a crowd! Retreats do not work on us from the outside in, but from the inside out, renewing our spirits and strengthening what remains. Retreats are not for the faint hearted – for most of us, if the truth be told, are not all that keen on being turned inside-out.

Yet look how the solitude worked for John, and even more so for Jesus.

Suggested hymns
Be still, for the presence of the Lord; Christian, seek not yet repose; God moves in a mysterious way; I hunger and I thirst

SS Peter and Paul, Apostles 29 June (or transferred to 30th) **Deliverance** Ezek. 3:22–27 or Acts 12:1–11; Ps. 125; Acts 12:1–11 or 1 Pet. 2:19–25; Matthew 16:13–19

'Then Peter came to himself, and said, "Now I am sure that the Lord has sent his angel and rescued me from the hands of Herod and from all that the Jewish people were expecting."' Acts 12:11

276

God's support

Both Peter and Paul knew the value of God's support. Peter was delivered from Herod, Paul from the Jerusalem Jews when his Roman citizenship gave him the right of appeal to Caesar's court instead. God would get both apostles to the place he wanted, no matter who or how many put stumbling blocks in the way.

And we, too, may think the outlook is bleak, and progress which we had counted on making is barred. But if God is having his way with us, he'll give us an alternative – a *better* – route. Think of Martha and Mary, devastated not only at their brother's death, but at Jesus' apparent lack of care in coming to help quickly. He had delayed only in order to give them a richer blessing.

Confidence

Peter and Paul had a lifetime of confidence-building. The elderly Peter would look back to those times on Galilee when he had cried out in fear at the sight of Jesus walking on the water, had clung to the side of his boat as the tempest threatened to capsize it; and how he had denied his Lord three times in Jerusalem on the night of Christ's arrest. Paul, too, would remember – recalling the Damascus road when the super-light of Christ had blinded him; and the time when the apostles had suspected him of trickery; the occasions when he had been tortured, arrested, stoned, beaten . . .

Yet God had brought the two apostles safely through – every time.

If we have confidence that God is greater than whatever is bugging us just now, we can go forward in the confidence that he will deal with the opposition – from inside us. We may be tempted to take the credit for victory – but if we do, the victory next time may be harder to get.

Quo vadis?

It is thought that both Peter and Paul were martyred in Rome around the year AD 64. Paul, at the end of Acts, has been in 'his own hired house' (AV) for two years. It is unlikely that his appeal to Caesar ever came to a hearing. According to tradition, Peter, at the outbreak of persecution, was advised by his friends to flee into the country. As he was leaving the suburbs, he met a man, and asked him: 'Where are you going?' 'I'm going to Rome – to be crucified, again,' was the quiet reply.

And Peter, overcome with shame, turned back and returned to the city to meet his death.

Suggested hymns
Father God, I wonder how; For the might of thine arm, we bless thee; Stand up and bless the Lord; They who tread the path of labour

St Thomas the Apostle   3 July   Unless...
Hab. 2:1–4; Ps. 31; Eph. 2:19–22; John 20:24–29

'The other disciples told [Thomas], "We have seen the Lord." But he said to them, "Unless I see the mark of the nails in his hands, and put my finger in the mark of the nails and my hand in his side, I will not believe."' John 20:25

Beyond belief
It was what Thomas wanted more than anything else: to see his Lord again. But he had both feet so firmly planted in gravity, science told him that resurrection was impossible.

When we are in shock, we can say and think very strange things. Not so very long before, Thomas had witnessed the raising of Lazarus (John 11:16) – yet this was different, perhaps because he had seen Jesus die so terribly convincingly on the cross.

Yet Thomas had stayed with the disciples. It probably gave them some comfort in their grief, to reminisce about the three years of ministry they had shared with Jesus.

Glorious belief
A week later, Thomas was still with them, so there was no shortage of witnesses when Jesus – gently but comprehensively – turned unbelief into certainty. 'My Lord and my God!' It was the first time in the gospels that Jesus had been called 'God'.

It would not be the last.

Did Thomas realize, as Jesus quoted back to him his protestations of the previous week, and invited him to 'check it out' on all counts, that Jesus *knew* what had been said? This shows us that the resurrected Jesus is a witness to all our conversations. A plaque (sometimes worked as a sampler) that our grandparents often had hanging on the wall, read:

> *Christ is the Head of this house,*
> *The unseen Guest at every meal,*
> *The silent Listener to every conversation.*

Missionary to India

Thomas is believed to have taken the gospel to India, where in parts Christians are still known as 'Christians of St Thomas'. A gospel bearing Thomas' name was discovered near Nag Hammadi in 1945, portions of which had been known for some time. It is thought to date from the fourth or fifth century, and includes the following logia:

> 'Jesus said, "Whoever has known the world has found a corpse; and whoever has found a corpse, of him the world is not worthy." '(*Log. 56*)
> 'Jesus said, "Come to me, for easy is my yoke and my lordship's gentle, and you shall find repose for yourselves." ' (*Log. 90*)

Thomas found repose in believing, that night in the upper room – for Jesus was no corpse in a sepulchre, but very, very much alive.

Suggested hymns

God of glory, God of grace; Judge eternal, throned in splendour; Thee we adore, O hidden Saviour; Thou art the way, by thee alone

St Mary Magdalene   22 July   Believe Me!

Song of Sol. 3:1–4; Ps. 42; 2 Cor. 5:14–17; John 20:1–2, 11–18

'And [Christ] died for all, so that those who live might live no longer for themselves, but for him who died and was raised for them.'
2 Corinthians 5:15

'Apostle to the Apostles'

In the early Church, Mary was known as 'the Apostle to the Apostles' – the woman privileged to see her risen Lord on Easter morning, and who ran to tell the others. It was a far cry from what she had been before Jesus had come into her life: a harlot of Magdala, which was a byword for crime.

But Jesus had restored her purity – in the euphemism of the day, 'casting seven devils' (i.e. the lot) out of her. And her gratitude had kept her loyal to him.

The world's memory

But there would be those who still pointed the finger, raised the eyebrows, whispered behind her back (or even to her face): 'The harlot, don't you know – Mary of Magdala . . . !' For the world has a better memory for sin, confessed or otherwise, than God has. The world, in its perversity, would rather watch a person careening down the road to hell, than be turned right-way-round by Jesus and heading for heaven. Even after confession, conversion and acceptance by Jesus, Mary would have to live with people's memories.

Our memory recall

How is our own memory recall? Poor for past sin confessed and repented of (whether our own, or others')? Good for the new life, new hope, new courage and perseverance of post-repentance? May we be as generous, on this count, with others, as we pray God will be with us. If God was not a merciful God of love, Mary Magdalene would not have been at the sepulchre that morning, and Peter might well be wallowing somewhere in hell, in the remorse of his denials.

Disbelief

So Mary ran, breathless, with news that her Lord's body was not in the tomb – and then, that he had risen. The first truth was provable, the second took the disciples nearly all of Easter Day to believe; it took, moreover, a personal face-to-face meeting with Jesus, since the disciples refused to believe the ecstatic Mary.

Credibility quotient

How is our own credibility quotient? Are we such folk of our word that others trust us as speaking the truth? Not too many of

us can share the purple past of Mary. But we all join her in proclaiming the truth of Christ's resurrection. How is our news
received? With apathy, disinterest, animosity or with gratitude
and faith? If we were convincing ourselves of this truth, how
would we need others to tell us? With conviction, quiet faith and
awe?

It was not Mary's fault that the disciples did not at first believe
her. And when we, too, meet disbelief, let us not get weary of
telling – and let us resist the temptation to water down the truth
to a level that the world regards as unbelievably true.

Suggested hymns
Breathe on me, Breath of God; Magdalene, thy grief and gladness;
O thou not made with hands; O thou who camest from above

St James the Apostle   25 July   High Office
Jer. 45:1–5 or Acts 11:27–12:2; Ps. 126; Acts 11:27–12:2
or 2 Cor. 4:7–15; Matthew 20:20–28
*'About that time King Herod laid violent hands upon some who belonged
to the church. He had James, the brother of John, killed with the sword.'*
Acts 12:1, 2

The first apostle martyr
James was the first of the twelve to be put to death, probably in
the year AD 44. Herod Agrippa was so pleased with the effect
that this death had on the Jews, that he considered taking Peter
out of the picture, too.

James ('the Great'), son of Zebedee and brother of John, had
been one of the inner circle of Jesus' disciples. Called by Jesus
while mending nets in the family's boats on Galilee, after Christ's
ascension James became head of the Church in Jerusalem, and
thus a prime target for anti-Christian persecution. Such are the
dangers still of high office. Yet someone has to stick his head above
the parapet; someone needs to lead and to be seen to be leading.
James' martyrdom sent shock waves through the Jerusalem
Church.

Who is willing?

Perhaps we have difficulty in filling the Chair or the senior offices on our committees, councils and synods. Whether out of false modesty or reluctance, or because there is actual or potential strife among members, a recalcitrance sometimes allows vacancies to remain.

James had headed the Church in Jerusalem for around fifteen years of struggle and tension. His death, premature though it was, saw the Christian community well established, if not comfortably so. Many of the members were to travel out from Jerusalem on ever longer missionary journeys; but this movement was largely in the future at the time of James' execution. Yet the groundwork had been laid – and the disciple who had once asked for a place of honour in heaven, had been spared any further hassle on earth.

When life is hard

While we are not to seek for easier lives, we can at least have confidence that, whatever the degree of Angst we suffer, God will not allow it to be too much.

But we can always opt for too little Angst. Satan's always ready to oblige.

We don't know how many more church members were arrested with James; possibly his was the only martyrdom in the strike; but Herod would hope that this would encourage the others to recant.

On James' festival, let us give thanks for a man who stood up and stood out, for Jesus. There will be at least one James in our own church community. Let us give him all the support we can.

Suggested hymns

Captains of the saintly band; Firmly I believe and truly; Not for our sins alone; Sow in the morn thy seed

Transfiguration of our Lord   6 August
Shekinah Glory   Dan. 7:9–10, 13–14; Ps. 97;
2 Pet. 1:16–19; Luke 9:28–30

'And while [Jesus] was praying, the appearance of his face changed, and his clothes became dazzling white.' Luke 9:29

Encouragement

The Transfiguration was a blissful moment of encouragement – for Jesus as well as his disciples. For this short time, our Lord enjoyed some of the *shekinah* glory he had known before his incarnation. The disciples were startled, awed, nonplussed – because it was a new experience for them. But it was gloriously familiar to Jesus. It would give him new heart for his mission. In effect, God was saying: 'Not long now, and you'll be back once more in glory.'

To the disciples, it was a glimpse of the glory that Jesus would eternally purchase for them at Calvary; an experience that in the short-term they must keep to themselves; but after Jesus had ascended, then they would be able to share the Transfiguration glory in their preaching and teaching. 'If it were not so, would we have told you?'

Otherness

It is easy to think of *shekinah* glory as belonging to Jesus – harder to take on board the fact that this glory was shared by the disciples on the mount; easy to believe that the departed souls are still living and active – harder to believe that they still preserve recognizable bodies that are somehow beyond the laws of chemistry and physics. The divide between this world and the next was temporarily demolished at the Transfiguration. Perhaps it is normally not so wide as we imagine.

Following God's lead

Those who are involved with Satanic and occult practices claim to know a lot about the spirit world that has no foundation in the Bible. But God has given us a remarkable number of glimpses and hints in Holy Writ, and we can safely accept these and meditate on their significance. The 'other' world is there, and it is contactable – but unless the contact is initiated and authorized by God, we should leave well alone. Let us not spoil the glimpses he allows us with unjustifiable meddling.

Our glory glimpses

God is not looking to us to crawl our way miserably to a death that leads to dark unknowing. When he gives us glory glimpses (and, being no respecter of persons, he gives them to all of us at some time or another), he wants to encourage us to thrill with excitement, to gain new courage, to strengthen our faith. The positive goodness and light of God's glory glimpses are as far removed from Satan's dark occult deviations as it's possible to imagine. Let's take a leaf out of Joshua's book, and boldly affirm: 'As for me and my house, we will serve the Lord.'

Suggested hymns
Bright the vision that delighted; In days of old on Sinai; 'Tis good, Lord, to be here; To God be the glory

Assumption of the Blessed Virgin Mary
15 August   **How Can It Be?**   Isa. 61:10–11 or
Rev. 11:19–12:6, 10; Ps. 45; Gal. 4:4–7; Luke 1:46–55

'Then God's temple in heaven was opened, and the ark of his covenant was seen within his temple; and there were flashes of lightning, rumblings, peals of thunder, an earthquake, and heavy hail.' Revelation 11:19

Assumption or Dormition?
While in the West the Latin Church has observed this festival of Mary's Assumption for less than two hundred years, in the Eastern Church the Dormition (Falling Asleep) of the Virgin has been celebrated for much longer. With advances on the ecumenical front, an increasing number of Protestant churches are including this festival in their calendars as a Marian observance, though some stop short of calling it the Assumption.

Did Mary die a natural death, and is she buried somewhere on earth? Or was she really assumed bodily into heaven? Christians in general have no problem with accepting the assumptions of Enoch and Elijah: after all, there is biblical support for both. But this is not the case with Mary. It is strange that the death/assumption of both Mary and Joseph are shrouded in mysterious silence. Was it deemed irreverent to record such details of a couple whose lives had been so bound up with that of Jesus?

Cherished as a mother
However we celebrate today – and whatever we believe of Mary, let's honour her as the most special woman in Jesus' life – can we not reverently believe that our Lord, who cherished his mother so

dearly, would take as much care of her at death as he had in life? Is it not possible to believe that he would not let Mary's body see corruption? Could we but turn back history's page, and excise the appalling anti-Marian Protestant revulsion of the Reformation, perhaps we should have been less divided on the place of Mary in Christian belief.

> *To live and not to love thee,*
> *Would fill my soul with shame;*
> *When wicked men blaspheme thee,*
> *I'll love and bless thy name.*

> J. Wyse

Committed service
We know that, after the ascension of Christ, Mary opened her house to the Church, and was much involved in its earliest days in Jerusalem. At Calvary, Jesus had given her into the care of the disciple whom he loved (probably John); thus the two would seem to have started perhaps the first 'house church' congregation. John lived to a good age, and yet is silent in his writings as to the end of Mary's life. Whether she was assumed or buried does not detract one iota from our worship of Christ – nor need it influence our appreciation and understanding of Mary's unique role as *Theotokos*. Wherever her body is, we can be sure Mary is being cherished by her Son in heaven, as she is cherished in our hearts today.

Suggested hymns
For Mary, Mother of the Lord; Ye who own the faith of Jesus. And from *Celebration Hymnal*: I'll sing a hymn to Mary; Mary Immaculate, Star of the morning

St Bartholomew the Apostle   25 August
(transferred from 24th)   Coming Alongside
Isa. 43:8–13 or Acts 5:12–16; Ps. 145:1–7; Acts 5:12–16 or 1 Cor. 4:9–15; Luke 22:24–30
'You are those who have stood by me in my trials, and I confer on you, just as my Father has conferred on me, a kingdom . . .' Luke 22:28, 29

A cynic believes

As soon as he had been won over by Jesus, the disciple Philip went and found his friend Nathanael (believed to be Bartholomew) and invited him to come and meet the Lord. But Nathanael was cynical about the veracity of anyone who came from Nazareth. Jesus knew how to cut through cynicism. 'Before Philip even spoke to you, I saw you under the fig tree,' Jesus told him. And as the truth dawned, that no ordinary person in the blinding Palestinian sun could penetrate the thick shade of a fig tree from a distance, Nathanael's cynicism melted into an affirmation of Jesus as Son of God and King of Israel. Once converted, he remained a loyal – if largely unrecorded – member of the Twelve.

Bishop Eusebius of Caesarea mentions a certain Pantaenus of Alexandria, who, in the late second century, went to India ...

'and the story goes that there he found, in the hands of some persons who had come to know Christ in that land, the Gospel according to Matthew, which had anticipated his arrival; for that Bartholomew, one of the apostles, had preached to them and left behind the writing of Matthew in the actual Hebrew characters, and that it was preserved up to the said time.'

Eusebius, H.E. *V.10:3*

Standing by

In our text today, Jesus is paying tribute to those who have stood by him in the difficult times. It's easy to come alongside a friend when life is good, but the testing of friendship comes when trouble arrives. His friends had stood the test, and Jesus showed his appreciation of their loyalty.

There must have been something very special about Bartholomew-Nathanael that encouraged Jesus immediately to reveal that he could see beyond normal sight. Usually, he kept his 'otherness' hidden, particularly at a first meeting. Did he want Bartholomew in his team so badly, that he needed an immediate decision, even overturning the man's cynicism? Why did he make it virtually impossible for Bartholomew to refuse? We do not know; it is part of the freedom that God reserves, to deal with individuals in different ways.

'I saw you'
And we can be sure that he will work like this today. Some of us take a longer time to come to full belief, while others declare immediately for Christ. Nathanael's case shows that a 'snap decision' can also lead to a lifelong commitment; we should not be afraid of making up our minds fast (nor of having God make our decision for us, on occasion).

Today, despite our vaunted freedom, wouldn't we probably have set about recruiting our mission team by preparing a set of formal application forms – a series of set questions, perhaps with a blank half-page for the candidate's individual comments on why he/she considered him/herself eligible for the position. And of course we'd need references – and short lists – and interviews – and mileage expenses, assurances, guarantees . . .

Jesus' way was much simpler – and look at the candidates he selected! Well, they may not have made it on to our short lists or selection conferences – but our Lord called them the salt of the earth.

If life is more complicated today, it's not God's fault.

Suggested hymns
A charge to keep I have; Lord, it belongs not to my care; Put thou thy trust in God; Will you come and follow me

Birth of the Blessed Virgin Mary
8 September   **Theotokos**   Mic. 5:2–4; for the Psalm: Judith 16:13–16; Rom. 8:28–30; Matthew 1:1–16, 18–23
'Now the birth of Jesus the Messiah took place in this way. When his mother Mary had been engaged to Joseph, but before they lived together, she was found to be with child from the Holy Spirit.' Matthew 1:18

Prayer for Mary
We know far more about the birth of Mary's Son, than about her own. According to legend, her parents were Joachim and Anna, and the festival of her birth has long been celebrated on this day in both the Eastern and Western Churches. The Eastern Orthodox Church has a beautiful liturgy for Mary's Nativity, which includes this prayer:

What is this sound of feasting that we hear?
Joachim and Anna mystically keep festival.
'O Adam and Eve,' they cry, 'rejoice with us today;
For if by your transgressions you closed the
  gates of Paradise to those of old,
We have now been given a glorious fruit,
Mary the Child of God
Who opens its entrance to us all.

Thy nativity, O Theotokos,
Has brought joy to all the world;
For from thee has shone forth
The Sun of Righteousness, Christ our God.
He has loosed us from the curse and given the blessing.
He has vanquished death and bestowed on us eternal life.

By thy holy nativity, O most pure Virgin,
Joachim and Anna were set free from the reproach
  of childlessness,
And Adam and Eve from the corruption of death,
Delivered from the guilt of sin,
Thy people keep the feast and sing:
'The barren woman bears the Theotokos,
  the Sustainer of our life.'

Be renewed, O Adam, and be magnified, O Eve;
You prophets, dance with the apostles and the
  righteous;
Let there be common joy in the world
  among angels and mortals
For the Theotokos is born today of
  righteous Joachim and Anna.

Nunc Dimittis

It is not possible that the Anna who approached the young Child
and his parents when Simeon was pronouncing the *Nunc Dimittis*,
was Mary's mother. The old Anna in the temple had been a widow
for much of her eighty-four years; but there is a mystery in her
presence at the Purification – a mystery that may be solved one
day when we meet her face to face.

   Meanwhile, let us give thanks for the blessed union of Joachim
and Anna, which God used to give us our *Theotokos*, our Mother

of God and the precious woman whose *Fiat* was to usher in the Saviour of the world.

Suggested hymns
Ave Maria, O Maiden, O Mother; Daily, daily, sing to Mary; Immaculate Mary! Our hearts are on fire; O purest of creatures! (All from *Celebration Hymnal*)

Holy Cross Day   14 September   Cross of Light
Num. 21:4–9; Ps. 22; Phil. 2:6–11; John 3:13–17

'At the name of Jesus every knee should bend, in heaven and on earth and under the earth, and every tongue should confess that Jesus Christ is Lord, to the glory of God the Father.' Philippians 2:11

Helena's discovery
In the fourth century Helena, mother of the Emperor Constantine, is believed to have discovered the true cross of Christ, during excavations in Jerusalem. A church erected on the site of the present Holy Sepulchre was dedicated on this day, AD 335, since when it has been observed as Holy Cross Day.

In his *Letter to the Emperor Constantius*, of AD 351, Bishop Cyril of Jerusalem writes:

> In the days of Constantine your father . . . there was discovered the wood of the cross fraught with salvation, because the divine grace that gave piety to the pious seeker vouchsafed the finding of the buried holy places. But in your time, your Majesty, most religious of Emperors . . . are seen wonderful works, not from earth any more, but from the heavens. The trophy of the victory over death of our Lord and Saviour Jesus Christ, the only-begotten Son of God, I mean the blessed cross, has been seen at Jerusalem blazing with refulgent light! For in these very days of the holy feast of Pentecost, on the seventh of May, about this third hour, a gigantic cross formed of light appeared in the sky above holy Golgotha stretching out as far as the holy Mount of Olives. It was not seen by just one or two, but was most clearly displayed before the whole population of the city. Nor did it, as one might have supposed, pass away quickly like something

imagined, but was visible to sight above the earth for some hours, while it sparkled with a light above the sun's rays. Of a surety, it would have been overcome and hidden by them had it not exhibited to those who saw it a brilliance more powerful than the sun, so that the whole population of the city made a concerted rush into the Martyry, seized by a fear that mingled with joy at the heavenly vision ... not only Christians but pagans from elsewhere sojourning in Jerusalem; all of them as with one mouth raised a hymn of praise to Christ Jesus our Lord, the only-begotten Son of God, the worker of wonders. For they recognized in fact and by experience that the most religious creed of Christians is *not with enticing words of wisdom, but in demonstration of the Spirit and of power* (1 Corinthians 2:4), not merely preached by men, but having witness borne to it by God from the heavens.

Looking to the Cross
There must be few churches where the cross is not to be seen – in wood, brass, silver, embroidery or stained glass. At St Matthew's Church, Morley, is mediaeval glass from the ruined Dale Abbey, showing the story of the *Invention of the Cross*. In the Lady Chapel at Hereford Cathedral, and in Holy Trinity, Edale, can be seen stained-glass windows representing the cross as *green*, still growing and in leaf.

May we reflect on the growing, ongoing efficacy of the cross' sacrifice today.

Suggested hymns
Beneath the Cross of Jesus, I fain would take my stand; Cross of Jesus, Cross of sorrow; In the Cross of Christ I glory; When I survey the wondrous Cross

St Matthew, Apostle and Evangelist
21 September   **A Mixed Welcome**   Prov. 3:13–18; Ps. 119:65–72; 2 Cor. 4:1–6; Matthew 9:9–13
'When the Pharisees saw this, they said to his disciples: "Why does your teacher eat with tax collectors and sinners?"' Matthew 9:11

In at the deep end

Matthew (Levi) would remember his call with mixed feelings. Jesus had shown him kindness, concern and understanding; but the Pharisees could only criticize rudely – *very* rudely, as it was Matthew's house (Luke 5:29)! The office of tax collector was seen by the Jews as being an accommodation to the Roman force of occupation. Jesus did not enter into an argument, but merely called Matthew away from the toll booth to follow him. He was after the man, not the money; the witness, not the work. As was his custom, he chose a man who was in lawful employment, and no idler. The fact that 'sinners' (of unspecified nature) were at the meal, speaks well for Matthew's hospitality and generosity – and surely, after all, the choosing of the guest list is the prerogative of the host! It is also to the credit of the disciples that they did not allow these critics to dilute their acceptance of Matthew into their team.

The past put behind

Just as Mary Magdalene put her past behind her, and responded to the goodness that had healed her from her addiction to vice, so Matthew drew a line under his tax collecting. Later, Zacchaeus was also to turn a shady past into a brighter future, after he had met up with Jesus. He, too, gave Jesus generous hospitality – on demand (Luke 19:5)! Our Lord has many ways of consolidating his approach!

At the meeting of our eyes

> *Jesus, stand among us . . .*
> *At the meeting of our eyes*

we sing, in a modern hymn. But when we have asked him to come – when, spiritually speaking, we look at him in each other's eyes, what are we prepared for him to do?

Indeed, we are not prepared, because he will never tell us what he is going to do. He has been taking people by surprise for two thousand years, and he's not in the business of change. We need to have faith enough to say, with Job: 'Though he slay me, yet will I trust in him' (Job 13:15; AV). Remember, this was the same man who affirmed, way ahead of his time: 'I know that my redeemer liveth, and that he shall stand at the latter day upon the earth' (Job 19:28; AV)!

Life can never be the same again, once Jesus has looked us in the eye. And the more we meet him, the more – spiritually speaking – our feet won't touch the ground.

Are we willing to take the risk of such excitement?

Matthew was. And millions more.

Suggested hymns

I heard the voice of Jesus say; Jesus, stand among us; Take up thy cross, the Saviour said; Will you come and follow me

St Michael and All Angels   29 September
'Who Is Like God?'   Gen. 28:10–12 or Rev. 12:7–12; Ps. 103:19–22; Rev. 12:7–12 or Heb. 1:5–14; John 1:47–51

'And [Jesus] said to him, "Very truly, I tell you, you will see heaven opened and the angels of God ascending and descending upon the Son of Man."' John 1:51

Seven archangels

This festival has been kept since the fifth century, when a church in Rome was dedicated to St Michael on 30 September, the celebrations beginning on the previous evening. Michael's name means 'Who is like God?', and he is best remembered as being the victor in a great battle with the Devil (Revelation 12). In addition to Michael, the Bible mentions Raphael and Gabriel, but we need to go to the Book of Enoch to find the names of all seven archangels:

And these are the names of the holy angels who watch. Uriel, one of the holy angels, who is over the world and over Tartarus. Raphael, one of the holy angels, who is over the spirits of men. Raguel, one of the holy angels who takes vengeance on the world of the luminaries. Michael, one of the holy angels, to wit, he that is set over the best part of mankind, and over chaos. Saraqael, one of the holy angels, who is set over the spirits, who sin in the spirit. Gabriel, one of the holy angels, who is over Paradise and the serpents and the Cherubim. Remiel, one of the holy angels, whom God set over those who rise.

Enoch, XX.1–8

The Valley of Judgement

Enoch also enlightens us as to the angels' function in the Judgement at the End of the world:

> And I looked and . . . saw there a deep valley with burning fire. And they brought the kings and the mighty, and began to cast them into this deep valley. And there mine eyes saw how they made these their instruments, iron chains of immeasurable weight. And I asked the angel of peace who went with me, saying: 'For whom are these chains being prepared?' And he said unto me, 'These are being prepared for the hosts of Azazel, so that they may take them and cast them into the abyss of complete condemnation, and they shall cover their jaws with rough stones as the Lord of Spirits commanded. And Michael, and Gabriel, and Raphael, and Phanuel shall take hold of them on that great day, and cast them on that day into the burning furnace, that the Lord of Spirits may take vengeance on them for their unrighteousness in becoming subject to Satan and leading astray those who dwell on the earth.'
>
> *Enoch, LIV.1–6*

As we celebrate Michael Archangel's feast today, can we praise God for giving us such a strong force as spiritual backup?

We cannot fathom such strength – but thank God it's on our side, and not for the opposition!

Suggested hymns

Angel voices, ever singing; Around the throne of God a band; Ye holy angels bright; Ye watchers and ye holy ones

William Tyndale, Translator and Martyr

6 October **God's Word For All** Prov. 8:1–11;
Ps. 119:89–96; 2 Tim. 3:12–17; John 17:6–8, 14–19

'Indeed, all who want to live a godly life in Christ Jesus will be persecuted.' 2 Timothy 3:12

Opposition from the Church

William Tyndale (*c.* 1494–1536) studied at Oxford and Cambridge, and had a burning ambition to give the English people the Bible in their mother tongue. For too long the church services had been in Latin, which most folk didn't know; and many priests seemed determined to keep it that way. 'I will see that the boy following the plough knows more about the Bible than you do,' Tyndale told one objecting cleric.

It was not the best way of making friends, though Tyndale was to influence many people. He was forced to leave England, and to continue his translating on the Continent. A printer whom he employed to run off his first New Testaments was so impressed by the text, that he became a Christian and worked for nothing on the job.

The best of texts

Tyndale had seen the shortcomings of the Latin Vulgate, and he went behind this to the Hebrew (Aramaic) and Greek texts, in order to produce the best possible translation. He worked long and hard, and soon the first of his New Testaments were shipped to England. The vindictive priests (mainly in the episcopacy) pounced on as many as they could, and destroyed them. Undeterred, Tyndale started work on the Old Testament. It was a mammoth task, and before it was completed he was betrayed by a sixteenth-century Judas, and executed.

Within a few years of his death, his text was accepted for use in all English churches. Now, indeed, the plough boys could hear the word of God and understand it.

We know that the English clerics were fearful of Lutheran influences creeping into the Church, but this surely cannot excuse their desire to keep the understandable word of God away from their congregations.

Tyndale's text proved so acceptable that ninety per cent of the Authorized (King James) Version of the New Testament is Tyndale. More recently, Dom Henry Wansbrough paid generous tribute to the help Tyndale's text had afforded him in his preparation of the New Jerusalem Bible.

So diligent – so young

To work so hard, and die so young, is surely tragic. Yet look at what Tyndale, under the direction of the Spirit, achieved! As we give thanks for his life, can we glimpse the sheer relief and joy experienced by those who even today are receiving the Bible (or part of it) in their mother tongue for the first time: to be able to handle God's word, to mull it over, turn hither and yon through its pages, commit its precious truths to heart . . . One man, hounded from his homeland by the Church he was trying to help, murdered for giving the gospel to millions, did not die in vain.

Centuries later, D.L. Moody, the American evangelist, was to be told by a friend: 'I have yet to see what God can do with a man who gives himself wholly to him.' Moody bent his energies to one end, and thousands were converted through his preaching.

God has today a greater potential manpower than ever before. And we are part of it.

Suggested hymns
Fill thou my life, O Lord my God; Forth in thy name, O Lord, I go; Lord, speak to me, that I may speak; Strengthen for service, Lord, the hands

St Teresa d'Avila, Teacher of the Faith
15 October   **The Way of Perfection**   Wis. 7:7–15; Ps. 138; Rom. 8:22–27; John 14:1–7

'And God, who searches the heart, knows what is the mind of the Spirit, because the Spirit intercedes for the saints according to the will of God.'
Romans 8:27

A heavy cross
Teresa d'Avila (1515–1582) was a Spanish Carmelite nun whose catholicism was a combination of mysticism and down-to-earth practicality: a fusion of 'faith and good works' at variance with the purely Roman catholicism of the day. She travelled widely in Spain, founding many religious houses for men as well as women, inculcating a spirit of *working faith* in her novices. Dogged by ill health, constantly harassed by the clerical hierarchy, Teresa went on her way – not too calmly, for she had a quick tongue, and was not averse to berating even God. She nevertheless found time to write two classics that are still valued today: *The Way of Perfection*, and *The Interior Castle*.

She died of exhaustion on 4 October 1582 – the day before the calendar was reformed. October lost eleven days that year, resulting in her festival being celebrated on the 15th.

Woman of prayer

Teresa wrote a number of prayers, one of which – her bookmark – has become the bookmark prayer of many Christians:

> *Trust in God.*
> *Let nothing disturb you,*
> *nothing afright you.*
> *All things are passing;*
> *God never changes.*
> *Patience achieveth*
> *all that it strives for.*
> *He who has God*
> *finds he lacks nothing.*
> *God alone suffices.*

And one of her prayers of dedication:

> *Govern all by thy wisdom, O Lord, so that my soul may always be serving thee as thou dost will, and not as I may choose. Do not punish me, I beseech thee, by granting that which I wish or ask, if it offends thy love, which would always live in me. Let me die to myself that so I may serve thee; let me live to thee, who in thyself are the true life.*

Our own dedication

Opposition from other Christians, ill health, a sometimes recalcitrant work-force – the way of Teresa was no bed of roses. Yet her dedication and devotion touched many lives, and her writings live on. As we reflect on how our own dedication is being lived out, we may perhaps ponder which facets of our lives may still be influencing others for good, four centuries or more after *our* deaths.

Who knows? The news may even catch up with us, wherever we are at that stage.

Suggested hymns

Give me oil in my lamp; Peace, perfect peace, in this dark world of sin; Teach me, my God and King; They who tread the path of labour

St Luke the Evangelist   18 October
A Good Friend   Isa. 35:3–6 or Acts 16:6–12a; Ps. 147;
2 Tim. 4:5–17; Luke 10:1–9[10–11]

'During the night Paul had a vision; there stood a man of Macedonia pleading with him and saying, "Come over to Macedonia and help us." When he had seen the vision, we immediately tried to cross over to Macedonia, being convinced that God had called us to proclaim the good news to them.' Acts 16:9, 10

Missionary doctor

Our reading picks up the point in Acts where the 'we passages' indicate that Luke has joined Paul full-time in the missionary work. We don't know whether Paul, feeling the aches and twinges of an ageing frame, considered it would be expedient to have a doctor on board (Paul was no hypochondriac, but he could recall his vicissitudes and the impact they had made, in his letters and preaching) – or whether Luke had volunteered his services.

> *There's a cry from Macedonia,*
> *Come and help us! The light*
> *of the gospel bring;*
> *Oh, come! Let us hear the joyful*
> *tidings of salvation;*
> *We thirst for the living spring.*
>
> *Oh, ye heralds of the cross,*
> *be up and doing!*
> *Remember the great command,*
> *Away! Go ye forth and preach*
> *the word to every creature,*
> *Proclaim it in every land.*
>
> *Fanny J. Crosby*

The beloved physician

In good times and in bad, Luke proved to be a good friend. Paul speaks of him as 'the beloved physician', and at one time there was only Luke who was there to support him in prison. If indeed Luke wrote the Third Gospel and Acts, we can probably believe that he had spent some time with Mary, for his Christmas stories have an intimacy and delicacy that suggest her influence. Luke, according to tradition, died in Boeotia at the age of eighty-four, having completed his gospel in Greece.

Did he intend to write a third book? Acts finishes quite abruptly, leaving us wondering whether Paul's appeal to Caesar was ever heard, how long he stayed in Rome, whether he ever reached Spain as had been his longing (Romans 15:24).

Shared ministry

Ministry by its very nature needs to be shared; Jesus recruited a standing committee of twelve, but he had an enlarged team of seventy out in the field. Paul's inner circle consisted of stalwarts like Barnabas, Silas, Mark and Luke. If we try to go it alone, God may give our ministry rich blessings; but sooner or later he will give us physical as well as spiritual backup, and even greater blessings. One man under God can move a mountain; two or more can tackle the Karakoram Range.

On occasion, we may feel that our well established ecclesiastical structures are more of a hindrance than a help; but the Body of Christ functions best with *all* its members – even though some of us agree to differ in the plethora of committee, council and synod meetings that are sent to try us!

Suggested hymns

Can I see another's woe; Help us to help each other, Lord; Thine arm, O Lord, in days of old; When I needed a neighbour

SS Simon and Jude, Apostles 28 October

Essential Building Blocks Isa. 28:14–16; Ps. 119:89–96; Eph. 2:19–22; John 15:17–27

'In [Christ Jesus] the whole structure is joined together and grows into a holy temple in the Lord, in whom you also are built together spiritually into a dwelling place for God.' Ephesians 2:21, 22

They only serve . . . ?

While we know relatively little about Simon and Jude, we can be sure they did more than just 'stand and wait'. Simon is known as 'The Zealot' – perhaps because of his enthusiasm for the gospel, but more likely because he was a member of the Zealot party either before or after he joined Christ's disciples. Jude was unfortunate in having a name so similar to the betrayer's (he is often called Thaddaeus), that he was relegated to the 'last option' so frequently in the Church's intercessions, that he became known as the patron saint of lost causes! He was either the son of a James (according to Luke) or the brother of one (according to his own, very short, letter), or he could have been both.

In the seventh century, a church where the relics of Simon and Jude had been deposited was dedicated on 28 October, which has been celebrated as their joint festival ever since.

Stones for the temple

As possessors of the Holy Spirit, entempling our mighty Advocate, we form stones in the Great Temple, the Body of Christ. We may have prominent positions, or be so hidden that only our Builder knows we are there; but every stone in the Temple is vital and appreciated by God. If we drop out of our allotted place, we are missed: the engagement we fail to keep, the task we conveniently or inadvertently forget, the meeting we don't attend, the opportunity we lose, the comfort we fail to bring, the letter we don't write . . . we are missed. If only we were more conscious of our crucial place in God's Temple, perhaps we'd not go missing so often.

When Thomas absented himself from the meeting of the disciples, late on that first Easter Day, he had to face a week of unknowing, of deliberating, doubting and disbelieving, before Jesus put him out of his misery at the meeting he did attend.

Our word, our bond

It boils down to the honouring of one's commitment at baptism. We know we are not, cannot yet be, perfect – but the Christian way is the way of doing the best one can, and offering our lack to God's abundance. A beautiful prayer that concludes the Office of Compline runs:

> To thy mercy, O Lord Jesus Christ, I commend this imperfect Service, which I have offered up to thee; would that it were more worthy of thine acceptance; but let the great worthiness of those prayers, which thou didst offer in the days of thy sojourn on earth, atone for the weakness of my prayers and praises, and offer them up in union with thine own, for therein

is abundance to supply my lack: who ever livest to make inter-
cession for us, our Mediator and Advocate.

Suggested hymns
Crown him with many crowns; Father, I place into your hands;
Prayer is the soul's sincere desire; Teach me, my God and King

All Saints' Day 1 November New Creation
Wis. of Sol. 3:1–9 or Isa. 25:6–9; Ps. 24:1–6; Rev. 21:1–
6a; John 11:32–42
*'Then I saw a new heaven and a new earth; for the first heaven and the
first earth had passed away, and the sea was no more.' Revelation 21:1*

Forward planning
The saints of old looked forward, to the time (or timeless state)
described in Revelation. If there was nothing for which to hope
after death, their lives – our lives – would be in vain. For all saints,
in every age, it is the hope that Jesus has given us that sustains
and provides us with our reason for living and for dying.

They gaze at us, from stained glass or illuminated manuscripts,
in impassive, serene holiness, their glory shining out and redolent
of an existence we only glimpse from time to time. But we *are*
given such glimpses, because God in his love and mercy seeks to
keep alive and vibrant our hope of eternal life.

East and West
We can read the martyrologies of centuries past, and discover
saints whose names have long since been dropped from our calendars. We can travel east and find the Orthodox Church celebrating
the festivals of a multitude of saints of whom we have never heard.
We can even motor through Cornwall and learn of yet more saints
with the loveliest of names, yet little known outside that county.
And as we add to our knowledge of these saints, this vast, unseen
'cloud of witnesses' should give us an ever increasing thankfulness, that these giants of the faith (whom most would not have
called extraordinary in their lifetime) have fought the good fight,
have finished the course, and are even now here as our spiritual
backup, to help us by their example, courage and love.

Semen est sanguis Christianorum

The fiery Tertullian – who had sighed after patience but never obtained it – thundered in righteous anger against the persecutors of Christians: 'Kill us, but the blood of the martyrs is the seed of the Church! The more seed you sow, the more the Church will grow!' He was so right. History has shown that the Church does not die under persecution: it may take a battering, but it comes back stronger than ever. Like a cork in the water, no one can keep a Christian down. Multiply one cork by all the Christians in the world (including the saints in the Hereafter), and you have an unsinkable, irrepressible force that is more than a match for the Devil.

All Saints

ALL saints – eastern and western, famous or little known – are honoured today, as the Church Triumphant in heaven gives the Church Militant here on earth cause for encouragement. Many of those saints knew far greater dangers, hardships and agonies than we do. They cleared the final hurdle, in the strength of Christ.

And so can we – but only in the strength of Christ.

Suggested hymns

Around the throne of God a band; For all the saints, a noble throng; For all the saints, who from their labours rest; Let all mortal flesh

All Souls' Day   2 November   They Are With God

Lam. 3:17–26, 31–33 or Wis. 3:1–9; Ps. 23 or Ps. 27; Rom. 5:5–11 or 1 Pet. 1:3–9; John 5:19–25 or 6:37–40

'Blessed be the God and Father of our Lord Jesus Christ. By his great mercy he has given us a new birth into a living hope through the resurrection of Jesus Christ from the dead, and into an inheritance that is imperishable, undefiled, and unfading, kept in heaven for you.' 1 Peter 1:3, 4

A thousand years of remembering

In 998, Abbot Odile of Cluny initiated the observance of All Souls, though the Western Church as a whole didn't take it over until the thirteenth century.

It is a time for memories: the memory of God's goodness in

giving to us, for a longer or shorter time, beautiful lives and loves and laughter: memories of those who may not have made world headlines, but who have left us a legacy and example to follow – a challenge to be saints in our time.

Sands of time
They have left their mark, the souls whom we honour today. The sands of time still carry their record. We tell the young ones today of their deeds, and recall their words with pride. We hope the young ones of today will, in their turn, remember to tell the next generation.

But when we reach the Gates of Heaven, we shall not be asked about these dearest ones. We shall need to answer for *ourselves*. And surely the best tribute to their memory will be what we have been, and what we have done to further the work of God's Kingdom on earth. We have had opportunities they did not have – yet their lives and examples have counted towards how we have met and used our openings. The seed sown by the faithful departed is the harvest we are reaping now.

They are in God. And we also are in him.

Can we grieve, when the Almighty is so kind? Well, yes, we may shed some tears, and the ache inside may still be there. But God understands, because – not so very long ago, on a day in Bethany – his Son wept in sympathy with those he loved (John 11:35).

Not the end
Death is not the end for Christians; it is only an intervention; and God's hand is firmly on life's tiller. Much of what makes life recognizable and meaningful here continues Hereafter, yet time, space and gravity seem not to operate in that life – which gives us the (as yet) incomprehensible mystery of departed souls being further than the furthest star, yet closer than they ever were on earth.

In fact, we are probably wrong in calling these souls 'departed'. As Jesus told his disciples: 'I am with you always' (Matthew 28:20).

Suggested hymns
Days and moments quickly flying; For ever with the Lord; My soul, there is a country; There is a land of pure delight

A SERMON FOR HARVEST
THANKSGIVING

May the words of my mouth, and the meditations of our hearts, be now and always acceptable in thy sight, O Lord our Strength and our Redeemer. Amen.

'Jesus said: "But as for that [seed] in the good soil, these are the ones who, when they hear the word, hold it fast in an honest and good heart, and bear fruit with patient endurance."' Luke 8:15

How fast are we holding on to the word of God? Does it impact on every circumstance, every decision we have to make, every meeting that God arranges? Or do we catch ourselves worrying about anything before we remember God's word? For although the Bible was written thousands of years ago, it has a word for every situation. *Every one.* If we lose sight of this truth, we have let go of the word of God.

But seed doesn't stay for ever, hidden in the decorative, sealed packets. Before it can bring forth a harvest, it needs to be ventilated and sown. Where are we sowing our seed? Here a little, there a little? Helping, sharing, comforting, healing, preaching, teaching, supporting, encouraging, contributing – making way for God in others' lives is seed-sowing at its best. The harder we work at the sowing, the more seed God will provide to keep us in business. There are millions who are spiritually starving for lack of this seed.

'Oh, surely not!' sneer the cynics.

Make the connection, you who wish to scoff! What is the seed but the word of God? What is the word of God but Jesus? What is Jesus but the bread of life? What stands between a soul and starvation?

God, for his part, has undertaken a constant supply of seed. We Christians pray every day in the prayer our Lord taught us, for bread: for ourselves and for others; it is *our* Father to whom we pray. St Teresa d'Avila composed a beautiful prayer on this 'harvest petition' that is so well known we often take it for granted.

> First our Lord prays
> that we should be given this bread every day;

and he continues:
Give it us today, Lord,
repeating the name of his Father.
This is what he is saying to his Father:
that as the Son has already been given
to us once, in that he died for us,
so he is ours henceforth
and will never be taken away from us again
until the end of time:
so he remains with us,
and upholds us day by day.
Eternal Father,
we cannot value too highly
the humility of your Son.
With what treasure did we buy him?
We know that thirty pieces of silver
were sufficient to sell him,
but there is no price adequate to buy him.
He is wholly one with us
inasmuch as he shares our nature;
but being Master of his own will
he lays it before the Father
so that, since our nature is also his,
he is able to give something of his nature to us,
and thus he says: our bread.
He makes no distinction between himself and us;
but it is a distinction we make ourselves
in not giving ourselves
to the service of his Majesty
every day.

This is the crucial difference between sowing on the natural, and the supernatural, scale. The sowing of the word of God is constant, continuous – because its benefits are everlasting: we are investing in and for eternity. Is it too much to ask? No, God never demands of us more than he knows we can give.

There is an anonymous beatitude:

> *Blessed is the man who is too busy*
> *to worry in the daytime –*
> *and too sleepy to worry at night.*

Such a seed sower will not come with empty hands to the harvest store at his life's end.

Worry is the greatest single cause of poor sowing and bad harvests: worry about whether the time is right, the weather is propitious, the seed is viable, the soil is wrong . . . On the spiritual scale, worry means that we have taken our mind off God's work and efficacy, and on to our disinclination and inadequacy. Dr W.E. Sangster, the well-known Methodist preacher, used to say: 'If I trust, I do not worry; and if I worry, I do not trust.' We can't do everything (at bad times, it may seem as though we can't do anything), so we need to trust God to do what we cannot do. But there is one thing God cannot do – or at least that he requires our co-operation to do – and that is to have the *will* to sow his seed. He provides the seed – who among us can claim to be without the word of God? He provides the opportunities for sowing: even a life of solitude on a remote island gives unlimited opportunities for a seed-sowing prayer ministry. He gives all the strength he knows we need. What more is required to kick-start the sowing, but our willingness to get out there and do our best?

A Harvest Thanksgiving focuses our thoughts on the natural seeds and what this earth produces. Despite our advanced technology, there are great inequalities between nations who produce too much and sometimes waste the excess, and nations who cannot or will not produce enough for their needs, and who either starve or are forced to accept help from others.

It's now exactly one hundred and sixty years since the first Harvest Thanksgiving service was held. It came about in this way.

Miss Kuczinski was governess to a family in the Cornish town of Morwenstow. Writing in her diary one day, she remarked: 'Mr Hawker, our vicar, is slightly cracked, but he is a very clever old soul.' Within a short time, she had married the clever old soul, becoming the second Mrs Hawker when he was sixty years old. In October 1843, the Revd Stephen Hawker opened the first Harvest Thanksgiving with the words:

'Let us gather together in the chancel of our church on the first Sunday of the next month, and there receive the bread of the new corn, that blessed sacrament which was ordained to strengthen and refresh our souls. Let us remember that, as a multitude of grains of wheat are mingled into one loaf, so we, being many, are intended to be joined together into one, in that holy Sacrament of the Church of Jesus Christ.'

If someone came to our door asking for food, would we send them away hungry? Sowing seed on the spiritual front is all the more worthwhile because it not only fills a requested need, but also takes the initiative: 'Preach the word in season, out of season,' St Paul commanded Timothy (2 Timothy 4:2; AV). If we wait for folk to declare their need, we'd be waiting in some cases for ever. The need of the world for the word-seed of God has never been greater.

And the time for sowing starts NOW.

In the name of the Father, the Son and the Holy Ghost. Amen.

A SERMON FOR REMEMBRANCE SUNDAY

Destruction   Ezek. 37:1–14; Ps. 51; Mark 13:1–8

'As [Jesus] came out of the temple, one of his disciples said to him, "Look, Teacher, what large stones and what large buildings!" Then Jesus asked him, "Do you see these great buildings? Not one stone will be left here upon another; all will be thrown down."' Mark 13:1, 2

Don't be alarmed

Jesus could look into the future, barely forty years away, and see the Romans laying siege to Jerusalem, throwing up great ramps of soil while the emaciated Jews watched from the walls in sullen defiance. He could see the first soldiers storming the scanty defences, torching the temple, breaking into houses where the corpses of starvation victims were piled, and recoiling in horror. He could see Masada, Machaerus and all the beautiful palaces of the Herodian family, being invaded and burned to the ground.

And yet he calmly said: 'When you hear of wars and rumours of wars, do not be alarmed, this must take place' (Mark 13:7).

Remembering

Each Armistice Sunday we gather to remember, with our black mourning coats and the bright red poppies. The 'war that was to end all wars' had ended only twenty-one years before another, even worse, conflict erupted to involve most of the world – since when there has been hardly a month without a war of sorts in one country or another.

We haven't yet become used to the agony, the carnage and the waste. We still cannot view war calmly. Perhaps we never shall – never should. That calmness was the prerogative of Jesus, who could see further than the bloodshed and destruction, to where it was all heading. Too often we can see no meaning, no reason for war. The randomness, chaos and devastation make no sense. The remembrance to some degree is cathartic, but the anguish is still there.

John McCrae's verses

A Scots-Canadian medical officer with the First Canadian Army Contingent, Dr John McCrae (1872–1918), wrote verses of deep pathos and yet of hope, at Ypres, on 3 May 1915. From the window of the field hospital where he was working, he could see red poppies growing in profusion. Reflecting on the painkilling properties of the morphine extracted from poppies, to him the flowers symbolized the everlasting rest of the fallen.

In Flanders fields the poppies blow
Between the crosses, row on row,
That mark our place; and in the sky
The larks, still bravely singing, fly
Scarce heard among the guns below.

We are the dead. Short days ago
We lived, felt dawn, saw sunset glow;
Loved, and were loved, and now we lie
In Flanders fields.

To you from failing hands we throw
The torch; be yours to hold it high.
If ye break faith with us who die,
We shall not sleep, though poppies grow
In Flanders fields.

In 1918, as McCrae himself was dying, he asked that poppies should be laid on his grave. Three years later, the first Poppy Day was held in Britain, and has been observed ever since.

The danger is not that we shall forget the sacrifice of so many for so many, but that we *only* remember. Remembrance is important; we owe it to our dead, and in a way it also helps to lessen our grief and any guilt we may feel at our not having given an equal sacrifice. But were those who died fighting only for short-term freedom? Were their hopes not also on a better world, where swords will be beaten into ploughshares, and spears into pruning hooks? Jesus has promised that the End will come when this supernatural peace will take over – but only when we have published the gospel in every nation (Mark 13:10; Matthew 24:14).

Saving the rainforests is important; so is the reduction of CO_2 emissions, the abolition of leaded petrol, the wastage of fossil fuels, and a thousand other worthwhile schemes to try to halt the rape of the environment. Rebuilding towns and cities after the iron-mongery of warfare has knocked them about, is essential for morale and commerce. But even this is secondary to the evangelization of the world.

To the last, the Jews hoped that God would miraculously intervene, and either strike down the invading Roman armies, or turn them back. When he did not, many of them simply took their own lives in despair.

When we consider the serried rows of white crosses in far too many cemeteries in far too many countries; the many Rolls of Honour; the medals awarded posthumously and treasured by families across the world . . . we can, if we're not careful, also give way to despair. The futility of warfare is something that the Devil uses to persuade us that nothing is worth anything any more.

But we have a gospel to proclaim.

A Lord to love.

And a Kingdom to inherit.

Our lead-free cars, solar heating, 'green' lifestyle, even those rainforests we've done so much to save, will all have to be left behind one day. Only our imperishable temple, indwelt by the Holy Spirit, will survive. There will be a new heaven and a new earth (Revelation 21:1); and surely the best tribute we can pay to those whom we are remembering today, is to work towards this: to have our sights set on bringing about not merely a better world (here), but *the* better world (Hereafter).

A prayer

Almighty God, from whose love in Christ we cannot be parted, by death or by life; hear our prayers and thanksgivings for those whom we remember today. Fulfil in them the purpose of your love; and bring us, with them, to your eternal joy. We give thanks today, O Lord of hosts, for all that makes our common life secure; for the peace and freedom we enjoy; and for the opportunity that is ours of building a better order of society for those who are yet to come. We remember with pride and gratitude those who fought and died to make this possible; and we pray that the memory of their sacrifice may inspire in us the resolve to seek your kingdom and to do your will for the world of our day; through Jesus Christ our Lord.

Suggested hymns
O God, our help in ages past; O valiant hearts; Rejoice, O Land, in God thy might; Christ is the world's true Light

The Mission to Seafarers
A world mission agency of the Church of England

Earning a living at sea, bringing food to our tables and resources for our industry, is one of the most dangerous jobs in the world. On average 10 ships and 25 seafarers are lost at sea every month. Pirate attacks on merchant ships are on the increase with hundreds of assaults each year – sometimes resulting in loss of life.

Through a network of chaplains, lay staff and volunteers, the Mission has a presence in 300 ports around the world, caring for the spiritual and practical welfare of seafarers and their families.

If you would like to share in God's work among seafarers by joining our worldwide team of chaplains or our voluntary service scheme for young people, by supporting us in prayer, or by inviting a preacher or speaker to your parish, please contact us at:

The Mission to Seafarers
St Michael Paternoster Royal,
College Hill, London EC4R 2RL
Tel: 020 7248 5202
Fax: 020 7248 4761
Email: general@missiontoseafarers.org
Website: www.missiontoseafarers.org
Registered charity no: 212432

Caring for seafarers around the world

Notes

Scripture Index

Subject Index

Notes

Selected Index of Authors and Hymn writers

Notes

Notes

....
....
....
....
....
....
....
....
....
....

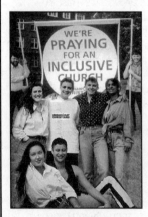

Notes

Notes